CRAZY IS MY
SUPERPOWER

CRAZY IS MY
SUPERPOWER

HOW I TRIUMPHED BY BREAKING BONES, BREAKING HEARTS, AND BREAKING THE RULES

AJ MENDEZ BROOKS

ILLUSTRATIONS BY ROB GUILLORY

CROWN
ARCHETYPE
NEW YORK

All rights reserved.
Published in the United States by Crown Archetype, an imprint of the
Crown Publishing Group, a division of Penguin Random House LLC,
New York.
crownpublishing.com
crownarchetype.com

Crown Archetype and colophon is a registered trademark of Penguin
Random House LLC.

Library of Congress Cataloging-in-Publication Data

Names: Brooks, A . J., 1987– author.
Title: Crazy is my superpower : how I triumphed by breaking bones,
    breaking hearts, and breaking the rules / AJ Brooks.
Description: First edition. | New York : Crown Archetype, [2016]
Identifiers: LCCN 2016027302 | ISBN 9780451496669 (hardcover) |
    ISBN 9780451496676 (pbk.) | ISBN 9780451496683 (ebook)
Subjects: LCSH: Brooks, A . J., 1987– | Women wrestlers—United
    States—Biography.
Classification: LCC GV1196.B76 A3 2016 | DDC 796.812092 [B]—dc23
    LC record available at https://lccn.loc.gov/2016027302

ISBN 978-0-451-49666-9
Ebook ISBN 978-0-451-49668-3

Printed in the United States of America

Book design by Lauren Dong
Illustrations by Rob Guillory
Jacket design by Jake Nicolella
Jacket photograph by Anthony Tahlier Photography, Inc.
All interior images courtesy of the author.
Thank you to Celeste Bonin and Eve Torres for contributing photographs for
the insert.

10 9 8 7 6

First Edition

FOR EVERY GIRL
WHO NEEDS A HERO
AND DOESN'T YET
REALIZE
SHE WILL BECOME
HER OWN.

CONTENTS

1. DROWNING BARBIES   1

2. MAD LOVE   21

3. A PLACE CALLED HOME   37

4. SWALLOW ME WHOLE   61

5. A STEP-BY-STEP GUIDE ON HOW TO TURN INTO YOUR MOTHER   73

6. LIE TO ME   99

7. THE ROBIN HOOD OF THE EXPRESS CHECKOUT LANE   119

8. BORN AGAIN   135

9. I WANT TO BELIEVE   159

10. HELLO, SUNSHINE   177

11. NO ONE WANTS TO HAVE SEX WITH YOU   191

12. EXTRA WHIP   215

13. GIRL ON GIRL   245

14. CRAZY CHICKS DO IT BETTER   259

ACKNOWLEDGMENTS   269

CRAZY IS MY
SUPERPOWER

CHAPTER 1

DROWNING BARBIES

W ould you like to join the rest of us?"

I look up from the intertwined fingers resting in my lap and into the eyes of a pissed-off second-grade teacher. I was certain if I sat incredibly still in my desk at the back of the classroom I would not be visible to the naked eye. I am rail thin and the approximate height of an average Cabbage Patch doll, so it is not outrageous to think it would be possible. The entire class has dragged their chairs into one large circle for "story time," an hourlong activity in which Miss Cahill will read Dr. Seuss while twenty kids try and fail to hold their pee. At seven years old, I already know I am too old for this crap. I consider making a run for it, but I am not exactly an athlete. I have the type of asthma that requires me to be so well acquainted with my inhaler it is covered in Lisa Frank puffy stickers. Combined with stubby legs that can only move in short bursts covering little distance, I would get nowhere very slowly. Imagine an overencumbered Chihuahua who has been frightened by a firework. I am that nimble.

I have been alive for seven years and have spent the majority of that time avoiding group activities. I sit in the back row of every classroom. I bring nothing from home to school bake sales. And I preemptively run at the flying balls during dodgeball, just to save everyone the time and effort. I would rather control the crowd than play among it. The only story-time experience I have ever enjoyed was last year, when I swiped Stephen King's *Cujo* off my first-grade teacher's desk and began reading it aloud during recess. My classmates were a spellbound audience while my teacher found it absolutely adorable, thus teaching me two valuable lessons: If you pretend that you know what you are doing, a large group of people will blindly follow you. And, if you are cute enough, you can get away with stealing.

"Are we going to be graded on this?" I answer a question by asking a question.

With a look of confusion, Miss Cahill folds the readied book in her arms. "No. This is a group activity. It is meant to be fun, April." She pronounces "fun" in a way that implies it is extremely painful.

"If we are not being graded, I'd rather have fun by myself," I reply while searching for my scented markers and dolphin-emblazoned Trapper Keeper. With the warmth of a bikini in January, Miss Cahill cups my hand in hers and leads me against my will into the group. "I don't know how you do things at home, but in school you have to learn how to follow the rules, like a good girl."

This doesn't seem like sound advice to me. For one, "be a good girl" sounds like the coax of someone trying to lead me into a windowless van. But I have also gathered some very valuable knowledge. Grown-ups are mostly lying pieces of shit. I am a straight-A student, my homework is always completed, and I am even a frequent winner of John F. Kennedy Elementary School's "Student of the Month" award. They gave me a ribbon. My picture is tacked to a goddamn bulletin board. And homegirl is going to talk to me like I'm a problem child? My parents taught me that the "rules" of school were to get good grades and to try to not get stabbed on the way home. (We lived in a sketchy neighborhood, but that's really just solid advice for anyone.) It doesn't quite add up that despite my skill I would not be considered "good" unless I quietly agreed to find something fun just because everyone else did. Is that truly what makes a "good girl"? Not her level of performance or intelligence but her ability to follow along? To listen without questioning? Well, there must be something wrong with me because I question everything. In fact, I cannot listen to an adult complete a thought without interrupting them with at least three follow-up questions.

At the pediatrician's office:

DOCTOR: You're going to feel a little pinch . . .
ME: Wait! Why? You said this was a checkup.
DOCTOR: Well, I have to take a sample of your blood.
ME: WHAT ARE YOU GOING TO DO WITH MY BLOOD?
DOCTOR: I'm just making sure you are healthy. I'm doing it to help you.
ME: So you're going to help me by hurting me?!
DOCTOR: *Sigh* You probably don't have diabetes . . . *puts away needle*

But each and every time I question an adult, I am treated as if I have just used crayons to draw a swastika on my forehead. Adults do not understand how to navigate my inquisitive nature. They instead label me as a "smart-ass." (But both parts of that word make me smile, so I wear that particular scarlet letter with pride.) I ask so many questions, the grownups in my life have begun to just straight up lie to me. I know "The Magic School Bus" is not going to pick me up in the morning if I go to bed on time, like my father would like me to believe. NJ Transit is not operated by Ms. Frizzle. I know, despite my mom's repeated claims, that pointing at someone is not sign language for "your mother is dead." It's just rude. This exaggeration seems a little extreme. I know that my grandma is lying when she says that if another girl runs her hands through my hair it means she is putting a hex on it to fall out. I asked my friend Jamielee why she tugged at a strand and she said I just had a Cheerio stuck in it. I am also certain most second graders are not well versed in the dark arts. But that's only because I have checked out the same book on witchcraft seven times from the public library and I am still not Sabrina. I know that sitting in a circle listening to an adult tell me a story will not be fun. Adults lie. I want to see the words for myself.

I wonder, if I were to ask very politely, would Miss Cahill consider reading some of Chris Claremont's *X-Men* instead. Certainly everyone would be as emotionally stirred by the "Dark Phoenix Saga" as I was. So moved by this story arc, every night after finishing all my homework, I would sit down with my Barbie dolls and joyfully reenact Jean Grey's suicide.

"She could live as a god, but it is more important she die as a human!" I would scream while Cyclops Ken watched in horror. Then I would go off script and throw everyone a much-needed pool party, filling a large Tupperware with water and bouncing the dolls inside of it. But just when they would begin to have some fun in the sun, several of Barbie Rogue's guests would slip and fall into the deep water, screaming, "We can't swim! Our legs don't bend that way!" The X-Men are never off duty. If they couldn't save all the drowning Barbies before bedtime, I would store the container of submerged dolls inside of the freezer until the next morning. Then I would use telekinesis, and often a kitchen fork, to rescue them from their icy prison. I tried to convince my friend Nikita of this game's merits, but she promptly cried about it to our teacher. Like any rational child, I scribbled "I HATE NIKITA" onto a piece of paper and taped it to the top of her desk.

With a growing mistrust of adults and distinctly different interests from my classmates, it is clear that I didn't entirely fit in. You might ask, *Where does a young freak go to find acceptance and commonality?* Mistakenly, I looked to my family. My brother and sister knew I needed them and thus made me pay gravely for it.

LITTLE RASCALS, BUT LESS CHARMING

I am the youngest of three children. Erica is two years older than me and likes to call me "the baby." This nickname may sound precious, but imagine someone saying it with equal fervor as a racial slur. Because that's how she means it. I am the bane of her existence. My sister went through a particularly impressive "Gerber Baby" phase—the period of time in which a child is so cute, every stranger suggests they should star in commercials. With jet-black ringlet curls, deliciously chubby cheeks, and a playful outgoing nature, Erica was the fawned-over center of every room. I, on the other hand, had a head the size of two full-grown humans, thin flat hair, and the body of a slug. Combine that with the resting bitch face I emerged from the womb sporting, and I was substantially less cute than Gerber Mendez. But I had something she didn't. Health problems. I was a preemie who had to spend weeks upon weeks in the hospital, and if there's anything people drool over more than a cute baby, it's a baby with a sob story.

When I came along, I unknowingly stole all her thunder and made an immediate enemy. But now, as a second grader, I like to believe a lot of Erica's disdain is really just a required part of the sibling process, much like the pair of hand-me-down gray sweatpants we have each been forced to wear. Erica likes to punch me square in the temple while I sleep because that is what was done to her, and she is just respecting tradition. It may also have something to do with the fact that my idea of "sharing" a bed includes spreading my limbs like an underwater starfish and breathing directly into her mouth, forcing her to protectively sleep in the fetal position facing the wall. We will share a room and a bed until we are in college, and then, pathetically, a great many times after that. Our tension can really just be chalked up to forced proximity. After spending the school day separated from each other, we can actually be quite pleasant.

3:15 p.m.
ERICA: That Barbie you're drying off from the torture chamber is really cute.
ME: Wow, thank you. Do you want to borrow her?

4:00 p.m.
ERICA: This doll's hair is perfect. Thank you for letting me borrow her.
ME: I barely use her. Sometimes she's Jubilee if I'm desperate. Would you like to keep her?
ERICA: Oh my God, yes. Thank you!
ME: Anytime!

4:30 p.m.
ME: Why are you cutting my doll's hair off? You said you loved it.
ERICA: Well, now she's my doll. And I told you her hair was perfect for cutting.
ME: Oh, okay, that's fine. Have fun!

4:32 p.m.

ME: I'm pretty sure you didn't mention the cutting part.

5:15 p.m.

ERICA: Are you jealous of how great my new Barbie's new hair looks?

ME: Uhhh, no. I told you I didn't even use her. I barely even liked her. And her new hair doesn't really look that . . . oh, wow, that looks really good . . . How did you do that?

ERICA: You should've asked me to cut it while she was still yours. Do you want to borrow her?

ME: No.

5:20 p.m.

ME: Hey, Eri, can I borrow your new doll?

ERICA: No.

5:30 p.m.

ME: Hey, Eri, can I borrow your new doll now?

ERICA: Nope.

5:40 p.m.

ME: Hey, Eri, I'm gonna need my doll back.

ERICA: What? You didn't even like her! You just want her because she's prettier now!

ME: I never said that! I love her! She's my favorite doll!

ERICA: I'm telling Mommy!

8:00 p.m.

ERICA: Maaaaaaaa! AJ ripped my doll's head off and left it under my pillow!

ME: If I can't have her, no one can!

After a few hours of existing within ten feet of each other, my and Erica's peace would inevitably unravel and we would find a reason to come to blows. And thanks to the coaching and encouragement of our parents, we knew how to throw a solid punch.

We lived in several rough neighborhoods all over northern New Jersey, one time witnessing a group of kids in an actual knife fight. In these cold, gray, concrete cities—where the streets were lined with low-income housing tenements, dollar stores, struggling bodegas, corner drug dealers, and sometimes unwrapped condoms I would unknowingly kick around with my siblings' unbridled encouragement—this was not the scariest thing we would witness while walking home from school. But it would certainly convince our parents to start cultivating our self-defense skills.

Standing us in the center of the living room, our parents would pit us against each other to see who was paying the most attention to Daddy's "bob and weave" lessons. It was basically Baby Gladiator. Erica and I would use these newly acquired skills on a nightly basis. But my full strength was saved for my brother, Robbie.

Robbie is four years older than me, which is just enough of an age gap for him to be deeply ashamed of our being related. While I often get in trouble for whipping novelty-sized pens at Erica's dome, leaving blue ink-stained splotches in the center of her forehead, it is Robbie for whom I save the really painful stuff. Ours is an unrequited love. My brother was the coolest kid I knew. So cool, in fact, I believed we couldn't possibly be blood related. I came to this conclusion after holding my almost see-through, pasty-white arm next to his naturally tanned face and accusing him of either stealing all my melanin or being a Filipino stranger's love child. He promptly told me the truth—that I was always so sick because I was adopted from a third-world country's Dumpster. Robbie would cut his own hair into a flattering mushroom helmet, could throw his skinny body off the top bunk bed without breaking anything (almost every time), cursed with reckless abandon, and embraced the foreign concept of "having lots of friends." He skateboarded on rooftops, Rollerbladed while holding on to the rear bumpers of strangers' cars, and had the sweetest Pog collection this side of the Hudson River.

(From left to right) Erica, a slug, Robbie

The only thing I didn't like so much about him was his undying hatred for me. Maybe it was because I refused to put his comic books back in the sleeves after reading them, or because I borrowed his clothes without asking—wrinkling every shirt by tying them with a hairband at the back to fit my smaller frame. Perhaps it was because I could not control my snort laugh despite his continuous warnings that people would confuse me with a retarded pig. Or maybe it all led back to that fateful day when a viewing of WWF's Saturday Night Main Event turned tragic.

At the time, Robbie was the world's biggest professional wrestling fan. Pro wrestling was monstrously popular among boys in the 1990s due to its larger-than-life personalities, soap-opera-like story lines, and heroes ripped straight off the pages of a comic book. (If you really don't know what professional wrestling is, why did you buy this book? Did you lose a bet? Do I look that intriguing on the cover?) And while during the day it brought Robbie physical pain to share the same air as me, he never seemed to notice when I sidled up next to him on the carpet in front of the TV while WWF programming was on. The first week I got away with encroaching on his pro-wrestling pastime I was sure it was a fluke. But the next week it happened again. And then again. Every week I would quietly join Robbie, cross-legged on the floor in the darkened living room, the bright lights of the tiny TV glowing against his captivated face. So enamored by this real-life world of superheroes and villains, he didn't seem bothered by me joining in on the fun, and occasionally he even spoke to me! "Doesn't Macho Man Randy Savage remind you of Wolverine? Man, he's the coolest," Robbie would say in my general direction while keeping his eyes fixed on the television screen. "Oh, yeah, they're both the coolest. Macho Man should be Wolverine for Halloween! Do you want to get friendship bracelets?" Perhaps I was a bit too eager and this would be my undoing. In an attempt to keep the party going after the last match's bell rang, I brought into the living room Robbie's WWF trading card collection and the plastic miniature wrestling ring our dad had found while Dumpster diving. The toy ring was missing one of the ropes it originally came with, but it still had its center WWF logo sticker, so I cherished it nonetheless. "How do you play with these cards? Do you want to make them fight in the ring?" I asked like an idiot lamb to slaughter. "You don't play with those cards! You collect them!" Robbie was red with rage, lunging at me to remove his prized possessions from my dumb, dumb hands. Somehow in the struggle, a 1987 Miss Elizabeth Topps card was irreversibly bent. "You . . . you bent her . . . MISS ELIZABEEEEEEETH!" Robbie screamed with the fire of a thousand Puerto Rican suns. Miss Elizabeth was not only Macho Man Randy Savage's manager but also the love of Robbie's life (second only to Winnie Cooper). I done fucked up. "I will make you pay for this for the rest of your life," he creepily promised. And Robbie was a boy of his word.

If there was a closet in any room I was alone in for more than five minutes, Robbie would somehow manifest inside of it and violently burst out. If it wasn't the closet he terrifyingly emerged from, he was under the bed or sometimes magically flattened within the sheets. One time he emerged from deep inside a laundry basket while I was sitting on a toilet. The boy was committed. He not only took pleasure in giving me tiny, but very real, heart attacks, but thoroughly enjoyed waving a white flag and then proceeding to stab me in the eye with it. Robbie knew how much I enjoyed playing games on his Sega Genesis and chose to bribe me with it. "If you stop talking to me for one hour, I will play *Bubsy* with you for two." *Bubsy* was basically Sega's cat version of *Super Mario* and brought me so much joy I would work up tears to convince my brother to let me play it. At the end of my silent hour Robbie would then change the rules and promise to play IF I could find the *Bubsy* cartridge. I would search tirelessly for forty minutes before he quietly snuck out the door to go skateboarding with his friends.

And thus I saved my strongest punches for Robbie's head. I would sometimes try to beat him to the literal punch, hiding behind doors to catch him off guard. But it never worked. Robbie was a CQC expert before he hit puberty and would somehow always manage to evade my swings, punch me in the gut, and leave me doubled over writhing for air each and every time. Ours was a literal blood feud.

You might be asking, *What kind of home would create such tiny monsters?* Well, clearly, a broken one. My family was dysfunctional, to say the least. First of all, we were never well off. We were never even middle class, or lower middle class. For most of our years together, my family was poor. Oliver Twist, "please sir can I have some more" kind of poor. There were rare times when we experienced short windfalls, like when a relative would lend my parents rent money or a lawsuit against the apartment complex in which a ceiling collapsed onto my sleeping father paid out a few grand, but that money would be spent frivolously and swiftly. Most of the time, making ends meet was nearly impossible. Our extended periods of poverty were not something I noticed right away. Before I began socializing in school, all I knew of the world was contained between the walls of whatever tiny apartment we lived in. I just assumed all people moved every few months with whatever belongings could fit in a backpack. My dad jokingly called us "gypsies," and even though I didn't know the definition of the word, I really liked the way it sounded. I thought every family shopped for free dented cans at a food bank. My mother tried to explain that this particular food was free because other people didn't want it, whether it was close to expiring or donated. I couldn't wrap my head around the fact that any logical human would not want a can of SpaghettiOs for any reason. And it was a step up from rationing week-old leftovers among four people, while my dad resorted to eating canned dog food to leave more for the rest of us. The fact that most of my toys were rescued from the Dumpster or found in garbage cans in front of neighboring apartment buildings didn't seem dirty to me. If some other kid couldn't appreciate the bike with tassels, training wheels, and popped tires my dad proudly salvaged for me, I sure as hell was going to.

The first time I realized there was any negative connotation to being poor was when a girl in school commented on my lack of clothing. "Do you just REALLY like that shirt or something?" she said, referring to one of the three tops I wore on a continuous rotation. Before that moment I didn't think there was anything wrong with having one pair of jeans, sharing T-shirts with my sister, or waiting two years to get a new pair of sneakers that actually fit. I didn't even care that the one pair I owned matched my brother's and sister's and came from the bargain section all the way in the back of Modell's. But in this moment, I questioned myself. Not only did teachers expect me to act a certain way, and kids expect me to play a certain way, but now I was expected to dress a certain way? What the hell? "Your mom really liked my shirt last night" was my only comeback, albeit a solid one. I didn't know what it meant, but my brother assured me it was a safe bet to go with some variation of a "your mom" joke should the need ever arise. And that has been my attitude toward style ever since. *My Target tank top isn't name brand enough for you? Well, I fucked your mom.*

I learned to never really give a damn about my style out of necessity. I was always going to be the kid who shared clothes with her sister, and all five of those items would undoubtedly come from the "irregulars" bin at Walmart. So instead of trying and failing to fit in based on something as trivial as clothing, I embraced what I had at my disposal. Never learning my lesson, I would steal my brother's sweatpants, cut up my dad's Hanes T-shirts, and proudly wear my title as "the tiny weirdo in baggy clothing who always looks angry." I basically had the same aesthetic every day from first grade well into high school:

cheap shirt, boy's pants, and a snarky attitude. And guess what happened? People ate that shit up. My lack of giving a damn was somehow interpreted as being a casual, "no-fuss" kind of girl. What was once primed to become a source of insecurity became the basis of others' attraction to me. Because, remember, if you are confident enough, idiots will blindly follow you.

Bullshitting my way out of being discovered as the poor kid in school became a necessary evil. I became Alcatraz-like guarded, having to always be on the lookout for cracks in my constructed walls that would expose my hardships at home. And thus the human Pez dispenser of desperate explanations was born. When I couldn't afford to pay for a field trip, I blamed it on my strict parents not trusting the school system to keep me safe. If I didn't have lunch to bring to school, I just pretended I was nauseated and didn't feel like eating. When a teacher asked why I was late to school, I'd tell them I overslept, when really my siblings and I had just walked a few miles because we couldn't afford the city bus. If a friend asked to come to my house after school, I told her my mother was a werewolf who ate visitors on sight. There was no way in hell I was bringing anyone home with me.

At seven years old, I am actually not allowed to call our apartment "home." My mother doesn't like it when I get too attached to a place and has to repeatedly remind me that it is "where we are staying for now." She's right, because it technically is not ours. We stole it.

My mother's sister agreed to let our family of five move in with her, her husband, and my younger cousin. Normally, when my parents owed months in back rent, instead of finding a way to pay it, they found a cheaper apartment in another town and quietly moved us there faster than you can say, "lost security deposit." But this time, our landlord was one step ahead of them. Escorted by law enforcement, we had to pack what we could carry and leave the premises in under an hour. With nowhere to go, my mother begrudgingly turned to her younger sister for help. Housing eight people was a lot to ask of a modest two-bedroom apartment. Imagine trying to squeeze into a child's one-piece bathing suit after eating a whole pizza and you are twenty-eight. It was a tight fit. The concept of a stocked fridge and hot water was so foreign to our family, we abused the privileges and became a nuisance. We were less the Six to their *Blossom*, and more the Urkel to their *Family Matters*. Understandably, we wore out our welcome in a few short weeks. But so desperate to be rid of us, instead of kicking us out, my aunt and her family simply packed their belongings and moved to another state. We had been welcomed in, allowed to share their food, and eventually forced them out of their own home. We were straight-up pilgrims without the scurvy. Now upon entering the apartment, life returned to our normal.

After school one day, I ran into the bedroom I shared with Robbie and Erica to change out of my one good pair of pants. The freezing apartment made it painful to have any skin exposed, so the process had to be a quick one. Once the utility bills became my parents' responsibility, the heat was cut within two months' time. It was deemed a nonessential, as my parents believed gas and electricity were the top priority. We could easily combat the cold air and showers by wrapping up in quilts and boiling water to bathe in. But without gas we could not make rice for dinner, and without electricity we could not find out who shot Mr. Burns. I declared myself a child prodigy upon figuring out that sleeping in my bulky winter coat practically guaranteed I would not wake up with the sniffles.

I opened the drawer I had claimed in my aunt's abandoned

dresser to search for something to cover my goose-bump-riddled legs. But before my hands left the metal pulls, I screamed bloody murder.

"Ahhhh! Robbie, you piece of shit!" I yelled as I stared into the eight eyes of a startlingly realistic toy spider. The nauseatingly furry beast, as large as the entirety of my upper body, was just casually chilling between a gray sweatshirt and floral-patterned cotton briefs. I had mistakenly opened up to my brother about how scary I found the movie *Arachnophobia* and was now being tormented for my vulnerability. A classic mistake among the Mendez children was to get wrapped up in the rare harmony of a late-night gab session. After our parents had fallen asleep, we would sneakily turn on *Late Night with Conan O'Brien* and muffle our giggles by pulling the bedsheets over our faces. High off heavy-eyed laughter and the adrenaline of staying up past our bedtime, Robbie, Eri, and I would spend hours baring our souls to one another. In the morning, when the positive vibes of delirium had worn off and we returned to enemy territory, we would naturally blackmail each other with the newfound juicy secrets.

"If you don't get out of the bathroom right now, I am going to tell Ma you want to be an ice cream truck driver when you grow up," Erica once threatened.

From behind the barricaded bathroom door I questioned her betrayal: "They make people so happy! And they get to eat all the ice cream they want! I could live in the truck next to the Push Pops! You said you understood!"

"Eri," Robbie calmly interrupted with his own barter, "if you let me go to the bathroom before you, I won't tell Daddy you wish you were one of the kids on *In the House* so 'sexy' LL Cool J could be your nanny."

It was essential I begin plotting my revenge for the spider surprise while Robbie's guard was still down. But first, I would have to work up some tears if I was really going to get him in trouble with our mother.

"Maaaaaaaaa! Look what Robbie did!" I burst out of the room and into the foul-smelling kitchen. When my aunt was here, it always smelled like lasagna, her homemade dish of choice. She made it so often the fridge was continuously overstocked with leftover trays I would pick at dozens of times throughout the day. Now the fridge's only consistency is a box of baking soda and a forty-ounce of Budweiser.

"Slow down, chiquita. The oven door is open," my mother warned while adjusting the oven knobs. Still wearing her medical scrubs, she was in the middle of her daily routine. After working an eight-hour day as a home health aide, a certified caregiver appointed to the homes of terminally ill or senior patients, Ma would arrive home an hour before we did. She would put on a pair of her plastic surgical gloves and scrub the kitchen counters, the inside of the refrigerator, and the bathtub. Next she would sweep every room and fold any item of clothing not in the laundry hamper, though sometimes she would fold those too. Then she would turn the oven on high and open its door in an attempt to add some much-needed heat into the apartment. As I approached, she was standing guard to make sure nothing dangerous happened. Before I could bury Robbie with some Oscar-worthy waterworks, Ma grabbed my father's attention. "Roberto, can I talk to you?"

"Yes, Jan?" he responded, putting an agitated emphasis on her name. My father always says my mother's name like they are in a sitcom taped in front of a live studio audience and she is the quirky sidekick. "Yes, Jaaaaaan." "What is it, Jaaaaaan?" "Oh, Jaaaaaaaan." Part of the reason for that could be my dad always seems overwhelmingly tired. Like he is carrying the weight of the world on his shoulders and my mother just asked him to hold her purse. He pulled up a seat at the kitchen table, knowing exactly what she wanted to talk about.

"Did you get any side jobs today?" My father was a mechanic. A "side job" was what my parents called any extra work my dad could find outside of the shop that employed him. Scheduled hours at work were inconsistent, and the majority of our spending money came from random neighbors who needed a tune-up or strangers on the road with a busted tire. Dad would occasionally make some business for himself by only finishing half the work necessary on the shop clients' cars. He would then "run into them" later in the week, offer his private services, and be able to pocket the money on the sly. Ingenuity at its best.

"No, Jan." Dad was tired of having the same conversation every day. "I'm doing the best I can."

"Then what are we going to do?" she worried. "I don't get paid until Friday, and your kids probably need to eat something before then."

I pulled up a chair, figuring I could complain about Robbie once their "talk" was over. It normally took about five minutes. Revenge could wait five minutes.

"I'm sure they ate their school lunch, so relax. I'll figure something out for tonight." I missed my aunt's Sega Genesis. For depriving me of Disney's *Aladdin*, the game, she will never be forgiven.

"So you don't have money for dinner but you have money for a forty?" Ma made a good point, I thought as I made the giant spider dance across the table. "I clean up some old guy's shit every day and you can't find one side job?"

"Drop it, Jan!" Dad shouted, standing up with such a powerful jerk it knocked his chair over. I couldn't help but think it was impressive how he slammed their bedroom door closed at the exact same time Ma snapped the oven's shut.

"Do you wanna know what Robbie did?" I began, but it seemed she couldn't hear my words as she walked over, laying a hand roughly on my head.

"Everything is going to be okay," Ma almost whispered before leaving the room.

My mom is one of those adults who lie.

CHAPTER 2

MAD LOVE

Janet Acevedo and Robert Mendez first locked eyes when they were fifteen years old and Robert was beating a man half to death inside a phone booth. Naturally, they fell in love immediately. Products of the New York City projects, they sensed a kindred spirit within each other. Both came from violent homes, enduring physical abuse from emotionally withholding parents. Both experienced the tragedy of loss: Janet losing her father when she was only eleven, and Robert losing all three of his brothers. They quickly became each other's whole world. When Janet got pregnant at sixteen, they were kicked out of their homes and disowned by their families.

They married and moved to New Jersey before Robbie Jr. was born. Without any formal schooling, Robert used his prodigy-like knowledge of automotive engineering to get odd jobs at various local body shops. Janet spent the next few years raising Robbie; their second/only planned baby, Erica (completely appropriately named after the *All My Children* character Erica Kane); and the best mistake they ever made: me.

I am named April, after the month I was supposed to be born in, and Jeanette, representing the Spanish version of Janet's name. I was born prematurely in March, but my parents had already bought an "April" license plate keychain at a gas station and were determined to see this thing through. I am only called April Jeanette when I have pissed someone off. Which is often. But for the most part, my family refers to me as AJ, a tongue-in-cheek nickname given for my penchant to shout things like "Why does Robbie get to have a penis and I don't?" and "If I ever get boobs, I am going to chop them off with a kitchen knife!"

In school, I am the kid with the cool parents. They curse like sailors on leave, have ink, and use hip slang like "Yo, that's fresh, son!" when talking to my friends. They are attractive and young. So young looking, in fact, several male teachers nauseatingly tell my mother, "You must be April's sister." When bringing me into school late one day, a teacher genuinely scolds my mother for skipping class, "You girls better get moving before I tell your teachers where you are!" "She's my frickin' mom!" I have exclaimed more times than I would like to admit.

My friends are insanely jealous Janet and Robert are my parents. They assume every night we have ice cream for dinner and go to bed at three in the morning, coked out of our minds. And some of that envy is certainly warranted. I have the fun parents that take us to R-rated movies, say things like "That teacher can go fuck herself" when I get a 95 instead of a 100 on a test, and who will encourage me, at age fourteen, to get a tattoo (I will decline, stating, "I feel like one of us needs to think rationally about this"). But having the "fun" parents can have its drawbacks.

Fun parents can be found sitting on the stoop of their low-income housing complex, listening to a boom box with some of the building's teenage dropouts. A child of fun parents has to call these cool cats inside at 11 p.m. because it is time for bed and the child has an English test in the morning. Fun

Janet Acevedo, MILF circa 1983

parents hand out high fives for solid disses. Erica would serve
me with such classic lines as "Your cheeks are so fat; you look
like you're storing nuts for winter." To which Fun Dad Robert
would delicately respond, "Oh, snap, do you need some aloe
for that sick burn?"

Fun parents accidentally spend the rent money on a new
pair of sneakers for themselves, and when their youngest child
scolds them for it, fun parents respond by saying, "Stop being
jealous of my fresh kicks." And when the landlord would inevitably come banging on our door for the money now being
worn on their feet, Fun Mom Janet would flippantly instruct
the family, "Just be really quiet and he'll think we're not home."

Fun parents party hard. I would often awake in the middle of the night, sick to my stomach from questionable fumes

invading my nostrils, to find my dad smoking pot and drinking in the kitchen with some of the older teens in the neighborhood. I was a bit perturbed to see their supply spread out
on the same place setting where I ate my morning Farina. I
hated the way these kids looked at me when I passed them in
the street, like they held a secret of mine in their hands and
it was a plaything. More than anything, I felt a burning envy
that my dad paid so much attention to children who weren't
his. They got so much of his time and got to see a side of him
he tried to keep hidden away from the rest of us. My jealousy
would give way to pure, unfiltered rage upon finding out from
my brother that drugs and alcohol cost actual money. Every
time I opened our refrigerator to find nothing but a forty-
ounce Budweiser, I would ugly cry to Erica. It was around this
time I began to realize that my parents did not have their priorities straight.

At some point my father began dabbling with drugs a little
stronger than weed, and we all got to experience the fun side
effects together. One early morning, around three o'clock,
Dad had wandered into our bedroom, dragging his feet on
the carpet and eventually stopping in the center of the room.
At the sight of a sliver of light entering the darkened room,
I bounced up in bed, calling out to him. "Daddy? Are you
okay?" I wasn't sure he heard me. He stood unnervingly still
for several minutes and then slowly made his way over to the
foot of our bed.

"I thought you were ignoring me. Is everything okay,
Da—" Before I could finish my sentence, he had grabbed ahold
of the bed's footboard and begun shaking it. Something about
the way it moved did not please him. I tensed up as he then
began kicking it. It started off gently, like he was checking
the footboard's tire pressure. But slowly the wallops became
faster and more forceful. I tried to shake Erica awake, but she

can—and has—slept through several of my openhanded slaps. Pulling the comforter over my face as a shield, I pretended to be asleep while he finished punishing the footboard for an unknown offense. The next morning, I pulled Ma aside to tell her what happened, but she didn't seem too worried about it: "Oh, baby, relax. He was probably just trippin' balls."

Having the fun parents really just meant having an extra pair of siblings. I began to feel the need to pick up the stress slack. Growing up in my parents' care meant growing up together. They weren't carefree because they were purposefully negligent or dismissive of responsibility; they just didn't understand what was traditionally required of them. They were forced into the duties of adulthood at sixteen, but that didn't make them adults. It made them teenagers who had to find a way to get by with no experience or assistance. They were children raising children. What were new experiences to me more often than not were new to them as well. We would have to learn how to navigate life together. And in that way, we were, unsettlingly, equals.

There was also no need to coddle. If my parents experienced pain, we all needed to experience it with them. I learned this when Dad didn't come home one night. We would eventually learn he was arrested, but for forty-eight hours his whereabouts were unknown. When I cried to Ma trying to get answers, she responded, "I think the asshole left us. I knew this would happen. Don't waste your tears on a man who just takes off, baby."

Living alongside us meant no one stepped up to take the reins. We all pulled together. When there was a heavy downpour, instead of being a shelter from the storm, we all got drenched. We were not shielded. We were not protected. We were expected to protect ourselves, and too often expected to protect our own parents.

ALL IT TAKES IS ONE BAD DAY

Ma would often boast that she was a "loud Puerto Rican," like it was a badge of honor. She and Dad would get into shouting matches so loud our upstairs neighbors would bang on their floor to get them to shut up. When that did not work, and the fights escalated into "who can throw more furniture" matches, the local police would inevitably end up at our door.

One fight was so extreme that Dad actually did take off. He wandered around New York City, eventually pawning his wedding band to "buy a drink." When he returned two days later, sans wedding band, Ma was a wrecking ball. Robbie, Erica, and I huddled together, barricaded inside of our room, playing The Game of Life on the itchy carpet.

"They're throwing things again," Erica worried. "That big cop said last time was their final warning."

Robbie's patience with the noise was wearing thin. "Good. I hope they both get arrested. That'll teach 'em."

"No!" I screamed. "Do you think Ma and Daddy are really gonna go to jail?"

"Not if you do something about it." Erica had her game face on.

"Me? Why me?"

"Because you're the baby." (There it is.) "You're the cute one! They can't say no to you." She rested her arm on my shoulders to make the persuasion all the more convincing. She knew this approach worked. Anytime my brother and sister wanted to stay up past their bedtime or wanted some of our parents' stashed candy, they would employ my gift of cute, boosting my ego in the process. Occasionally I would be recruited to handle the dirty work of inserting my cuteness into one of our parents' fights, but never had one sounded this scary. "You got this," Erica assured me.

Taking a deep breath, I prepared to peer through the bedroom door. Opening it just enough to fit an eyeball through, I could tell Ma and Dad were nowhere in sight. Cautiously, I entered the living room. It was a war zone. Chairs were flipped. A stereo was crushed in the center as if it had been stepped on by a giant. Loose sheets of paper littered every inch of the floor. I tiptoed through the mess, trying to not crinkle the paper beneath my feet too loudly. The shouting was now contained to the privacy of their bedroom. All I had to do was knock on their door and ask them to stop making noise. They would understand I was just trying to protect them. The big cop did not look friendly, and I did not want him to come back here and take them away from us. I also didn't like how Erica kept wiping her tears and then used the same wet hand to spin the Life wheel. My turn was right after hers.

I tried to steady my shaky hand as I knocked on the thin wooden door.

"Go back to your room! You don't want to see this," Dad yelled from deep within his gut.

"No! Come in here!" I could hear Ma's voice farther away, like she may have been sitting inside of their closet.

I stood frozen as the yelling halted. There was no more banging against the wall. Maybe it worked. They could tell I was upset and decided to give it a break for the day. The silence was so welcome I didn't want to disrupt it and continued to delicately maneuver my way back. And then I heard gargling. It was faint and accompanied by gentle, rapid stomps. The kind Robbie would always do when he rolled on the floor laughing at me. After a few seconds, a deep gasp broke the silence.

"He's choking me! Someone get in here!" Ma screamed for help.

What was I supposed to do? I could run back to the room

and hide under the bed, like Eri and I did last time. It was so quiet and dark under there. Though we had never been to church a day in our lives, Erica and I decided to lie on our stomachs, hold hands, and pray for the yelling to end. It hadn't worked then, and it probably wasn't going to work now. No one, besides nosy neighbors, was listening.

Daddy probably wouldn't hurt her. Sometimes Ma could be overly dramatic. If I just pop my head in, I will find that everything is okay.

When I pushed the door forward, I saw Dad holding the TV set above his head. He was preparing to send it crashing down on top of Ma, who was cowering in a ball on the floor. Without thinking, I burst into the room. I ran to her shaking body and threw all thirty pounds of me on top of her. Dad froze, but for a split second I met the gaze intended for my mother's eyes, and it sent fire through my chest. He threw the set against the wall, making the loudest series of booms and bangs I have ever heard. It sounded as if a truckload of fireworks had crashed into a brick wall.

"Please stop. Please stop." I could not stop my mouth from repeating this over and over. But when I finally dared to look up, I saw Dad was gone. The distant slam of the apartment's heavy front door comforted my trembling body.

"You're such a good girl," Ma cried while scooping me into her arms.

Later that night Ma and Dad were cuddling in bed like nothing happened that day. When they called me over, I hesitantly approached. For once I did not find it icky to see them in an embrace. It was a welcome sight. I crawled into their bed and Dad pulled me between them. I was an AJ sandwich and they were the bread.

"You're a tough little thing. Do you know that?" Dad asked. I had never been called tough before. In fact, Robbie called me a "weakling" every time I cried during *Beauty and the Beast.*

"You think I'm tough? Really?"

"Do you know how many fights I've been in? I've knocked out jerks twice my size. They've all been little bitches. No one has ever stood up to me like you did today."

My insides were warm. I was as radiant as a Glow Worm. This moment felt rare, like I would never have both of my parents so proud of me ever again.

I am thirty-six pounds and I am invincible. I have always been a straight-A student, proudly hanging my own stellar report cards on the refrigerator door. The rousing reception to my academic excellence I build up in my mind and entirely anticipate never actually comes to fruition. Looking back now, I understand that my parents were justifiably too preoccupied with working painfully long hours at their grueling jobs to perfect the backflips I fully expected to see in response to my good grades. But at the time, it was demoralizing. It felt as if my parents couldn't see the golden child my teachers had built me up to feel like. But lying squished between them while they praised my toughness made any desire for a report card parade melt away. In this moment I had their admiration and it was for the last thing I would have ever guessed. I was frail and skinny, weak and asthmatic, awkward and uncoordinated. My brother and sister made sure to remind me of these traits on a daily basis, often while pushing me over. The last thing I ever thought I could be was strong. Jean Grey was strong. Miss Elizabeth was brave. Princess Toadstool was tough. April Jeanette Mendez was a fucking spaz. I needed to cement my parents' new vision of me. I craved nothing more than to see the warm, addictive eyes of parents who felt proud. I was told I had accomplished something no grown man was able to. I would find a way to accomplish it again.

STEP 1: TEST YOUR MIGHT

Erica was obsessed with baby dolls. And since I could fit into most of her Waterbabies' clothes, she would just cut out the middleman and carry me around instead. While she rocked me in her arms like an infant, we would joke that she was my new mommy, "Except I don't yell as much" she would say, laughing. One day, karma would bite us in the ass for our shit talk. While swinging me around, Erica's hands slipped apart and my miniature skull came crashing to the ground. As my head contacted the apartment's linoleum floor it made a nauseatingly sharp crack ring through the room. We both froze in fear. Erica stared wide-eyed at me, waiting for my inevitable full body ugly cry, but mostly making sure she hadn't just killed me. As the tears welled up in my throat, it hit me that this was an opportunity to test my might. "I'm okay. I AM OOOO . . . KAAAAAY!" I smoothly said as I stood up and immediately fell back down on my ass. "Well, you don't look okay." Erica looked worried.

She nervously checked the apartment to see if Ma had heard my brain go splat, but she was busy scrubbing the kitchen countertop down with Ajax. As we tried to tiptoe past her, playing it as cool as two very guilty cucumbers, Ma whipped around, noticing something amiss. "I'm okay!" I shouted in response to no one's question. She raised an eyebrow. "Your hair is . . . very messy." She was getting suspicious, but she wasn't entirely sure why. Ma was in what we called her "cleaning mood," intensely scrubbing every inch of the apartment to a germ-free finish, and the sight of my unruly hair drastically conflicted with all her hard work. "I can fix this. Go get me a brush and I'll fix your hair."

I scurried to the bathroom to find the one round brush the Mendez women shared and began to feel light-headed. "I'm okay," I repeated to myself. When I returned to the kitchen, Ma was sitting in a dining chair, her plastic gloves removed, and motioned for me to stand in front of her, facing out. "I don't know how you girls play for your hair to get this messy," she mumbled as she attempted to move the brush through my hair. But on the first stroke it got stuck on a large knot. "April Jeanette, when is the last time you combed your hair? It's full of knots! And why is it so dirty?" In an instant her demeanor changed and she became enraged. She had just spent two hours cleaning to find her daughter was the real-life Pig-Pen. I winced as her stroke became rougher and rougher, unsuccessfully trying to loosen the bird's nest resting on my scalp. With a strong flick of the wrist, the brush finally made way, its teeth ripping through to the other end. As I stared at the ground in front of me, trying to focus my eyes, I noticed what looked like a small pony's tail fall to the ground. I thought it was strange, but my mother continued to furiously tug at my locks and I didn't want to disturb her until she was done. But then another disturbingly large hunk of hair floated to the floor in front of me. "Umm, Ma. Is my hair falling out?" This question seemed to snap her out of her trance-like determined brushing. Looking down, she let out a horrified gasp upon finding her hands covered in blood. "What the fuck did you girls do!?"

"Erica dropped me and now I'm bald!" I screamed while the severity of the situation began to dawn on me.

"I'll get a towel! I just mopped this floor!" She hurriedly wrapped a towel around my head. "Wait, I just washed these towels! Goddammit!" My mother did not do well in stressful situations.

"Do I have to go to the hospital?" I tried to focus her.

"No! No hospitals. We'll just leave that wrapped for a while. Pretend you just washed your hair. How long have you been bleeding?" She began pacing, visibly flustered.

"I don't know! You were the one brushing my hair. Who doesn't notice they're ripping someone's hair out?"

"Jesus, I don't know! Who doesn't notice their own head is cracked open?" She began hyperventilating. "I'm gonna have to take you to the hospital and then do you know what's gonna happen? The state is gonna take you away. They're gonna think I did this to you and . . ."

While using one hand to hold the towel in place around my head like a snake charmer, I grabbed her forearm with the other. "It's okay. I'm okay. Really, I'm fine." Three lumps of foot-long bloodied hair strewn across the tile begged to differ. "Really?" She exhaled. "Okay, good. You must have a really tough head."

Yes! There it was again! And all it cost was a few bald spots for a year!

STEP 2: KNOW YOUR LIMITS

I was fascinated with my newfound strength. This was the first time I had seen how much blood was really inside of me. I had soaked a bath towel through, lost my hair, and somehow convinced myself it didn't hurt. I was sure I had willed myself into being okay. Could this be my very own superhero origin story? Sure, it wasn't as cool as gamma rays, but I was convinced something special was afoot. Naturally, I wondered what other kind of damage I could withstand.

When a shouting match with Erica inevitably ended with me in tears, I thought I had the perfect amount of rage-filled adrenaline to test the resiliency of my skull again.

"If you don't shut up, I'm gonna smash this cookie tin on my head!" I threatened an understandably perplexed Erica.

"I want to see you do that. Why would I shut up?"

"Because I'm gonna tell Ma you did it again. Remember how mad she got last time?"

"Dude, go for it."

And with that, I smashed the hard, circular lid of a sugar cookie tin against my forehead. But it didn't hurt. Had I whiffed and hit air? Or was my head just tougher than I had ever imagined? I rapidly and forcefully banged it against my forehead twenty more times just to be sure.

"Maaaaaaa!" Erica screamed. "AJ's a psychopath!"

I had not entirely thought this one through. Within an hour an enormous goose egg appeared. It looked as if a grapefruit was trying to force its way through the skin of my forehead or I was in the process of transforming into a unicorn. I decided inflicting pain upon myself was not the way to prove my toughness. I was going to have to start inflicting it on other people.

STEP 3: SHARING IS CARING

In the third grade I got into my first fistfight in school, and I have never looked back.

The majority of my friends in school were guys, because most girls at the time didn't want to talk about my theory that Princess Peach kept getting kidnapped because she just liked the attention. One day, a boy shared his Gameboy with me and an older kid decided to make fun of it. "Why are you guys sitting so close? Are you doing hand stuff under the desk?"

I was insulted. Not only did this sad excuse for a class clown make me feel uncomfortable for hanging out with a boy, he sullied my sacred Tetris time. How dare a child so dumb he had been left back a grade three times in a row try to make me feel inferior? But instead of coming back at him with "I do hand stuff with your mom," I just wildly swung my teeny tiny fist at his temple. Before he could blink, it connected with a dull thud, almost knocking him off his chair. I thought I saw some of his third-grade mustache instantaneously fly off. "Can't you take a joke?" he yelled, tears welling in his eyes. My small hands had normally felt weak and ineffective when used against my siblings, but with the power of indignation, it was a mighty hand of justice. Why had no one ever told me violence was the key to solving problems? That felt like a serious lack of communication. A boy twice my size had tried to bully me and I made him frickin' cry. Word quickly got around the whole school that tiny AJ was a low-key violent menace. I felt drunk with power. Eagerly I awaited the next opportunity to swing for the fences.

When Billy stole my Play-Doh during recess and used it to artfully mold a green penis, I swung. When Omar followed me home because he had a crush on me, I made him regret it. When Helen said she could hit harder than I could, we spent fifteen minutes of our lunchtime welting each other's bodies to try and win the argument. And when Javier called my father a "junkie," I convinced two of my guy friends to hold him down while I placed an actual bucket over his head and repeatedly kicked it. I was getting a bit out of control. It got so bad, teachers started to hear tales of my volatile nature. They couldn't believe their star student could be living such a double life but decided to give my father a heads-up just in case.

"Do you have any reason to believe April would be prone to violent behavior?" one concerned teacher asked Dad when he picked me up from school.

"Absolutely not. April's a good girl," he assured her.

As we walked off school grounds he turned to me and asked, "Did they deserve it?"

For a second I was confused, until I saw that exciting, familiar glow of pride shine from his eyes. "Hell, yeah, they did." I smiled as Dad held his hand out for a high five.

CHAPTER 3

A PLACE CALLED HOME

Growing up, my greatest desire was to be able to breathe. I felt like my world was in perpetual motion, my breath trapped anxiously in my throat. I wanted nothing more than to sit still. Exhale. And rest my tired eyes in that elusive place called home.

My family experienced being evicted almost twenty times. Almost twenty different buildings, twenty different bedrooms, twenty different ceilings when I opened my eyes in the morning. Every time I woke up, I hoped that it had all been a bad dream. That I would get out of bed, open the door, and be inside of a real house. With furniture that wasn't someone else's trash. With clothes hanging in a closet instead of pre-emptively readied in a packed duffel bag. But that hope would never be realized. Instead, every day we lived in fear of having to leave on a moment's notice. It seemed once a month we would struggle to find the next place to safely sleep. Eventually my parents tired of the struggle and made the decision to move in with Robert's parents in Rincón, Puerto Rico.

Meeting my grandparents at the age of nine for the first time was a shocking experience. They were unlike any of the city slicker adults from my mother's side of the family in New

Jersey or New York. I had been told they once visited when I was a baby, but any memory of that meeting must have been lost alongside the story my mother likes to tell of baby me pooping in the bathtub and shouting "M&Ms!"

Grandma Anna and Grandpa Jesus were islanders and farmers. Their massive farm in Puerto Rico, over fifty acres of rolling fields, was home to dozens of cows, chickens, roosters, and a two-thousand-pound bull that acted like a puppy. Every morning, with the gentle bull walking beside him, Grandpa Jesus would pick grapefruit off one of the dozen colossal grapefruit trees and gather eggs from the chicken coop. Grandma Anna would hand-squeeze juice and whip up omelets, and the seven of us would eat breakfast together like a cheesy sitcom family. I loved every second of it.

My grandparents were pretty hard-core. The two-floor farmhouse we all shared was built with Grandpa's very own hands. At seventy years old, he maintained a sprawling farm and preferred to lift cement blocks over his head rather than sit in a rocking chair. Grandma was a stone-cold killer, perfectly exemplified by the day she found out one of her roosters had roamed over to a neighbor's farm. Taking this as the ultimate sign of betrayal, Grandma walked him the half mile back home, holding on to his feet and completely ignoring his blood-drawing pecks at her hands. "You never betray a Mendez woman" she instructed me in broken English and proceeded to chop his head off with a machete. I wish she would've also instructed me to look away. We had rooster for dinner that night, and I decided I would stop naming the farm animals. Poor "Home Boy" never saw it coming. Coincidentally, I would be a vegetarian for the next thirteen years, but at least I had learned a snappy catchphrase and a swift solution to disloyalty that would terrify all future boyfriends.

Dad promised this move was only temporary until he could

get some money together, but I was in no rush. Life in Puerto Rico was magical. A video rental store in town had a Cruisin' World arcade game, and my grandparents had a seemingly endless supply of quarters. Robbie saved up his quarters to buy *Mortal Kombat 3* and *Samurai Showdown*, and we lost hours in those games delivering brutal deaths to each other.

When I wasn't gaming, I actually enjoyed going to school, mostly because of the dress code. Our new school required us to wear uniforms. For once it was normal and accepted to wear the same few items of clothing every day. And I look pretty rad in plaid.

Each morning I would secretly climb the farm's trees with Robbie and Erica in tow. When I would inevitably fall into a red ant hill, and require about a hundred spots of calamine lotion all over my ravaged legs, the secret was out. But that didn't stop me from continuing to play the role of Tarzan every day. Having spent all my years in concrete jungles, I was simply astounded by the majestic, lush trees in actual nature. I couldn't believe anything that wasn't man-made could ever be so tall. In the afternoons I would scour the pea plants for rotted pods that were bound to be inhabited by beautifully colored caterpillars. I would collect a rainbow's assortment of the sticky bugs and line them up on my dresser, giving each a name and backstory. "Cher lives with Dion and their best friends are Kitana and Mileena . . . son of a bitch, that lizard is eating all of them! It's a massacre!" I was learning about the circle of life pretty hard and fast.

Every night I would lie on the cool cement of the front yard and stare up at the sparkling sky. I had read about light pollution in my science textbooks, but it was hard to believe there were millions of stars hidden to us busy city dwellers. Here, in the miles of open fields and farmland, the dark sky glittered with diamonds. Every night I was joined in my stargazing by three stinky, transient dogs: Bobby, an all-white twenty-pound pit bull mix; Pitusa, a miniature pinscher mix named for a local furniture store; and Leal, a monstrous part dog, part Clydesdale whose name fittingly meant "loyal" in Spanish. Grandma had taken in the strays a long time ago and converted them to faithful farm dogs. They would wander from home, exploring the hills of Rincón, but would never travel too far. She would cook bowls of chicken just for the pups and let them sleep inside on cool nights. I wondered if that was how she saw us. Another clan of dirty strays she had rescued. It was in this shared dependency on the kindness of a practical stranger that I came to understand the little mutts. We all could use a good bath, and our ribs protruded a little from lack of nutrition. We were all wary of our surroundings, wondering when the rug would be pulled out from under us, forcing us to find a new place to rest our heads. But we were all so appreciative, so content to have the simplest comfort and sanctuary for as long as we could. We were rough around the edges, but that didn't make us worthless. Being a little damaged does not make someone broken. It just means they have better stories to tell and cooler scars. It was here, lying among ants on the dirty slab of concrete, that I found my soul mates. My furry, stinky soul mates. This was true happiness.

And that is why it absolutely broke my heart to learn we would be leaving Puerto Rico. After a short time, my parents had grown bored with the monotony, with the comfortable predictability of farm life. Wild horses would rather take the risk of running free than live in the safety of confinement. At the time, I couldn't understand this. I relished boredom. I lived for uneventful days of calm bliss. I did not confuse drama and chaos for passion and adventure. And I had dogs, dammit! Big, beautiful, loyal dogs that seemed to enjoy my company more than any human friend ever did. Leaving Puerto Rico felt like being ripped away from my first real [animal] friends, my first sense of peace, and my first real home. What were they rushing back for? And more importantly, what would be different for us this time around?

ANYWHERE BUT HERE

After six months in Puerto Rico, we moved back to New Jersey in the winter, I assume to make the transition as painful as possible. Walking through bustling, crowded streets was a stark contrast to the tranquil isolation I had become accustomed to on the island. But I was determined to make the best of it. We still had our Sega Genesis, and I tried to re-create the bloody magic. "Let's see if we can beat Shao Kahn with Sindel this time! I bet she's pissed at him for bringing her back from the dead." I tried to pitch a gaming session to Robbie, but he wasn't having it. "We already beat the game ten times. Let it go." Robbie wasn't taking the return to the city well either. He too had trepidations about our parents adjusting to paying bills again, and he seemed to wistfully pine for the island's adventures. "I'm going for a walk," he said as he snuck out of our new, empty apartment. Erica and I tagged along. We had all gone on numerous walks together through the mountainous roads of Rincón, catching bugs and feeding stray dogs along the way. I was sure we could find some sort of similar escapades on the Jersey sidewalks.

About ten minutes into our excursion we were almost run over. The car, speeding out of a McDonald's parking lot, honked at us for getting in its way. While a stream of expletives flew out of Robbie's mouth, Erica noticed a gray cat at the far end of the lot. "Do you see that? That poor baby!"

"What is it doing out here all alone? It's so cold out!" I was not yet familiar with the concept of resilient stray city cats.

To me this was a Bobby or a Pitusa, just waiting for a kind stranger to take her in.

"Let's take her home! We'll hide her under the bed for a couple of days so we can prove Ma is faking when she says she's allergic." This plan seemed foolproof. Robbie finally found something that excited him, we were about to have an awesome new pet friend, and we were about to get a solid burn on our mother. It was a good day.

Carrying the chubby cat inside of his jacket, Robbie successfully snuck her past Dad, who was on his way outside for a smoke. Now we just had to figure out how to get her into the apartment without Ma noticing. His arms having grown tired from smuggling a wriggling cat inside of his clothes, Robbie placed her down in the building's main vestibule. "What do we name her?" he asked the group.

"How do we even know it's a her?" I pondered.

"I didn't see a cat dick," Robbie responded.

"Eww, don't say dick," I yelled.

"It's called a penis," Erica helpfully chimed in.

"Eww, that sounds even worse!" I yelled again.

The cat began to nervously pace around the tiny, enclosed foyer.

"You need to grow up," Robbie mocked.

"You're thirteen!" I mocked back.

"You both need to shut up and name the damn cat," Erica helpfully chimed in again.

The cat gently pawed at the glass door.

"What about Bobby II?" I was a genius.

"That's the dumbest fucking idea of all time." Robbie was mean.

The cat aggressively pawed at the glass door.

"How about Bobbi with an 'i'? That'll make it a girl's name." Erica was on a roll.

The cat backed up and then ran full speed at the glass door. Its tiny cat skull made a loud wallop upon contact.

"You guys are both so stupid she's trying to kill herself to get away from you!" Robbie had enough. He reached down to try and pick Bobb(y? i?) back up into his arms, when she surprisingly turned to face him, springing onto her hind legs. Making a hiss that would frighten a boa constrictor, she exposed her claws. The cat swiped at the air like Baraka performing a combo. Her tiny, scary paws viciously sliced through the air as fast as she could move them.

"She's trying to kill us!" Erica screamed as we all simultaneously flattened against the claustrophobic room's walls.

"We just wanted to help, you ungrateful dick!" Robbie yelled as she swiped in all our directions. She was a blender's blades, and we were the food desperately clinging to the sides of the plastic. We were going to be a bitch to clean off. Inching along the wall, he managed to reach the entrance's door handle and push it open. The cat darted out, and presumably would've flipped us off if her little cat paws were capable. I quietly looked around in astonishment. Oh, is that how it's gonna be, New Jersey? I see you. Clearly, our transition back to civilization was going to be rougher than I thought. What we needed was a way to ease that transition. What we needed was a pet. Preferably one who wouldn't kill us.

Admittedly, during this time, my dad had his faults. I wasn't sure if being impetuous enough to move us away from his parents and a guaranteed roof over our heads was one of these faults, or if it was a brave, independent choice that should be admired. But what I know for sure is his most admirable quality is his love for animals. I feel like his devotion to all things furry and feathered was somehow passed down in my DNA.

While others see pigeons as flying disease-ridden rats, he is the kind of guy who finds one flying low to the ground, notices it has an injured foot, and takes it home to nurse it back to health. He even converted an eyedropper into a baby bottle to feed it water. When our own parakeets, Rocky and Cindy, were on their way out to that great big birdcage in the sky, he improvised cribs out of shoeboxes, so they would have a comfortable place to spend their final days. One apartment we lived in had a fenced-in parking space behind it. When I came home one evening, I found a minihorse wandering inside of it and damn near crapped my pants. "Why is there a horse out back?! And who shrunk it?" I asked, bewildered. "He just needs somewhere to stay for a few days," Dad calmly explained while really explaining nothing at all. Dad's love for animals far exceeded his means to properly take care of them, but his heart was always in the right place.

Dad's greatest soft spot is for dogs. Any pup could turn the burly, tough guy into mush. If he saw a stray dog wandering the streets, he would find a way to scrounge up some food scraps for it. Several times he would open our home to pit bulls who needed to be fostered for a few months. Even though we didn't have much in the way of food or square footage, he found a way to share it with animals in need. On one trip into Manhattan to score some drugs, he found out his dealer was participating in illegal dogfights. The dealer introduced him to a pit bull puppy he was planning on raising and training to participate in the brutal, unconscionable bouts. Appalled and heartbroken, my dad immediately offered the asshole fifty dollars to take the dog home with him. Hungry for cash, he quickly accepted, and a sixth member officially joined the Mendez family.

Mugsy Mendez was a chubby little guy with a giant melon head, a black-and-white-tuxedo-patterned coat, and a white stripe running down the center of his forehead, nose, and chin. We called it his racing stripe. He was the first puppy I'd ever had, and he was an adorable, chaotic handful. At first he terrified me. His penchant to nibble at exposed toes would cause us to warily wear sneakers at all times, even immediately after stepping out of the shower. You never knew where or when he would pop up and snack on your feet. He had boundless energy. One afternoon I brought home a handful of schoolmates to show off my new pup, and he spent a whole forty minutes chasing all five screaming kids in a circle.

But eventually his undeniable cuteness wore me down. I had missed cuddling with Bobby, Pitusa, and Leal and it was as if little Mugsy could sense that. His first week at home, while I sat cross-legged on the floor doing my homework, he gently crawled into my lap. He curled into a small, cuddly ball and was snoring in ten seconds flat. I stared at the warm, precious soul making piglet noises. All snuggled up, trusting in the safety of my lap. In an instant, I fell head over heels in love. I thought of the life that was originally laid out in front of him, a life of violence and pain—a life my dad had saved him from ever being forced to live. How could any human with a functioning brain and heart ever think of being so cruel to something with so much trust and unconditional love to give? I stroked Mugsy's velvet smooth fur and silently promised to protect him from pain for the rest of his life. I had heard a song on TV a few hours earlier, and in this moment it popped back into my head. As I caressed the sleeping pup I sang,

> *"You are my sunshine, my only sunshine.*
> *You make me happy when skies are gray.*
> *You'll never know dear, how much I love you.*
> *Please don't take my sunshine away."*

Mugsy viciously cuddling me and Eri. Also Exhibit A that I am a starfish sleeper.

Mugsy snored in approval. For the next fifteen years, this would be our special lullaby.

Another quality I truly admire in my father is his ability to treat every human as equal. I always wondered how every person in the neighborhood knew his name and would joyfully greet him as he passed by. Even the homeless, huddled in an abandoned convenience store's entranceway, would wave and shout out "What's up, Rob?" as we walked the street. He would always tell me to smile and greet them back. They would occasionally loiter around our apartment building, waiting until he came outside to smoke. If he had a spare dollar, they knew he would give it to them. And if not, he would at least always gift them with a lit cigarette. Like most kids who hide a parent's carton of cigs in a microwave, I loathed the fact that my dad smoked. I resented anything that could possibly hurt him and take him away from me. But the fact that he would try and make sure there was at least one extra smoke in the pack in case one of his displaced acquaintances asked for it was possibly the most adorably generous action I have ever seen in my life. Robert Mendez can really have a heart of gold when he wants to. He would talk to a bum on the street in the exact same manner he would the president of the United States. It's just who he naturally is. It's who we should all be. No one is less human than anyone else. It was an invaluable lesson I took with me throughout my life. The president of any corporation I've worked for gets the exact same smile and greeting as the janitor who mops the building's floors. Do me a personal favor and try this in your life. You have no idea how much it'll mean to someone who too often feels invisible. Everyone just wants to feel seen.

I know this because my family would eventually be home-less as well. Our worst fear in coming back to the States, that life would return to the chaotic struggle it had always been, came true. Within a year we were evicted from our apart-ment, yet again. There was a shared coin-operated laundry room that led to the apartment we were being thrown out of. Laying some disassembled cardboard boxes on the roach-filled ground, the five of us and a growing pit bull hid in the back of the room, trying to formulate our next move. We quietly watched as men broke down and removed the bunk beds my mom had proudly purchased after working hours of overtime in a nursing home. These uniformed men spent the afternoon dragging our sparse, but beloved, belongings out into the street with the rest of the garbage waiting for pickup. Ma strictly enforced a "no crying" rule, instructing that it was important to "have some pride" in these situations. But I couldn't help but break into a sob when I watched the pink bicycle Dad had once rescued from the trash returned unceremoniously to it. I looked over to see if Dad had noticed, and watched his eyes fill up before he blinked the weakness away. I tried to follow suit.

We slept hidden in the laundry room that night, piled on top of the broken cardboard slabs. But when we awoke, we found out we had not been as stealthy as we had thought. Covering every wall surrounding the washers and dryers were black streaks of spray paint. Written on the door to our old apartment was the cold message "Get Out Trash." The building's landlord called us out hours later, apparently having been notified by the tagger that vagrants had holed up in the laundry room. Dad stepped outside to talk to him.

"Okay, guys," Ma said. "Look really sad when he gets back in here. Take your shoes off. They threw your shoes out, okay?" At least Ma had a game plan.

"What's happening?" I asked, confused as to why Ma was pulling my socks off.

"Your dad is gonna see if he'll let us stay in the apartment tonight. You guys have to really sell it."

"Okay!" Erica was exuberant to be given an important assignment. But this felt like the opposite of "having pride," and the mixed messages were beginning to make my head spin, though that could've just been the fumes from the spray paint. The landlord walked back in with Dad, skillfully avoiding eye contact, and removed the padlock from the empty apartment's door. "Just one night," he warned, "and make sure you stay quiet." We spent the rest of the day throwing our bodies on Mugsy anytime he tried to bark. Though we had to sleep on the floor again, we were relieved to be behind a locked door. It really is the little things.

The following morning we piled into Dad's baby blue Monte Carlo and drove aimlessly around town. When a street seemed less crowded, Dad would pull over, turn the car's engine off, and sit silently. "What's the plan, Robert?" Ma would yell, inciting Dad to shout back even louder, "I'm thinking, Jan!" It seemed we were out of options. Borrowing money from their relatives and never paying it back had made us the black sheep of both the Acevedo and Mendez families. The last time one of my parents' siblings had opened their home to us, they ending up moving out in a burdened frustration. No one wanted to be the helpful sucker this time. While they fought, Robbie, Eri, and I would distract ourselves by playing "mule kick" with Mugsy. The backseat was uncomfortably close quarters, and the now fifty-pound pit had to lap hop on the three of us to fit. When he would settle into position, one of us would discreetly tickle the pad of his paw, causing him to instinctively kick his leg back—directly into the stomach of whoever was holding him. Winding your siblings is a solid way to pass the time.

At night we would find a street that seemed safe enough, and Ma and Dad would take turns with us kids getting some rest. I closed my eyes and tried to force myself to sleep, but every passerby would set my skin on fire. I could feel strangers peer into the car, wondering why five people and a dog were sleeping in a parking spot. I made the mistake of opening my eyes when particularly loud footsteps startled me. I locked eyes with a boy from my class who was walking past with his mother. He gave me a look asking, *What's going on?*, but I was frozen in embarrassment. His mother pulled him close to her side, shaking her head and breaking his judgmental gaze. That night I couldn't bring myself to sleep, but I closed my eyes tightly and pretended I was snoozing. In my head I repeated over and over, *This is not happening. I am not here. I am not here.*

I decided the hardest part about living in a car was knowing that I was missing the *Buffy the Vampire Slayer* season finale. This truly was my greatest concern at the time. While we drove around for days, I set my mind to daydream mode. For hours upon hours I would stare out the car's windows and imagine various scenarios in which I was Buffy, tortured by the memories of killing Angel (spoiler alert!), leaving Sunnydale in a Greyhound bus. At night, my fantasies would change.

At night, lamps would light up the living rooms of every home we passed. I would stare into those illuminated windows, catching only glimpses of the smiling families sitting on their comfortable couches or surrounding a dining table for dinner. I made a special note of how most people's furniture seemed to actually match, as if it were all bought in a set together, instead of a hodgepodge collection of hand-me-downs and street finds. I imagined myself in each home I stared into. I would eat their dinner. I would watch *Buffy* on their TV. I would sit in their fancy, coordinated living room, and I would be at home. "Home" was such a foreign concept, I wasn't sure if I was imagining it right. I couldn't put my finger on its exact definition, but I knew it felt warm and safe. It felt steady and dependable. It wasn't the crowded backseat of a Monte Carlo. Home was on the other side of each window, unattainable and out of reach. Home was anywhere but here.

One morning, my mom hopped out of the car to use a pay phone. She had been reluctant to ask her brother, the last remaining family member who would accept her collect calls, for help. But after some convincing, he decided to let us stay over at his house for a night. Ma was upset he was only offering a short twenty-four hours' access to his home, but I was thrilled to have a change of scenery, no matter how brief. As Dad began the hour-and-a-half journey to our uncle's house in the suburbs, he drove past our old apartment. Our furniture and possessions were still strewn about the sidewalk, a pile of "attempt and failure." From around the corner, a young boy pedaled my bike, now crudely painted white. "He has my—" I cut myself off midsentence, disappointed I had let myself get attached to something I knew I could never keep.

My aunt greeted us at the door of her beautiful two-story home. She was the only white person to marry into our extended family, and for that, she was an enigma to me. Did all white people have delicate, pointy noses? Did they all have houses instead of small apartments? And did all their houses have STAIRS? I was convinced stairs were the epitome of success. I made a mental note that if I could one day live in a house with stairs and matching furniture, I would have truly found home.

"I'm sorry, we finished all the dinner I made, but I'm sure I have something in here," she said while Robbie, Erica, and I sat around her kitchen table. We hadn't eaten much while staying in the car, and my stomach was aching with hunger pangs. Rummaging through the fridge, she excitedly let us know she did indeed have some Hot Pockets she could share. Fuck. Yes. Hot Pockets were like a rare and majestic unicorn. They were too expensive for my parents' budget, and on every trip to the supermarket, I would longingly push the cart past the frozen food section, staring at their flaky, cheesy goodness. She microwaved one for each of us and I inhaled mine in under thirty seconds. While I licked the crumbs and bits of cheese off my plate, she stared at me in a humiliating mix of shock and disgust. My body was in flames again. I suddenly knew why I had felt it in the car and why the burning fire encircled me once more. I was being pitied. Eyes were looking down upon me, like I was a sad, inferior creature. As if my unfortunate circumstances made me less than human. I immediately dropped the plate on the table. "Ummm," my aunt began, avoiding eye contact. "Do you want me to microwave you another one?" I felt disgusting. I was growing weary of being a dirty, pathetic stray. "No, thank you," I said while staring at my shoes. Gosh, I could've eaten twenty more, but the price of being pitied was not worth the reward. I silently promised myself I would never take anything from anyone ever again. I would never be pitied again.

My father spent our allotted twenty-four hours using his

brother-in-law's house phone to make some calls to various acquaintances. The good thing about being a mechanic who would fix a tire at any hour of the night, and take in whatever bird, dog, or minihorse someone asked, was that Dad had made a lot of friends who felt indebted to him. The next night was spent at a former client's house a few towns over from the apartment we had just left. Erica, Ma, and I crashed in the bedroom of the client's young daughter while Robbie, Dad, and Mugsy slept in his garage.

The night after that a man named Don let Dad know he could clear out some space in his home and we were welcome to stay there for as long as we needed to. My parents were ecstatic. However, that excitement quickly dissipated when we arrived to find out Don and his wife, Joann, were hoarders. I'm talking collectors straight out of the series *Hoarding: Buried Alive*. Every inch of their house was filled with items ranging from expensive antique furniture to worthless flea market finds, to thousands of trinkets that hadn't had their tags removed, to more than a dozen cats. And cat shit. God, there was so much cat shit. When traversing through the obstacle course to get to a furniture-packed bathroom, I would step on at least three piles of cat shit just on the way there. If the miles of useless furniture had been removed, there would have been five extra rooms for my family to comfortably stay in. But these hoarders had a serious problem. When Don told my dad he would make some space for us, he meant he would make room for a twin-size mattress, a moth-eaten love seat, and a space heater in his screened-in porch.

During the dead of an unforgiving New Jersey winter, my family of six practically slept outdoors. The armoires and shelves lining the screen walls of the porch were useful in blocking the frigid wind, but the temperature inside the porch was always painfully low. I looked forward to going to

school, just to be inside of four solid walls. To be able to take my winter jacket off. We would take turns huddling around the space heater while watching a black-and-white TV Don and Joann had surprised us with one evening. "Check out this great find!" It was slightly comforting to know someone other than my dad brought home Dumpster treasures.

Though we would all get sick on a weekly basis, we were grateful to technically have a roof over our heads, and we didn't want to mess it up. Ma would limit our trips inside to their first-floor bathroom. Since she wanted us to remain as unnoticeable as possible, my sister, my mom, and I had to all take trips to the toilet together so as to avoid multiple disturbances. We were allowed to go once in the morning, once after school, and once before bed. We would shower every other day to limit our use of their hot water. And we never shared their food. I would, however, sneak upstairs with Robbie before Ma came back from work, to play *Resident Evil* with Don and Joann's son. It was a mind-saving relief to have that video game to disappear into, if only for an hour. They did, kindly, invite us inside to have Thanksgiving dinner with their family, but I chose to finish my homework, sitting on the twin mattress, watching *Friends* in black and white, wearing my winter jacket. I would never take food from anyone again, I told myself.

After about five months awkwardly living in a screened-in porch, my parents had saved up some extra cash. It wasn't enough to put down a security deposit and first month's rent on a new apartment, but we were all stir-crazy Popsicles, so they decided to use it to move on. Packing into ol' Monte again, Ma tried to explain that we were headed to a weekly rated, extended-stay motel.

"So we're going to live in a hotel?" I had heard worse plans.

"No, baby, it's a motel. There's a big difference."

She wasn't lying. We moved into a room at the aptly named Hilltop Motel, a sprawling three-building establishment off the Jersey Turnpike, situated on the top of a tall, steep hill. The three-hundred-square-foot room we shared was a serious upgrade from Don and Joann's porch. For one, there were four solid walls. No longer would a simple thin screen separate us from nature. Almost as important to me was a color TV. A glorious color TV that didn't need bunny-eared antennae to get a proper signal and had at least ten different cable channels. I had heard about this magical invention called "cable TV" but had assumed it was an old wives' tale meant to make poor kids feel even shittier. I didn't know what HBO was but I knew I wanted to be a part of it. Particularly because my mother told me its content was way too graphic and mature for me. Oh, the forbidden fruit! There was also a small fridge, a microwave, and a round dining table for two, simple conveniences I had almost forgotten existed while camping in the snow. There was a bathroom a mere ten feet away from the table. I wouldn't have to ration my trips to avoid being a nuisance or have to navigate a minefield of cat poop to . . . well, human poop. But perhaps the most comforting of amenities the motel room provided were two whole, separate beds. I wouldn't have to sleep curled up on a cushion of a ratty old couch anymore. Dad, Robbie, and Mugsy shared one of the full-sized beds, and Ma, Erica, and I occupied the other. Ma thought Erica and I were too old to share a bed with boys, but I thought it was strange for a husband and wife to not want to sleep next to each other.

A typical day at the motel would go something like this. Dad would walk Mugsy around the parking lot and pick up some continental breakfast from the motel lobby. He would wake us up with single-serving boxes of cereal, eight-ounce cartons of milk, individually wrapped Honey Buns, and bananas. It was a feast fit for kings. After breakfast, I would brew some coffee and prepare for my long trek to school.

I had started drinking coffee around age seven and never looked back, probably because my body was too jittery to do anything but run in panicked circles. It was a habit that grew out of necessity. Having only tap water available for drinking, I desperately wanted to taste something with any kind of flavor and began experimenting with Ma's espresso grounds. I think starting with the hard stuff made me a customer for life. I also like to blame my childhood addiction for stunting my growth, because in height and stature, I still very much have the body of a seven-year-old.

The three Mendez kids would then pack up our backpacks with homework and pocketknives and head out for school. Dad had given us all the tiny weapons upon moving in because the motel grounds were a bit sketchy. The seedy motel attracted all sorts of unsavory characters and activity. We were told which rooms to avoid walking past, as it was understood by all residents that particular ones were designated "Buying and Selling," which was either a thin veil for drugs or a lesser-known *Property Brothers* show. Occasionally, while walking

The Hilltop Motel, many years later.

to the vending machine at night, Erica and I would get asked "How much?" by a random drunk. To be fair, the motel was littered with prostitutes roaming for customers. However, I question anyone whose taste leans preteen. Flashing lights and sirens shone through our windows on a weekly basis, but Dad told us as long as we kept the door locked and were aware of our surroundings, we would be fine. But just in case, he wanted us to be packing.

To get to school, we would walk down the quarter-mile-long steep hill with our backs leaned back so far you would think we were doing a bit, but really we were just trying to avoid tumbling down the hill face-first. The motel parking lot led to a thin sidewalk on the side of the highway. Cars would zoom past so close and so fast, I would just about jump out of my skin. After several blocks, our route to the NJ Transit bus stop would take us back up the hill for half a mile. After a forty-minute bus ride, we would then walk ten more blocks to school, and we'd reverse the process on the way back. Naturally, this grueling process began to wear on me.

I hated having to lie to my teacher about why I was late to school, but Ma reminded us if anyone knew we were living in a motel, the state would undoubtedly take us away. The goddamned state, again. I begged Dad to drive us to school, but he said he couldn't afford to fill up the Monte Carlo's gas tank and we should look at it as good exercise. I guess he was right, since I do credit these punishing walks for laying the groundwork for the monster quads I have today.

For a while I was unbelievably happy living at the Hilltop. Sure, I would loathe traveling from the interstate into town and back five days a week, and I knew those loud bangs in the parking lot at 3 a.m. weren't the firecrackers my dad pretended they were, but there was a sense of consistency, of dependability I relished.

We lived in the motel for close to two years. It was the longest we had ever stayed in one place. It seemed paying fifty bucks a week was way more achievable for my parents than paying monthly rent. We even had money to have Wendy's for dinner almost every night. Dad and Ma would walk down the highway to the adjacent Wendy's fast-food restaurant and, arriving back at the motel, give the secret knock on the heavy metal door to let us know it was safe to open. Opening the door to the dark parking lot and seeing the beacon of light that was Ma and Daddy holding bacon cheeseburgers, fries, and chocolate Frostys will forever be ingrained in the sparsely decorated "happy childhood memories" room of my brain.

And though I had lost all my toys after our last eviction, Dad had managed to find an enormous box of used green, yellow, and blue Legos in the motel's Dumpster. He proudly handed the box off to me and I was beside myself. I quickly poured them out onto the dining table and began building. When I finished my castle and had leftover Legos in the container, I wrote the names of my Barbies on small pieces of notebook paper, cut them out, and taped them to the back of the excess blocks. These blocks would now serve as my dolls; and the action movies, talk shows, and soap operas I had previously created with my Barbies could now continue.

I had almost forgotten what it felt like to create worlds, to use my imagination to find a place to escape to. I sunk hours into those blocks. When Dad came home with a *CosmoGirl* magazine he found in a client's car, I had even more to work with. This issue of *CosmoGirl* had a comic strip of a teen named CG, who would have various adventures in high school. Seeing this brought back comforting memories of my brother's X-Men comics and lit a fire in my belly.

I began filling my school notebooks with sketches of my own young female superheroes. Over time I began actually drawing out panels and creating continuous story lines for my teenage heroines. I would present the stapled-together pieces of notebook paper to Erica, and she would always give supportive, positive reviews. I had my first fan! When Dad noticed I had filled up the books intended for math homework, he bought me three CVS brand one-subject notebooks, all with green covers—my favorite color. No matter what your circumstance, if you provide kids with creative ammunition, they will blast holes into an oppressive reality and conceive limitless worlds.

I was beyond appreciative, and the outlet did wonders to soothe and streamline my mind, which for some reason had begun to grow increasingly erratic.

The first time I remember scaring myself was around 5 a.m. on a weekend. I woke up early because I really had to pee. While washing my hands in the sink, I glanced at the red flashing 5:01 on the nightstand clock. I looked at myself in the reflection of the wide mirror before me. In the blink of an eye, it was 5:08. Seven whole minutes had passed and my hands were still furiously moving under the stream of hot water. I jarringly pulled them out and noticed I had scratched little red lines into my knuckles. Since it was a Saturday, I was excited to hit the proverbial snooze button and go back to sleep for as long as I wanted. But when my head hit the pillow, I just lay there, wondering about my missing seven minutes. The scrapes on my fingers began to burn.

After waking up so early, I assumed I would be yearning for bed when 10 p.m. came around. But as the lights went off, and everyone closed their eyes, the fatigue I had felt all day faded away. I was wide awake. Squeezing my eyes did not force me to sleep as I had hoped. Counting the tiles on the ceiling only led to recounting the tiles on the ceiling. And recounting them, again. My eyes drifted from the ceiling to the peeling wallpaper beneath it. On top of that wallpaper were body-length mirrors. So many mirrors. On every wall. I wondered, *Why are there so many mirrors? Was it to give the illusion that the small room was larger? This room is pretty small. Smaller than I had thought during the day. Did it somehow get smaller? God, Ma is sleeping so close to me. I have no room to move. There is not enough space on this bed for three people. They're too close. Why are there so many mirrors? Was there someone looking through the other side? Could I get to that side if I went through the mirrors? Were all the reflections they held really just another world I could get to if I tried hard enough? Did other-dimension AJ just move? I didn't move! She is real! Why am I not breathing? I can't breathe!*

Before I knew it, I was wheezing deeply and rapidly, waking my mother.

"I can't breathe!" I managed to shout as she nervously looked around.

"If you can say 'I can't breathe,' you can breathe. Just relax."

But I couldn't stop the uncontrollable heaving of my chest. My fingers began to tingle, and my heart felt as if it was beating in my ears.

"Just relax," Ma said as she pulled me in, making me the little spoon. With the same shushing noises normally reserved for a fussy infant, she ran her fingers through my hair. My heart began to return to my chest. My breathing slowed. But I still couldn't fall asleep. I had to stay awake. My eyes had to stay fixated on the AJ in the mirror, just in case she made another move.

"Hey, Ma. I think I saw something in the mirror," I whispered to the groggy woman trying to lull me to sleep.

Without opening her eyes she shushed me again, "Shhhh. Go to sleep and stop acting crazy."

CHAPTER 4

SWALLOW ME WHOLE

I t might be hard to reconcile the fact that I wore denim booty shorts for a living with the fact that I don't have daddy issues. No, when I'm thirsty for a pity party, or blaming someone for my adolescent proclivity to fall in love with gay men, I fill up at the deep dark well of maternal abandonment. I truly believe Janet fought against her demons and tried her best to be an ideal mother. But over time, the façade of strength would crack. The guarantee of a traditional mom would slowly become unreliable.

As humans we are programmed to crave motherly comfort, despite ourselves. We want to be enveloped in protective warmth. To have an all-knowing blanket of safety who will stroke our hair and then rock us to sleep. An unconditional shelter from an unforgiving world. No matter how old we are, it is something our hearts will find a way to ache for. No matter how big and strong we grow, there will always be an innate urge to run to Mommy when we fear the monsters underneath our bed. But sometimes the person we depend on for that comfort becomes the thing we fear the most. Sometimes we just draw the short straw of uteruses.

My mother has been bipolar for most of her life. Janet was diagnosed with bipolar disorder when I was in college, but she clearly suffered from its painful effects for years before it could be properly identified. The disorder can be indefinable and mysterious, and it is often confused with depression. However, accidentally treating it with antidepressants does nothing but magnify the illness.

So what is bipolar disorder, exactly? In precise medical terms, it is a giant prick. An uncontrollable, malevolent force, it is a psychological disorder that causes unexpected, severe shifts in mood and reckless behavior. These cycling episodes of mania and depression affect day-to-day functions, destroy relationships, and can cause suicidal thoughts.

Ladies, imagine you are on the worst day of your period and then multiply it by seven . . . ty thousand . . . and you're in a sandstorm, naked, with scorpions crawling all over you, and there's a pissed serial killer somewhere in the vicinity, and also you're pretty sure your boyfriend is banging that chick Sheila from his office.

Oh, and guys, imagine the exact same thing, except instead of your period, your balls are delicately hovering over a rusty bear trap. And instead of Sheila, you suspect your lady is handing it out to Brad, that handsy personal trainer from her gym. Imagine trying to focus on all that emotion, discomfort, fear, insecurity, and paranoia, at the same time.

This is the tiniest insight into what a day, or even an hour, might feel like for someone going through a bipolar depressive cycle. And that's just half of it.

Mania isn't a lazy Sunday in sweats, either. Sure, it's all fun and games when the boost in morale inspires you to clean the entire house and start a small business in under an hour. But it's a slippery slope from there to spending two thousand dollars online ordering Victoria's Secret lingerie, trying to scrub the shower tiles so hard your fingertips start bleeding, and feeling so invincible you are tempted to run into oncoming traffic.

Janet's condition controlled her. Its onset occurring during her twenties, the disorder slowly consumed her, changing every facet of her personality, until eventually only remnants of the original woman remained. One of my biggest regrets in life is not noticing she was being eaten alive before it was too late. We were uneducated and naive about mental illness.

In fact, depression and anything of the sort, in the Mendez household, was perceived to be a creation of people who weren't strong enough to handle their own problems.

"Don't act crazy." That was the stock response I would get if I felt my mind begin to mold in dangerous ways. That was the response I got when I asked if talking to a psychiatrist might help the growing anxiety I felt. That is how Janet and Robert were raised, and it is the sentiment they would pass down to us, even while they fought their own demons. Sadness was weakness. Giving any force besides yourself power over your mind was the ultimate sign of ball-lessness.

I wish I would've known enough to call bullshit on that way of thinking. Bipolar disorder was not a choice my mother made. Had we opened our minds, had we done our research, had we paid attention, maybe we could've helped her. If mental illness is the greatest villain I've ever faced, then we were all its unwitting accomplices. The signs were there. We were just too busy being hurt to notice.

I would experience the fallout of my mother's illness more intensely than anyone else in the family. Always a strict parent, she was an enforcer of her standards for academic success and appropriate behavior.

I never minded her concern. I liked having a parent who would make sure I did my homework correctly. I was proud of having a mom who taught me to not squander my value on boys who weren't worth my time, especially while I should be focused on schoolwork and my future. But bipolar disorder tends to take who someone is at their core and multiply that essence by a million. It amplifies and distorts their traits—the good, the bad, the scary—into something unrecognizable.

I was my mother's premature baby, riddled with health problems, extremely undersized for my age, and hopeful to a fault. I was the fragile child she worried for the most. Her disorder would manipulate her concern into a fixation. It would transform it into something dark and dirty.

One weekend, all of us Mendez kids were home sitting in the kitchen with Ma. As the kids sat around the table, playing a game of "who can make who cry," I fired off a particularly uninspired diss at Robbie.

"You're ten, shouldn't you be taller?" As I gangster-leaned back in my chair, looking smug as shit, my brother shot back.

"You're six, shouldn't you be able to tell the time?!"

Ma stopped in her tracks and made her way over to us, laughing.

"That's not true, is it, AJ? Come on, what time is it right now?" Smiling, she extended her arm until her watch was directly in front of my face. I knew how to tell time, I was just occasionally an hour or four off. However, despite my ability to come within a day of the correct time, I was notorious for cracking under the pressure my mother presented.

"I don't know," I quietly responded, silently wishing someone would help change the subject.

"Stop playing. Where's the little hand?" She seemed to be more or less teasing me. Maybe I was safe.

"I don't know. Just leave me alone." This kind of back talk was a mistake. She was no longer laughing.

"I'm not joking around. What is the fucking time?"

"Game time!" my brother said, joining in. I always appreciated his inappropriately timed humor.

"That's it. Go to your brother's room," she snapped.

I couldn't tell what was happening. Was I in trouble? Did
she want to talk to me in private? Why Robbie's room? Because it was the closest? Looking back, I realize the answer
was because it didn't have any windows.

"Leave her alone!" Erica shouted, but it was too late. We
were on our way, hand in hand, to the privacy of a dark room.

"Go stand on the bed," she ordered. I felt like I was on a
stage in the middle of a play, but I couldn't remember any of
my lines. She tossed the plastic watch my way, and I didn't
catch it because not only could I not tell time, I was also a but-
terfingers. I was not shaping up to be the pick of the Mendez
litter.

"Pick it up. Look at it and then tell me what time it is."

"I don't want to. I'm embarrassed!" The nervous tears were
well under way.

"This isn't embarrassing," she insisted. "Embarrassing is
not knowing how to tell time when you're already in the first
grade! I'm so disappointed in you."

"You're embarrassing me!" I was a faucet.

"You want to know what embarrassing feels like? Take off
your shirt," she unexpectedly fired back.

Without questioning why, I pulled the T-shirt off. I quickly
wrapped my arms across my chest to alleviate some of the ex-
posure.

"Every time you can't answer me right, you're going to take
another thing off. That is the only way you are going to learn."

After several unsatisfactory responses, I ended up completely
naked, shivering and bawling, standing atop a crude stage like
a stripper during an afternoon shift, but more depressing. At
some point the panic engulfing me began to slip away. I couldn't

explain how I was doing it, but I started to feel less in the moment. Like it wasn't me who was stuck frozen in fear. It was like I was watching myself from a safe distance. It helped.

Instead of making my mother feel culpable for her method of parenting, I began to excuse it. Whether I was being directed to stand perfectly still facing a wall for two hours because of my sassy mouth, or being asked to present my back for overhand slaps for getting an 85 on a test, I would apologize like a meek little mouse. Then my mother would be stricken with guilt. She would console me and ask me if I understood why I had to receive the punishments I did. It was a sickening cycle with no end in sight.

"I'm sorry I was bad. I'm not mad at you for teaching me." I would make myself believe.

My mother found one thing more important than insisting I was on the Honor Roll, and that was making sure I would one day die a respectable virgin. As a teenage mother herself, she feared her daughters would go down a similar road if she didn't instill proper values and morals as early as possible. In an attempt to snuff out any ounce of sexuality before it grew, she hounded us several years before we even needed training bras.

While waiting for my sister's elementary-school volleyball game to start, I sat next to my mother on the gym's bleachers. I unwrapped a green apple Blow Pop, an award from my teacher for getting the highest score on a pop quiz. I was unaware of the severe connotations associated with a third grader holding a lollipop in her mouth for over thirty seconds, but my borderline pornographic behavior caused Ma to yank the lollipop stick out of my mouth, almost taking my front teeth along . with it.

"You're giving the wrong impression!" she scolded me as she cracked the hard candy shell against my head in front of almost fifty schoolmates and parents. When I attempted to pick the sticky green apple candy bits out of my hair, she snapped again, "You leave that alone. Maybe it'll teach you to not act so nasty."

At times, I felt I could do nothing right by my mother. I couldn't even walk right. Literally. There was a six-month span during the fourth grade where she would make sure to walk at least two feet behind me to monitor my gait. According to her, I walked like someone who had been having sex. I didn't even know what sex was in the fourth grade. I assumed it was whatever my sister made our undressed Barbie and Ken do, which was aggressively smash their boobs against each other.

To be fair, Ma was actually a bit more specific in her accusations, an actual reprimand including "You walk like you've had a dick up your ass." Which was immediately followed by, "Wait until I find out. You're gonna get it." Get what? I wondered. A punishment? A beating? An actual dick up my ass? Was that even a physical possibility? In a world where I could literally walk the wrong way, naturally I became terrified of my sexuality.

The idea of anything I did being misinterpreted as welcoming mischievous thoughts, as "asking for it," made me shun anything that exposed my femininity. I became an asexual slob, refusing to comb my hair and exclusively wearing sweatpants and oversize T-shirts.

In a way, it was incredibly freeing. I didn't have to be a girl. I didn't have to live by the female codes of conduct or the male standards of beauty. I didn't have to be anything but an amoeba in a Windbreaker. In another way, it was suffocating. I feared how I could ever interact with people in the real world. Boys spoke my language. We liked the same things, shared the same interests. I wanted to be friends with the boys in my class, but I was deathly afraid of my mother finding out.

"Your daughter has a wicked hard punch, man," a boy I had

punched in class told my parents after school. His delivery, his shit-eating grin and giggle, led my mother to believe that our scuffle was somehow inappropriate. Perhaps a love spat or a strange form of flirting. When we got home, Ma gave me a few good overhand smacks on my back before making me stand facing a wall in the kitchen for three hours while she interrogated me.

Her interrogations always consisted of me having to stand facing a wall, while she screamed every curse word in the book, until she could get the information she was looking for. Question after question about my sexual experiences: Did I ever kiss a boy? How many boys had I kissed? Did my whole class think I was loose? I couldn't win. I defended myself and yet still got in trouble.

At a routine doctor's visit later that year, I was stuck in a lose-lose situation yet again. When asked if I would be comfortable getting a vaginal exam, I met my mother's eyes. If I were comfortable, that would mean I must have experienced taking my pants off in front of men. If I refused to let him check me, she would assume I was hiding something. I denied him access (the first of many men) and found out my suspicions were right.

Furious at my refusal to be violated at age ten, she let me have it. "Do you know that I asked the doctor to check if you were still a virgin? I'm going to assume you're not until we go back there and you prove to me you still have a hymen."

Could parents actually ask a pediatrician to check for that sort of thing? I was dumbfounded. I felt violated and deeply terrified of ever returning to a doctor's office. Also, I was certain my hymen had already said good-bye to this cruel world during an ill-advised attempt to change a lightbulb while balancing on a wooden bed frame.

My body never fully got a grasp on the blooming process,

as evidenced by the fact that at age twenty-nine, I am still waiting for my boobs to kick in. At age thirteen, on the first day of eighth grade, I got my inaugural period. Because my mother believed if she withheld information about the maturing process, it would actually freeze her children in time, I was clueless as to what was happening to my body. I had read about menstrual cycles in health class but couldn't be sure what was happening to me was the same thing. I knew some amount of some kind of blood would fall out of somewhere when my hips were wide enough, but the details were fuzzy.

Maybe something had torn in my intestines and I was bleeding out. Perhaps I had been shot in the crotch on the way to school and hadn't noticed. It was a particularly rough part of town filled with very short hoodlums.

Our school nurse laughed at my concerns and gave me a Suzuki Katana made of cotton to casually sit on and waddle with for the rest of the day. When I got home, I hid from my mom. Television makes this out to be a warm and fuzzy moment, but we were far from a TV family, unless you count the family on *Breaking Bad*. After an hour of pleading my case, I convinced Erica to share the news of my newfound womanhood with my mother. Naturally, she found the timing incredibly odd.

If I started bleeding on my first day of school, that must've meant I met a boy in eighth grade, had sex at some point between history class and lunch, and the blood was actually from tearing my hymen. This was the actual thought process of a real-life human person. I was interrogated for hours, until she eventually retired for bed. That night, as my eyes grew heavy, I silently thanked the stars the situation hadn't ended any worse.

At 3 a.m., I snapped awake after feeling a presence standing over me. I tried to make sense of the intruder in my bedroom.

My sister and I shared a full-sized bed, but she remained unbothered and deeply asleep. As the fog lifted, I realized the figure was my mother. How long had she been there? What was she going to do to me? I looked over at Erica, peacefully asleep, and considered kicking her awake.

"Come with me," my mother whispered as she grabbed ahold of my wrist. Her grip was painfully tight as she shuffled me through the kitchen to the railroad apartment's only bathroom. Both our bodies squeezed into the small room, and I stared at her, confused and not fully sure I wasn't dreaming.

"Pull your pants down." She left no room to argue. But I tried.

"What are you doing? I'm tired, please let me go back to bed," I pleaded.

"You can go back to bed after you pull your pants down." This wasn't my mother speaking. Yes, she was often intimidating and her actions were questionable, but there was something missing in her eyes. Part of me wondered if she was somehow sleepwalking or just tripping balls. But a bigger part of me truly believed she was possessed. She held firmly to my wrist, jerking me closer to her face as she spoke.

"If you really have your period, I'll be able to tell by the blood. Pull your pants down, now."

In that moment I could feel myself begin to melt away.

It felt as if I was watching AJ as she loosened the drawstring to her Pokémon pajama pants, dropped them alongside her underwear to her knees, and exposed the mess between her legs. I could see the tears descend down her pudgy cheeks, but her face didn't move. They weren't tears of sadness or fear, but of quiet resignation. My mother seemed satisfied.

"Okay, then. Clean yourself up and go back to bed." She left the room, content with her findings, and I began to dry my eyes.

I tiptoed into my room and tried to get beneath the covers as quietly as possible. Watching Erica adorably snore, I cursed at her for not waking up. Then I inched my way toward her sleeping body, wrapped my arm around her back, and lay awake until the morning, my mind unable to shut off.

I knew that was not my mother who made me do those things. I wondered, could she also melt away from herself? Or had something vile, after years of closing in on her, finally gained complete control? If it could take over my mother, could it one day swallow me whole as well?

There's a recurring dream I have, where I am standing over my mother as she sleeps. She looks so peaceful and innocent, unsullied by the wickedness of her illness. After watching her for a moment, I notice it in the corner of the room. The darkness, preparing to engulf her. I know there's nothing I can do. It is waiting. It is too late. But it lets me say good-bye. I lean over and gently kiss her warm forehead. I hover there, close enough to feel her breath on my face. I look at this beautiful woman and whisper, "I love you, Ma. I'm so sorry."

CHAPTER 5

A STEP-BY-STEP GUIDE ON HOW TO TURN INTO YOUR MOTHER

As I got older Ma's transformation into a Lifetime channel movie villain continued. It was as if the more I learned about the real world, the more I became a part of it, the more she feared losing her grip on me. She had to find a way to hold on tighter.

Watching me like a hawk, Ma saw every move I made as a cause for interrogation. Every pimple was proof I was dirty. Every pound gained was a painful reminder of how pretty and skinny I used to be. Every male classmate who looked in my direction was the secret father of my nonexistent baby. It set my nerves on edge. I never knew whom I was going to get when I walked through the door. Would I get a smile from the vibrant woman cooking rice and beans while blasting Marc Anthony on her boom box? Or would I get the pissed-off crone wondering if I was home ten minutes later than usual because I had to give a quick BJ before catching my bus?

Even if Ma was in a good mood, there was no guarantee that wouldn't change an hour later. There was no way to tell what would set her off. She would spend most of the day locked away in her room, and each time the door creaked open, I would get a painful twinge in my stomach. My body was beginning to expect the worst as well.

I even developed a twitch. Every time I felt a hint of anx-
iousness creeping in, my neck would jerk my head from side to
side and push my chin forward. I had no control over it. Eventually it became as natural as a blink. I didn't think anyone
had really noticed it, but ol' hawkeyes did.

The second Ma pointed out my odd neck movement, its
frequency went off the charts. "Stop moving your head like
you have Tourette's," Ma would gently chide. The more she
would notice, the more it would happen, until one day she had
enough.

Making me step into the shower fully clothed, Ma turned
the showerhead on as cold as it would go and let me know I
could leave once I stopped twitching. Her method may have
been suspect, but it was surprisingly effective.

Though I had gotten my twitch mostly in check, I was
more uneasy being at home than ever. A slammed door here, a
loud drop of a TV remote there—even without words Ma was
making the plentiful hair on my arms stand at high alert. One
day as I was washing the dishes from dinner, Ma slammed the
freezer's door. I was so jumpy that the sound made me wildly
flinch. The two glasses I held in my hands collided, shattering
upon impact. I had smashed them together so hard the glass
crumbled into hundreds of tiny pieces, covering the entirety
of my arms and chest.

I held my breath and froze with my arms outstretched, half
because I was hoping Ma hadn't noticed and half because I was
covered in frickin' shards of glass. I didn't know what to do.
Luckily for me, Ma had indeed noticed and was already on her
way, washcloth in hand.

"You can't even do the dishes right? Why do you have to be
so fucking worthless?"

Ma had been harsh in the past. She had scared me and made
me cry. She had cracked me across the back or upside the head

to keep me in check, and I would have preferred those slaps to those words. She had never been that mean. She had never called me worthless. It cut deeper than the glass jutting out of my palm. A familiar frenzied look entered her eyes, and I feared what would come next.

She moved my arms from the sink to my side. Straightening my elbows and moving my palms out, making pieces of glass fall to the ground like a rain of diamonds. "It's all over the floor now! You got it all over the floor! I have to clean all of this! On top of finishing the dishes since you can't seem to handle such a simple job." As she muttered a stream of curses underneath her breath, she wet the washcloth and began to use it to knock the glass off my shirt and into the pile around my feet.

She moved the towel to my arms, roughly dragging it down the exposed skin.

"You're hurting me," I tried to plead, but she was focused on the mission at hand. Pressing the washcloth onto my arms just pushed the tiny pieces of glass into the skin. Moving the cloth dragged the shards down my arms, scratching the whole way.

When she was done, I was torn to ribbons. One piece of glass had been so strongly pushed into my flesh, it remained burrowed under the skin of my wrist three months later.

My nervousness at home was perpetual. I had the anxiety level of a Chihuahua taking Adderall during a thunderstorm. I needed to find a way to alleviate it before I shattered like broken glass. Robbie, noticing the bizarre wrath I was incurring, became kinder and more accepting of me than he had ever been before.

He actually invited me to use his new PlayStation. Having

saved months of checks from his first job as a cashier, Robbie rewarded himself with the gaming system he had coveted for years. Watching the PlayStation symbol grace the screen of the television was as close to a religious experience as I had ever had. Inviting Erica along for the ride, we all sat on his futon and played *Resident Evil: Nemesis* for hours on end.

The game's heroine was Jill Valentine, a petite brunette who could not only wear the hell out of leather, but also managed to wield a grenade launcher while fighting hordes of zombies. This was my kind of chick. Before I knew it we had sunk weeks into the game, beating it over and over again. It felt cathartic to blast zombies away into chunky little pieces. There was something about seeing this strong, stylized female lead holding her own and taking out the bad guys that spoke to me. It was like a comic book I could control and be immersed in.

Next we played *Metal Gear Solid*, and again I was graced with the presence of badass heroes in the form of gun-toting Solid Snake and Meryl Silverburgh. I loved escaping to this world, a world where I could be a capable powerhouse. I, quite literally, had the control. I had the power. When stress began to take its toll, I would escape to the worlds of *Tomb Raider*, *Final Fantasy*, *Need for Speed*, *Mega Man*, *Soul Reaver*, and *Silent Hill*. Screw the real world. I was no longer the fragile victim. Video games made me the hero of my own story.

Robbie even invited me to watch wrestling with him again. While we hopped around from apartment to apartment, I had lost interest in trying to keep up with the show. When I sat down and watched an episode with him, I was taken aback by how it all had evolved. No longer was the only female representation the demure, dainty flower Miss Elizabeth. The women who now graced my screen were muscular and overtly sexualized. They now competed inside of the ring instead of just valeting a male wrestler. They even mixed it up with the guys in intergender matches.

I was floored. I had thought spandex-wearing heroines had only existed within the pages of my comics or pixilated games. But here were real-life, flesh-and-blood ass kickers. Some of the women were jacked and tough as nails. The others were gorgeous blond bombshells. All of them were confident, interesting pieces of the show. I watched as they received brutal beatings and doled them out twice as hard. Robbie and I would sit down twice a week and cheer on our favorites: Eddie Guerrero, Chyna, The Rock, Rey Mysterio, Kane, the Hardy Boyz and Lita, Chris Benoit, and Shane and Stephanie McMahon.

On days as rare and glorious as a unicorn we would hit up the PlayStation for a couple of hours, turn on *Monday Night Raw,* and then create ourselves in the Create-A-Wrestler mode in the WWF's PlayStation game, *SmackDown.* I cherished this time with my brother.

I had been so scared of my surroundings, so unsure of myself. But in trying to help me out and take my mind off things, he inadvertently introduced me to exactly who I wanted to become. I wanted to be as brave as Jill Valentine and Meryl Silverburgh. I wanted to be as memorable as Aerith, as skilled as Lara Croft, as strong as Chun-Li and Kitana.

But I needed it to be real. I needed to experience the power and strength with my own hands in real life. The amazing women in the WWF were the closest to the leading ladies as I could ever get.

"I'm going to be a professional wrestler when I grow up!" I proudly announced to my mother at the age of twelve.

"That's not a real job, baby," she muttered, walking right past me.

YOU NEVER FORGET YOUR FIRST STABBING

As I was preparing to enter high school, Robbie was preparing to leave it. Mere months away from graduating, he was tired of his tumultuous life at home. Ma's erratic behavior had begun to rub off on Dad, and he too exhibited signs of change and increased violence. Robbie would always fall into something that would cause him to get smacked around by Dad. I remember crying my eyes out when Dad knocked a bowl of cereal out of Robbie's hands because he wasn't making enough eye contact while being yelled at. The tension between the Mendez parents and children was at an all-time high.

Erica had rebelled and discovered boys and parties. She made the mistake of staying out too late one night and Dad threw a mug at her head the second she entered the door. As she cowered, all curled up in a crying mess on the floor, Dad wouldn't back off. He kept yelling and yelling, throwing out nasty names that made my blood boil. I was scared he would hit her the way he smacked around Robbie.

I had enough. I was all hyped on my newfound hope to one day be my own Wonder Woman, and I figured now was a good place to start.

"Leave her alone!" I shouted with all my mousy might.

"What did you just say to me?" Dad was infuriated.

"If you want to hit someone, hit me!" I stupidly challenged. I had been watching so much wrestling I was sure I had figured out the trick to taking a punch was just gritting your teeth. I could do that if it meant sparing my sister. Plus, I was going to have to start getting physically tougher at some point. I considered this practice.

Dad power-walked up to me like a fuming bull, but I did my best not to budge. I clenched my teeth, thinking this was my moment to prove I could take a beating like the wrestlers did. I met his eyes and didn't flinch. This pissed him off. He reared back and punched clean through the closet door behind me, sending wooden splinters flying around my head.

"You're not my daughter anymore!" he yelled, storming off.

I didn't know what that meant. Did it mean I wasn't acting like myself? If so, good. I didn't like meek, Chihuahua AJ anymore. I needed to be stronger. Did it mean I was being disowned? As if I should be punished for not being afraid of a man with a balled-up fist? For standing up for myself and for another person? What kind of message was that to send to your own daughter? That cowering is a correct response?

Not only was I upset about all the possibilities, in a strange way I felt empowered. I was becoming a different person. And I liked who she was.

But Robbie was tired of cowering. He was also tired of moving around like gypsies and needed a way out. Unfortunately, my parents had no money and no plan to send him to college. Having average grades, he couldn't get the scholarships necessary to put him through school, either. And so, at the age of eighteen, he entered the army's Airborne Infantry unit.

A year later, 9/11 happened right across the river in New York. And my big brother was sent off to war. He had joined the army with the intention of finding stability, of escaping turmoil at home, and he ended up deep within it. Before he left for basic training, he surprised me with my very own PlayStation 2, the latest gaming system. "I'll kick your ass on it when I get back," he promised as I wondered how long it would be until I saw him again.

My rock was gone, and the apartment returned to constant hostile territory. I felt for my dad. He seemed to blame himself for pushing Robbie out the door. I knew Dad's violence wasn't representative of who he really was. He is the softie who brings home strays. He's not a bad person. The level of strain

Forcing human contact on Robbie after his
Army Basic Training graduation.

thrust onto our family when my mother began her downward
spiral was intense and more than anyone could handle alone.
Here he was trying to keep this roof over our heads while his
wife descended into a mysterious darkness none of us could
explain. I understood how the pressure and stress began to
break him too.

While I began my first years of high school, Robbie toured
Iraq and Afghanistan. In his care packages I would include
handwritten letters, decorated with colored marker drawings

because I figured he could use a little pop of enthusiasm in his day. I also thought it was essential to include match-by-match rundowns and detailed play-by-plays of every episode of WWF shows. I didn't want him to miss out on the story lines we had bonded over and were invested in. I probably should've figured he had more important things to worry about. "You don't have to write me seven pages about wrestling," he let me know on a brief, static-filled phone call home. "Just let me know if you ever grow into your giant head."

Without my brother around to bring me out of my shell, I withdrew into solitude. I felt weaker somehow. Like not having the only person who understood what I dreamed of becoming was somehow making it less attainable. Naturally, my snark multiplied.

I had found strength in standing up for myself once, and I continued to use my words as protection. "You've turned into a real smart-ass," Ma would say, as if that were supposed to be an insult. But the day I invited my dad to take a swing was the last time either of my parents hit me. It was as if my demonstration of nerve had earned some perverse respect.

Psychologically, my mother would continue to find new and exciting ways to torment me, but it was quietly understood there was no way to scare me physically anymore. In numbing my nerves, I began to believe my own strength.

I was proud to be a smart-ass. This smart mouth was going to build armored walls around me and keep me safe.

When the holidays came around, my mom wanted to drive into Manhattan for Christmas Eve dinner with her relatives. It had been quite some time since our little band of merry misfits had been invited, and coincidentally, it had also been some time since my parents last asked any of them for money.

Going to these family gatherings had once held a special place in my heart. When my parents couldn't afford to buy us Christmas presents, an aunt or uncle would bring a bag of extra toys to our family gathering and make sure the Mendez kids had at least one present to unwrap. I was so appreciative to receive my first childhood baby doll at one of these dinners, over twenty years later I haven't had the heart to get rid of it. Though I probably should, since it now looks like it's haunted.

Looking beat.

But the more dependent on them we became, the less they wanted to share their holidays. Having become a little ball of bitterness, I asked to be excused from the evening.

"We don't ever celebrate Christmas. We don't give each other presents. Why are we going to start now?" I made my case.

"Because these people are your family, and family is supposed to be together on the holidays," Dad tried to convince me.

"Is this the same family that let us live in a car?" I bit back.

"You know what," Ma interrupted, "just leave her home alone if she wants to be a little Grinch. I don't want you embarrassing me with your smart mouth anyway."

"The Grinch had a pretty sweet dog." I pushed my face against Mugsy's like we were posing for a cheesy Kmart photo op.

I was psyched. I had taken a trip to Hollywood Video and rented a VHS of *Akira*, Katsuhiro Otomo's sci-fi anime classic. My interests had now broadened to all things anime, and it was an essential part of the education.

"It's just you and me, Mugsy," I said as I popped the tape into the mouth of the impressive TV/VHS combo my dad had recently found on a curb, cuddling up with my little pup. Except by this time he wasn't really little. He was the size of a very small but very fat horse. Though he thought his overwhelming frame could still comfortably fit within my comparatively diminutive lap. He curled up across me, like one of those circus bears trying to ride a teeny bicycle. I began to stroke his fur and sing his favorite song, "You Are My Sunshine," and as he drifted off to sleep he felt twice as chunky.

I thought it was endearing Mugsy had convinced himself he was still the size of a puppy but frustrated that I would now be trapped underneath a boulder for the next few hours. Still, my night had to be miles ahead of a family function filled with phony smiles and stilted conversation. Even if my company tended to lick his own crotch in front of me, at least I knew it was company I could rely on.

I was sure Mugsy's fur released some kind of tryptophan, because every time he fell asleep on me, I would inevitably doze off soon after. As I strained to stay conscious and finish my movie, a loud bang snapped me awake.

We now lived in a basement apartment, which is just as dreary as it sounds. The subterranean abode would not only flood during a heavy rain, but its windows would also amplify all the noises of the all-too-close street they faced. I assumed someone had hastily thrown some garbage in a can out front and went back to watching my movie. But then the bang happened again.

Mugsy leaped off my lap in a single bound, scratching my legs through my sweatpants. In an instant he was snarling and barking at the door, letting me know he did not like whoever was on the other side. I looked through the peephole and was startled to see a man slumped over in the hallway. I watched as he used all his strength to throw his body against the door again.

Mugsy was in full-on guard dog mode, his instincts for protection kicking in. He was not about to let anyone come in and harm the lady who serenades him. But instead of letting the hundred-pound furry security guard handle his business, I irrationally worried about what the guy on the other side of the door might do to him. Upon further inspection through the peephole, his mouth was foaming and his eyes were almost inhuman. "Rooooooooooooobeeeeerrrrtttttoooooo," he gutturally shouted. Oh. So this was what one of Dad's new friends looked like.

I naturally assumed the guy was on drugs and began to dial 911, but he had stopped throwing himself at the door, seemingly giving up on his search for my dad. Moments later there was a crack against one of the front windows and I almost screamed in response. The man wasn't gaining entry through the front door, so he figured he would just pop in through a window.

My mind raced. This man would soon easily crawl into the apartment. I needed to protect Mugsy. I was home alone. What would Kevin McCallister do? Realizing I did not have access to marbles, let alone the time to properly set up an effective human trap, I found the next best thing. A steak knife. My dad let us know Mr. Pointy was easily accessible inside of a kitchen drawer, in his own words, *If you ever need to shank a fool*. Well, here was a fool. And he needed shanking. Mugsy wasn't about to grow an opposable thumb and do it, so I guess I needed to step up.

I watched as the stranger's hands successfully punched a hole through the window screen. My heartbeat pulsed inside of my throat. Luckily he was so out of it, he couldn't process how to unlatch the lock to slide it up. But his dry, dirty hands roamed around the inside of the sill, desperately looking for a way in.

"Rooooooobeeeeerrrrttttttoooooo," he continued to yell as if Dad would happily greet him at the busted window frame. I dialed 911 on the landline while my hands shook around the rusty steak knife. I was okay for now. The police were on their way. If he kept fiddling around the lock, I would scare him off with the knife.

As I tried to calm myself down I saw his hand bend around the frame and grab hold of the lock. Fuck this noise, I'm going in. Screaming at the top of my lungs, I wildly waved my weapon at his arms. He shrieked, seemingly noticing my brandished blade, but it did nothing to stop his hands from fiddling around the lock. He pushed the screen up, dropped his hands to the sill, and lowered his head through the foot-tall opening. He was going to try to wriggle through the small gap instead of just continuing to lift the screen the whole way. His cracked-out mind was doing me a favor. As his hands tried to pull the rest of his body through, I uncontrollably stabbed at them.

Somehow over my banshee screams I heard the blade connect with skin, a thick and wet sound that made me gag in return. It seemed to do the trick, and he retreated in a flash. Minutes later the police arrived to scold me. "You know, that giant pit bull would probably make a great guard dog if you didn't lock him in a back room."

Now, I'm not saying stabbing an intruder is the smartest, or safest, thing in the world, but I must admit, getting myself out of a dangerous situation using nothing but quick thinking and balls of steel certainly made me feel stronger than I thought I was.

I felt more in control. I felt safer behind the strength of my own hands. But over time, merely reading a comic, watching someone else's story unfold in a role-playing game, or dreaming of one day being a pro wrestler wasn't enough to drown out the anxiety anymore. I thought I had found a way to stop my twitch, but I really just somehow traded it in for full-on obsessive-compulsive disorder. I found myself having to crack each knuckle in a very specific order after finishing every homework assignment. Before leaving a room I absolutely had to rub both palms on every edge and corner inside of it. Of course, I would wash my hands right after because I eventually needed to wash my hands after I touched literally anything. The delicate skin on my fingers began to crack and bleed after a particularly handsy day. The hand sanitizer I needed to have in my pocket at all times would burn when applied to the fissures, but at least I knew the germs were gone.

I started having trouble sleeping. At first any creak or noise I heard when the lights were off would make me fear someone was trying to break in again. And when that chill of paranoia ran down my spine, it was soon followed by the nauseating memory of the squishy sound of popping skin. By around 2 a.m. I would finally fall asleep. But only a few hours later my alarm would go off and I would need to get ready for school. My body began to anticipate the early alarm, and I would wake up a half an hour before it, making my night of sleep even shorter. As time went on I would take longer to fall asleep, and instinctively I'd wake up earlier and earlier. Ultimately these habits met somewhere in the middle and I became a bona fide insomniac. I needed to take action. But only my make-believe worlds of crime fighters and saviors had been able to soothe the beast in my brain. So I decided to step it up. I had found strength in control, so now I would control the narrative.

For every video game or anime that ended in "happily ever after," I would open a notebook and write the "ever after." I was creating fan fictions before I even knew what "fanfic" was. I would continue the stories I loved so much so they would always be with me. I could make the heroines say what I wish they had said before. But that wasn't enough. I then started drawing my own characters and creating original stories. When I lay awake in bed, unable to sleep before school, I would quietly crawl out of it, prop a flashlight onto my desk, open a notebook, and enter the worlds created by my own hand.

When stress would overcome me, or I had a fight with my mother, I would take a pencil to a blank sheet of paper and create a new protagonist who would defend me from pain. Writing and drawing seemed to be doing the trick. My mind calmed a bit. I still couldn't sleep, but now I only had to push my palms against the corners of the desk before leaving the bedroom. It was progress.

Even though my mind was now preoccupied, my body was itching to join the game. I had curbed my loose-hand ways a while back, after Ma had found out I was punching randos in school. If only there was a way someone would just let me hit them. Not out of rage, but for practice. I promised myself I would become my own superhero and enter the world of professional wrestling when I was of legal age, but I didn't want to wait that long. And that's when having all guy friends really paid off. My friends were into wrestling just as much as I was, and after discussing our dreams of squared circle stardom, we decided we would just create our own wrestling federation. At lunch and after school we would all meet in the park and practice the moves we had seen on TV. Since I was the only girl, I was designated as the referee so none of the guys had to feel bad about clotheslining me in the neck. But they would let me try moves on them after their matches. I would jump off plastic slides with a flying cross-body and practice dropkicks in the softer patches of grass, and each of the boys was kind enough to let me try out forearms on their faces. It was so, deeply, stupid. There's a reason they advise kids "Do not try this at home." Someone would always end up breaking a finger or a nose, and dozens of times the cops were called to kick us out of the park. Apparently actual children didn't like playing on bloody monkey bars. Pansies. But I was hooked. I was inspired. I wanted to inspire. I believed I was meant for better things than car living, break-ins, and glass baths. I would create my own way out.

FUSHIGI YUGI

Erica had worked hard and scored some scholarships to send her to a good college. After graduating, there was practically an Erica-shaped hole in our front door. She was not as understanding of our parents' devolving ways as I tried to be—as I needed to be. She, like Robbie before her, just wanted out.

She picked a school that would not be easy for our parents to drive to on a weekend, and she never looked back. I was happy for her, but also scared of what being alone in this place would mean for me. I was basically Claire Danes watching Kate Beckinsale walk out of the Thai prison at the end of *Brokedown Palace*. Or maybe I was as angst ridden as Claire Danes in *My So-Called Life*. Whatever, I just wanted to be Claire Danes. I decided to formulate my own plans of escape. I wanted to go to a school that would encourage my blooming creativity. My grades were ideal, and I was in the top 10 percent of my class, but I enjoyed writing and creating more than science and math. When I started to look at colleges, I found amazing options all over the United States that would help me grow as an artist. But moving so far from home seemed an impossible task. I worried for my parents.

Living without Robbie and Erica had, in a way, broken their spirits. Sure, your average parent understands that spreading your wings and flying from the nest is a natural, healthy, positive part of life. But Janet and Robert were not your ordinary parents. They were dependent on their children. Not only did we serve to bring order, tranquillity, and rational thinking to decision making and everyday life, but my parents relied on us for the most basic of things.

Robbie and Erica used their meager savings from part-time jobs as supermarket cashiers to help pay rent. Janet used our Social Security numbers to open cable accounts and home phone lines when too many unpaid bills piled up in her name.

Erica shouldered most of the burden, acting as a surrogate mother to us all. She would organize the bills that came through the mail and try to remind Ma and Dad to pay them on time. She would carry heavy loads of laundry several blocks, all by herself, to the Laundromat in town so we would all have clean clothes for the week. She would work overtime at ShopRite to make sure I had a gift on my birthday. She was such a little adult at a young age.

Once, when she was around ten, she cut herself while

preparing dinner and walked ten minutes to a CVS so she could steal a Band-Aid. There was no way we had enough money to buy a whole box. Unfortunately, she was caught in the act, but a kindhearted CVS employee, seeing how bloody her little finger was, snuck one bandage out of the pack and told her to take it and run.

Janet and Robert felt safer knowing there was someone else around to carry the burden, even if those hands were ridiculously tiny. I knew I couldn't just take off and leave them behind. I decided to try to find a school I could travel home from, so I could take care of my parents.

My perfect match was NYU. New York University's Tisch School of the Arts became my dream school. Not only could I study writing, performing, filmmaking, and animation, I would only be one train and one bus ride away from home. Just in case. The only problem was NYU is expensive as hell. We had no money. This seemed like a pickle. So I did some research. I found out my grades could help me get some grants and scholarships, and our household income being only slightly more than that of our apartment's roaches would help me qualify for financial aid. Ma had spent so long ruining her children's credit scores, hers had ample time to repair itself, and she would be able to apply for loans to pay for the rest. Basically, the financial burden of education would be something I could worry about in the future, after graduating.

The problem was what was asked of me in the present. I was required to apply for early admission to enter Tisch, and should I be accepted, I would need five hundred dollars to hold my spot in the freshman class.

I needed to start making my own money. I sold my collection of WWF magazines on eBay. Three days a week I got paid under the table to clean the bathrooms at a local day care. Between that and my future obsession with cardigan sweaters, I had all the birth control I would ever really need.

But twenty-five bucks a week to clean up baby poop was not going to get me where I needed to go. I entered various poetry and writing contests and ended up winning hundreds of dollars in first-place prizes. Not only was I awarded exactly what I needed to hold my dream spot in school, I had some money left over to spend on anything I could dream of. I had never held so much money in my hands. The possibilities seemed endless.

Now I just needed to get accepted. All my friends, many also applying early to NYU, were discussing safety and backup schools just in case the stacked odds were too much to overcome. That seemed ridiculous to me. I knew exactly what I wanted, and there was no way I would let any other possibility enter the world even through thought.

Why did everyone want to play it so safe? If you are tightrope walking between two skyscrapers, the last thing you want to do is look down. I chose full steam ahead. At the beginning of my senior year, I decided to apply to only one school, my dream school. Unfortunately for me, my anxiety reared its ugly head, mutating into what I now know was a hatchling of depression.

But at seventeen, I had no idea what was happening. All I knew was that sometimes I would stay awake an entire night thinking about death. The death of my loved ones and of myself. I would horrify myself with worst-possible scenarios and begin the next school day exhausted and paranoid. Some days, I would actually get three full hours of sleep and wake up feeling refreshed. I would have a great day at school and come home full of positivity. But the rush of good energy seemed to come crashing down hard and I would lock myself inside of the bathroom, pretending to be showering, and cry for twenty straight minutes.

It started to scare me. I couldn't pinpoint this feeling growing within my chest and gut. I just knew that something felt . . . missing. And no matter what I tried to do to feel complete, the hole just seemed to swallow all attempts, growing bigger, stronger, emptier.

My health began to fail. Somehow my mind's ailments conjured themselves into a physical form. My asthma came back with a vengeance and I now required a bulky machine called a nebulizer to be strapped to my face for a few hours a day to help open up my lungs. However, I used those hours to perfect my Psycho Mantis impression. I would eventually miss over thirty days of my senior year. Sometimes this was because I felt ill; more often, it was because I woke up feeling like I was cloaked in a lead blanket. I couldn't peel myself off the bed. I couldn't dress myself. I dreaded the idea of opening the front door and moving within the world while I felt so damn heavy. My parents supported my decision to stay home, because it meant we could hang out and watch TV together.

The actual process of applying to NYU began to haunt me. I had filled out my entire application—which interestingly enough included my own *Metal Gear Solid* fanfic—but I couldn't find the strength to mail it out. For weeks it lay on the top of my desk, mocking me. There was no way I could actually make it into such a prestigious school. I was a poor kid from Jersey. Those spots would be reserved for the rich kids who could actually afford it. I bet they didn't have to mop floors and chase down bare-ass, crying three-year-olds who forgot their pants in the bathroom, just to pay the deposit.

Every day I would pass the glowing folder holding the dozens of pages of fastidiously prepared essays and documents. It would call out *SEND ME! Put a goddamned stamp on my face!* But I would ignore it. On the last possible day to mail it in on time to meet the early admissions deadline, I grabbed the folder on my way out the door. But first, I figured I would comb through, just to make sure my work was up to snuff.

While I perused the mountain of papers I felt my heart beat a little bit faster. Sweat slowly soaked through the fabric beneath my underarms. My chest tightened. *Oh shit*, I thought. Was I having an asthma attack? I grabbed my nebulizer and flipped its switch, holding the mask to my face. This was a really embarrassing way to go out—death by paperwork.

But then I felt tears fill up the inside of the plastic mask. An asthma attack doesn't usually make me cry like a baby who forgot her pants in the bathroom. Something was wrong and I didn't know what. Hearing the ruckus, Ma worriedly ran out of her bedroom.

"What's happening? Are you having an asthma attack?"

"I don't think so. I just can't stop crying. I don't know why I'm crying and sweating so much," I responded, confused out of my face.

"Fine. You can stay home from school today if it means you'll stop acting crazy," she said, then returned to bed.

Well, at least I had an out from school. But what was happening to my body? I assumed it must be the application. Was my body trying to warn me it was all wrong? The solution was clear. I was going to have to tear it all up. It was garbage. I would just simply redo the entire application in one morning and get it to the post office before the day's cutoff.

I don't know what muse or pixie was watching over me, but somehow I actually rewrote all my questionnaires and essays in one sitting. I mailed the application out on time and even made it to school by fifth period. And I have almost zero memory of how. It's all just one big blur of sitting too close to a Compaq monitor from Rent-A-Center and different bodily fluids.

While I was lying in bed wearing Pikachu pajamas and watching Kids WB cartoons on a Saturday morning, my dad handed me a big envelope from the good people at NYU Admissions. I was accepted into early admission for Tisch. "I got in! I got into NYU!" I screamed while jumping on the bed, reminding myself to leave the Pokémon pj's out of the retelling of this beautiful moment. "That's nice, baby," Dad calmly mumbled while patting me on the top of the head like I was about to get a Beggin' Strip. It was much too early in the morning to expect enthusiasm. But lack of congratulations aside, I had accomplished a goal. I was the only student in my high school to make it into NYU that year. I had absolutely no idea how, but I did it. And nothing could bring me down.

Two weeks later, something brought me down. I had been saving all my money in the top left drawer of my writing desk. I loved my writing desk. My mother had brought it home from a patient's house after the person died and would clearly no longer be using it. It had a hutch resting on top that I filled with books, comics, the growing collection of action figures I had purchased for myself, and taped-up drawings of my anime creations. It was the most special place in the world. I would sit at my computer or the kitchen table to do homework, but the writing desk was reserved for entering the dozens of worlds I had created. Its drawers were filled with full notebooks, sketchbooks, a possible ghost, and a wad of cash I had earned writing poems and stories atop it.

When the time came to send a money order in to NYU to reserve my spot for the next year, I opened my secret hiding spot. And saw nothing. My money had vanished. As a stream of expletives flew out of my mouth, I racked my mind for all the possible scenarios. Maybe our second pit bull, Kagome (whom I named after the school-girl heroine in the anime *Inuyasha*), had taken it as a chew toy. She seemed like kind of a dick. Maybe I had accidentally placed it into the wrong drawer after gently spooning it the other night. Or maybe, when you hear hoofbeats you think horses, not zebras. I knocked on my parents' bedroom door like the FBI during a raid.

"Where is my money? Did you take my money?" I questioned the particle wood door.

It swung open and Ma appeared. "Yeah, baby, you told me I could."

"Wha . . . but . . . I said you could have a few bucks if you needed it. Like for eggs or rice." I was midblubber.

"Well, I needed it for rent. We all live here, don't we? Would you rather we live in a motel again?"

There was no point in fighting. There are some people that no matter how heinous their actions will always find a way to rationalize them. I spent days sulking. Opportunity was so very close to my reach, but it slipped away as quickly as it came. I was back at square boned.

At school I confided in Mr. Donnelly, a teacher who ran the Peer Mediation group I was a member of. Basically we were the school's solution to fighting and bullying. If two kids got in some sort of tiff, instead of being yelled at by teachers, we would be brought in to help them communicate safely and find a peaceful solution to their conflict. (I know, I know, the irony.) Mr. Donnelly was sympathetic. He offered to call NYU and ask for an extension of my payment deadline. Maybe I would find a way to scrub enough toilets and mop enough floors to make the five hundred dollars I needed.

I sat in his office as he called the financial office, my fingers nervously interlocked. Everything seemed to be going well. His kind approach and apparent faith in me sealed the deal, and I heard him thank them for bending the rules just this once. But then the woman on the other end of the line asked if she could speak to me for a moment.

"Miss Mendez? We would be happy to give you a few more weeks to hold your spot, but can I be honest with you for a moment? I don't mean to sound insensitive, but this is a very expensive school. If you are having trouble affording five hundred dollars, maybe you should consider . . . other options."

All I wanted to do was hang up the phone and cry. Well, I also wanted to graduate from NYU and then use my diploma as kindling to burn her home to the ground. But mostly, I wanted to cry. Looking back, I understand her point. It made sense. But at the time it was just another adult, someone I was supposed to trust to have my best interests at heart, who didn't have any interest in supporting me.

A few days later, as I was fiddling through my locker, probably wondering if "joining the circus" was still a thing, my close friend and fellow peer mediator, Sophie, jumped behind me with a giant smile on her face.

"Guess what we did?" she practically sang. As I scrolled through my Rolodex of mean responses that would surely wipe her smile off her face, she pushed a giant manila envelope into my arms. "Mr. Donnelly and the Peer Mediation group got together and went to every classroom in school collecting money. A lot of it is in change, but we did it! We raised almost the whole five hundred dollars you needed!"

My heart was a messy blender filled with appreciation, embarrassment, swallowed pride, and pure, unadulterated joy. Though it physically pained me to have to rely on anyone, let alone strangers, for help, I couldn't help but feel deeply moved. Kids had done something kinder, braver, and more generous than any grown-up I knew. And there was not one well-off person in that whole school. We were all flat broke, so the fact that they shared what little they had to help one of their own succeed is enough to occasionally restore my faith in humanity.

This was it. This time, everything was going to be okay. I was so sure of it.

CHAPTER 6

LIE TO ME

N ew York City holds a special place in my heart. It was the first city I saw live wrestling, at the legendary Madison Square Garden. I was just about to turn seventeen and already steadfastly believed I would be a pro wrestler one day. But actually witnessing the spectacle in person, experiencing the electricity in the sold-out arena, really sealed the deal for me.

For a few hours I actually got to live within the reality of my dream. That night it was no longer an out-of-reach, distant fantasy. It was tangible. It was real. Getting a taste of it only made me want more. Every time I would picture myself inside a wrestling ring, I imagined performing in front of the raucous New York City crowd I had once been a part of. And since then New York City had represented the pinnacle of success. It was the path to escaping my past. It was the destination at the end of a long, arduous journey.

When I moved into a dorm room in the heart of NYC's Greenwich Village to start my first year at New York University, I felt like I was finally where I belonged.

My mother had complained that I packed my things like someone who had no intention of returning. As we both stared at my barren bedroom, it was clear my entire life was now jammed into boxes labeled FRAGILE. I tried to assure her I was just being prepared, making sure I had everything I needed. But she was right. A part of me was so desperate to be on my own, far away from the memories of childhood, that I was trying to cut ties.

I hoped that this was what my parents needed too. I was the last child living at home and the requisite responsibilities to the household were overwhelming for an eighteen-year-old. A college freshman's only concerns should be schoolwork and parties, and part of me wanted to run toward that future without looking back. I thought if I showed them tough love, and let them fend for themselves for at least a year, maybe they would grow stronger. I knew I would need to check in, to make sure they were eating and paying the bills on time, but I hoped they would be able to take care of things from now on.

Moving my belongings into the dorm was a bittersweet experience. I felt the weight of responsibility that came along with entering college. I was officially an adult. And that pissed me off. Because I never really got to be a kid. I felt like I had been saddled with duties and worry from as early as I could remember, and the door to a carefree childhood was now firmly closed.

But despite my concern that walking through my dorm room threshold meant entering the "real world," I knew I was prepared for it more than any of my schoolmates. I was certain the majority of attendees at the prestigious school, the children of privilege, had never had to survive on dry noodles or shank a fool on Christmas Eve.

Even though the room was musty, had no air-conditioning on a ninety-five-degree August afternoon, and consisted of gray cement walls as inviting as a women's penitentiary, I thought it was the most beautiful place on Earth. Within these four walls all that would be asked of me was that I get good grades. Here I would learn to harness my creativity, turn it into a career, and make a better life for myself.

I would try to make this home.

And for a while, that was exactly what it became. I was surrounded by everything I needed. I lived right next to beautiful Washington Square Park and would walk to class every day with a Cuban coffee in hand and a skip in my step. New York City in the fall is a thing of beauty. With red and orange leaves crunching beneath my feet, I would pass by whatever Will Smith or Matt Damon movie was filming that day on my walk through the city streets that make up the NYU "campus." I would sit among writers, performers, and artists and get actual school credits for activities that had just been beloved hobbies only weeks before.

A moment of epiphany came one day in a writing class when my teacher suggested the most important rule of prose was "Write what you know." Everyone has their own life story, she advised, and drawing from that was the key to original and authentic work.

My whole life, after every trial or heartbreak, I had told myself it had happened for some unknown, greater reason. That it was happening to me because I was strong enough to handle it and capable enough to pass on the lessons I learned. In a way, this felt like exactly what she was talking about. Writing and storytelling could be my way to catharsis. Also, my roommate didn't believe in television, so I could play my PS2 uninterrupted all day long. This was exactly where I needed to be.

When Robbie and Erica hit the age of eighteen, they embraced their independence much as a facehugger in *Alien* embraces an unexpecting face. They leaped toward their new lives without looking back. Erica was studying to get a degree in education. Her days were also fully occupied with sorority life and a long-term boyfriend. Robbie had been honorably discharged from the army's Eighty-Second Airborne Division. Two tours of duty, one in Afghanistan and one in Iraq, had left him with severe PTSD—post-traumatic stress disorder. On the army's dime, he enrolled in college in a distant suburb of New Jersey.

Neither had the time nor desire to come home for visits or check in with phone calls. They wanted to find their place in the world somewhere far, far away from any reminder of where their journeys began. They each wanted to create newer, happier versions of themselves, and that meant cutting ties with painful memories.

I understood how they felt, but I had been the one left behind to witness how their decisions affected my parents. In Janet's and Robert's minds, they had truly tried their best. And their efforts were rewarded with the sound of cartoon tires burning rubber as they sped away. Now that I was free to do the same, I began to feel tremendous guilt in building a life of my own, guilt for desiring that clean slate. And so the pressure I felt to take care of my parents only intensified. There was no one else who could do the job. I tried to make myself believe I could handle the burden of parenting my parents while becoming my own adult. For a while I was pretty good at the balancing act.

Every weekend I would take the train, followed by the bus, and travel for two hours to visit the parentals. I would finish my schoolwork in my old bedroom and help with chores around the apartment: cleaning, cooking, food shopping. Over time it began to feel like the chores at home were piling up. Every surface seemed dustier than the week before; the same dishes filled the sink. It was as if time hadn't moved while I was away at school for the week. When a class assignment would make it impossible to travel home, I would worry about how much work was piling up for me back in New Jersey.

What had changed? Why did my parents seem to be letting

things fall by the wayside? I became increasingly confused when upon entering the apartment one Saturday morning, my normally prickly mother greeted me with an all-consuming hug. The warm embrace took me aback, as tenderness had become a vestigial part of her ever-changing personality.

She enveloped me, letting her body slowly go limp on mine, for an uncomfortable length of time. As she ran her hands through my hair, her chin resting on my shoulder, I could feel the wetness of her tears begin to trickle down my arm. "What's wrong?" I asked. "Nothing. Just happy to see you," she meekly responded. I thought about that welcome-home hug on the entire trip back to school Sunday night. Something was very different about my mother.

I had gotten a job on a student-made film and wasn't able to return home for a few weeks while working on it. When I finally made it back to Jersey, I was horrified by what I saw when I walked through the door. Again Ma had thrown her weight against me, almost collapsing in relief to see me. And as she stroked my hair she whispered, "I used to have pretty, long hair too." I looked at the scalp nuzzling into my neck and saw it was littered with bald spots.

"What did you do?" I asked, alarmed.

It sounded as if a weakened child spoke using her mouth. "Sometimes I get a little nervous and I start pulling it out. Now it's all gone."

I didn't understand what was happening. All I knew was that it felt as if my mother was slowly melting away.

Each week she seemed smaller and daintier. Weaker and more vulnerable. The same woman who had scared the ulcers into my intestines was now a dog without bark or bite. When I questioned my father about her ripping patches of hair out of her scalp, he didn't seem too worried. "She's just sad all her kids left her."

The phrasing of this was grating. *Left her.* Children are supposed to grow into adults. The logical side of me knew that much. They are supposed to leave the nest and build lives of their own. I understood that Robbie and Erica had grown distant, and I felt bad for my parents, but it felt as if my dad was embracing the pity party a little too strongly. Parents should encourage their children to go out into the world and grow as humans, not make them feel guilty about it. Going to college is not a form of abandonment.

Somehow, their immature personalities had taken our development and natural life progression as a slap in the face, as an ungrateful insult. And now, along with the hard adjustment of life as a freshman in a challenging school, I was saddled with the responsibility of keeping my mother from completely falling apart.

"I think maybe she should talk to someone. Like a doctor. Or maybe a psychiatrist," I hesitantly told Dad, knowing it would not go over well. The Mendez family did not believe in psychiatry. They did not believe in mental illness. They would not allow their brains to be so weak.

"I don't ever want to hear you talk like that again." He brushed the subject off. "Your mother is not a crazy person."

I went home every weekend. My college friends would complain I didn't hang out with them or go to parties, and I tried to find any excuse other than explaining that I was too busy trying to keep my mother alive. We were eighteen-year-olds on very different wavelengths.

I lay awake at night, worried about what I would find when I arrived home each Saturday morning. In my heart I feared coming home to a dead body. Using the little money I had from part-time jobs, I bought minutes for a prepaid cell phone and made sure it was used for nothing else but calling my mother every single day. (Yeah, "minutes" were a thing, robot children of the future.) Though it was a decade ago, it was still pretty embarrassing to not have a real cell phone. Guys would ask for my number and I couldn't give it to them. Which was probably for the best since I was in no condition to share my bizarre life with anyone. "I spend my time reading, writing, and providing a twenty-four-hour suicide hotline for my mother. And what do you do?"

I was overwhelmed. Ma had begun spending every hour of her day curled up in bed, yanking at her hair and sucking on her thumb. She had devolved into a wordless, infantilized victim, and I had no idea how to help. During one visit, I discovered her entire body was now ravaged with bright red bedsores.

Was this my fault? Did I really abandon my own mother? Maybe if I hadn't gone to college, if I had stayed home and gotten a full-time job, she wouldn't be so broken.

That was the night my random crying fits began. While showering I spaced out and found myself crying in a ball on the floor of the bathtub. Throughout the school week all I could think about was the sight of those bedsores. My mother's body was beginning to fall apart along with her mind. I called Erica, hoping she could help alleviate some of the burden.

"She's just being dramatic. Like she's always been. Don't fall for it, AJ." She was in a rush to head out with her sorority friends and couldn't talk long.

I was filled with rage and envy. I was so mad at her for writing off this ordeal as an act, as if I was wasting my time worrying. But I knew in my heart something was deeply wrong. I was also painfully jealous. Erica was enjoying the college experience and had been for two whole years. She was finally getting to act her age, and though she deserved every second of it, I was envious I couldn't. I had grown increasingly isolated, every second spent only on schoolwork and momsitting.

I felt a crying fit coming on and hid inside the bathroom so my roommate wouldn't see what a mess I was. Running the water, I collapsed onto the bathmat, while simultaneously making a mental note to yell at my roomie for never vacuuming. I felt helpless. There was no way I was strong enough to save my mother on my own. But why did I always have to be strong? For once, I just wanted to fall apart and have someone else pick up my tiny pieces.

I felt so alone. I wasn't experiencing life the way other freshmen were. I could no longer take jobs on student films or attend club meetings, let alone spend time partying with my roommate. I was too busy mom-ing my mom.

Eventually, I became too busy to even sleep. With so much responsibility on my shoulders, my mind raced at night trying to find solutions. My insomnia returned stronger than ever. Some weeks I would spend a consecutive forty-eight hours awake. A fun side effect was once falling asleep while sitting at my desk in class. My giant melon of a head just crashed forward, forehead first onto the hard surface in front of me. My classmates' amused gasps woke me up.

But insomnia felt like a minor quirk to my personality. For the most part, I felt like I was doing my best to keep it together. I did begin exhibiting some odd behavior, though, besides face-planting in class. One afternoon I prepared to walk downstairs to the cafeteria to pack up a plate for the day. My financial aid package didn't provide me with a generous meal plan, only allowing me to swipe my card ten times a week. With no money to spend at the grocery store, I would have to make every trip to the cafeteria really count.

I would, naturally, get a take-out box because hungrily eating alongside hundreds of rich kids started to make me nervous, like every eye was fixed on me. Like every nose could sniff out the scent of poverty on me. I would ignore the judgmental looks as I piled three meals' worth of food onto one plate and scurry back upstairs to the safety of my dorm room. I would store the extra food in my small refrigerator for dinner that night and eat at my desk where no one could make me feel small.

One day as I readied to make the trip downstairs, I stopped as my hand reached for the doorknob. I pulled it back and sat on my bed. *Do I really need to eat today?* There were so many people downstairs, so many eyes that could burn into the flesh on my face. I thought about how hungry I was and decided, *Yes, of course I need to stock up on food for the day.*

So I stood up, walked toward the heavy metal door, reached out for the handle, and immediately jerked my hand back. Turning around, I walked back to my bed and sat down. I crossed my legs and began to shake them. Maybe I didn't need food after all. It's just food. It just fuels your body and gives you energy and . . . *Oh God, am I really going to starve myself to avoid human contact?*

I rushed the door, motivated to kick myself in the ass and stop acting so ridiculously, but as I reached the door I was frozen with fear. I could not, for the life of me, find the strength to open the door and enter the world. I was safe in these two hundred square feet of isolation. Opening the door meant seeing people, talking to people, being judged for scooping too much mashed potatoes onto my plate, listening to the card swipe guy tell me to smile more, walking past the lobby's security guards who probably thought I was a loiterer, and *Son of a bitch, I can't breathe!*

And so, over trying to decide to turn a door handle, I had another panic attack. Except this time I had no nebulizer to strap on my mouth, and no one around to calm me down. I turned the shower on as cold as possible and jumped in fully clothed. After a few freezing minutes, I had everything under control.

A few weeks later, while running to get to a class on time, I stopped in my tracks, distracted by a poster pinned to a bulletin board. DON'T JUMP! the poster implored. It listed the names and numbers of several school counselors who were available if anyone needed someone to talk to about their problems.

At the time, NYU had tragically lost several students to suicide. Over the past few years, almost a dozen students had jumped from their tall dorm room windows or over the railing in the high-rise library to their deaths. As a result, all the dorm room windows had been configured to only crack open a few inches, and the library railings had been barricaded. It made for a somber reminder of how stressful college, especially in a busy city, can be for some kids.

As I read the poster I thought of my mother. I wished I could find someone for her to talk to. But if I couldn't convince her to seek out help, maybe I could seek it out for her. Maybe by just relaying my mother's problems to a counselor I could be given advice on how to help her. Jotting down one of the phone numbers, I felt a small sense of excitement. Perhaps I had found the answers I was looking for.

Sitting down with a counselor for the first time was an awkward experience. I had talked to a guidance counselor in high school, but that was primarily about applying to college and why there were so many curse words in my poetry. I had never locked eyes with someone who was so interested in finding out what was bothering me.

In a way, I felt like I was ignoring everything my parents

had taught me. We weren't supposed to reach out to anyone for help. We weren't supposed to admit there was a weakness inside of us. I felt like I was betraying my mother by exposing her secrets to a stranger. But I didn't think I had any other option.

I kept trying to explain that this visit wasn't really for me, it was for my mom, but the counselor didn't seem to pay that any mind. Instead he kept asking me questions about myself. "How does that make you feel?" "What do you think that means?" "How is this affecting you?" I told him about my panic attacks and my insomnia, and I mentioned the sporadic crying but tried to explain that these were all just normal reactions to stress.

"They're not normal," he plainly put it. "I think you're experiencing depression. I would like to refer you to a psychiatrist."

I almost stormed out. How dare he assume I was broken. I was just trying to help someone else who really was falling apart, and maybe I wasn't handling it so well. This guy had known me for an hour's time and wanted to deem me crazy.

But as the session went on, I began to actually listen.

"Depression is not something you choose. It is a chemical imbalance, which can sometimes be hereditary. If your mother is indeed experiencing these symptoms, there's a chance you can be prone to them as well." He was so calm and matter-of-fact. I was a smart kid, but somehow I hadn't connected those dots. With certainty, I had decided my mother was experiencing some sort of mental illness. But if I would've taken the time, I could've noticed my own reflection in my mother's weary eyes.

Realizing the dark force swallowing her up was sizing me up for its next meal felt simultaneously like a ton of bricks had been lifted off and laid on my shoulders. I finally had answers for questions I didn't even know I had. But now I was left with more than just my mother's brain to worry about.

"If you have a deep cut, you go to a doctor and get a stitch. If you have a cold, you go to a doctor and get medicine. So what makes having something wrong with your brain any different?"

No one had ever explained it to me like that. So simply. So nonjudgmentally. I felt like an idiot for wasting so much time being too ashamed to recognize what was happening in my own head. For so long I had denied what I was feeling out of fear. I didn't want to accept that something could be wrong with me. I didn't want to feel different. All I needed was for someone to explain that there didn't have to be any shame in taking care of yourself.

But now I needed to figure out where to start. Convincing my parents to see a doctor would be an uphill battle. Convincing myself was even harder. But nevertheless, I made an appointment with the psychiatrist he recommended. I was terrified of what other dark spots on my brain this doctor would shine a light on. But the school was willing to pay for the sessions, and getting free treatment seemed like an offer, no matter how terrifying, I couldn't refuse.

IT'S DANGEROUS TO GO ALONE

The first time I went to see a psychiatrist I was dressed like Carmen Sandiego and was just as determined to not be found. Walking into the waiting room, wearing a hat lowered so dramatically it covered my eyes, I was on edge and deeply embarrassed. What if I saw someone I knew? Would that mean they were crazy too? Should we politely ignore each other? Or was there some sort of existing acknowledgment in the psychiatric community, like a gang sign we could flash to each other?

Maybe it was pointing to the side of the head and making a circling motion with the index finger while crossing the eyes.

I was sure the office receptionist, growing numb to the revolving door of Nutter Butters, was greeting me with apathy. When she handed me a clipboard without making eye contact and robotically instructed me to "Fill this out and give it to the doctor," I instead heard "Oh, great, another Looney Tune. Is Nurse Ratched on call today?"

Trying to get a lay of the land, I scanned the empty waiting room, reading every cheesy advertisement for antidepressants. *Once I get this depression under control, I'll finally be able to jump rope in an open field,* I thought. Between the cold receptionist and the overwhelming amount of trite "Life is better on drugs" flyers, I wanted to bolt. But entering the psychiatrist's office, decorated in soft white tones, potted orchids, and two plushy couches, I calmed. Noticing a box of tissues resting on a coffee table between the love seats, I snorted, thinking it was sort of presumptuous and honestly a little vain to believe each patient would fall into a sobbing revelatory mess in his company.

The doctor entered the room with a smile. He was warm and welcoming, which, considering how the nerves I was feeling made my body uncontrollably shake, was clearly essential.

"How would you describe your family?" was the first can of worms he asked me to open. I thought about the question for close to thirty seconds, opened my mouth, and immediately imploded in tears. Perhaps I would be in need of that tissue box after all.

For the next forty minutes we discussed my unconventional upbringing and the pressure I was still feeling. Going to a school counselor, though helpful, had ultimately felt like a sterile, clinical experience. "You are sick. Go get help" was the essential theme of the visit. And that was what I was expecting out of this session as well. But something about being in a cozy room across from a person who genuinely wanted to help was surprisingly comforting.

The psychiatrist suggested I see a therapist to continue exploring all the feelings that were bubbling beneath the surface. I hadn't realized that a psychiatrist's main focus is diagnosis and treatment. I would have to move forward with a therapist if I wanted to focus on sorting out my muddled mind. He officially diagnosed me with depression and wrote a prescription for antidepressants.

Leaving his office, I felt a sense of relief. I had a tangible enemy to fight now. This was probably what my mother was suffering from as well. And though finally having some answers made me feel ten pounds lighter, I was brought back down to earth by the impossibility of my next steps. It was hard enough having to walk into one cold office and bare my goose-bumped soul, but having to do it for the third time with a whole new medical professional was a lot to ask of someone just starting to experiment with treatment.

Even more terrifying was the small plastic bottle I picked up from a corner pharmacy. The tiny pills rattled around inside of it like a musical instrument. I wasn't sure how I felt about being medicated. Having a father who had been arrested multiple times for drug possession, finding only Budweiser in the fridge while my stomach growled, and witnessing firsthand the scary altered states of users had made me resentful toward any kind of drugs and alcohol. At the age of ten I had promised myself I would never touch them, and at eighteen I had stayed true to that promise. But could a prescription given by a medical professional, a stitch to an unseen wound, be thrown into the same category? I wasn't sure.

Tackling the easier task first, I made an appointment with

the therapist the psychiatrist had recommended. And thank whatever god might be real that I did.

First of all, the therapist's receptionist was much kinder. The waiting room was decorated with hilarious inspirational art, not unlike the "Hang in there!" kitten-holding-on-to-a-tree-limb poster I have as my laptop screensaver. The therapist was quirky and sweet, and again, I felt safe.

Giving therapy a chance was one of the best decisions I have ever made. I had never had someone's complete focus and attention before. I had never been asked how I felt about being in the situations I had been dragged through in life. For the first time I felt like I was allowed to break down. I didn't have to be the strong leader of the Mendez clan. I didn't have to hold everything together. I handed the reins over to someone else and allowed myself to melt into an almost euphoric defenselessness. I found the one place on earth it was safe to let my guard down.

The therapist suggested I start a journal. Each week he planned on giving me a different essay assignment I would bring into the office to read aloud. He said it would be like an exercise for my emotions, which were apparently a little pudgy. The homework ranged from writing "a letter to my past self," to "a letter to my future daughter," to "a list of things I wish I could yell at my mother," to "a list of things I am ashamed of." At first this seemed just as corny as the inspirational quotes framed on the wall behind him, but I actually came to find them surprisingly helpful. I also enjoyed cutting out letters from magazines to tape a hodgepodged "DIARY OF AN UNFIT MIND" across my journal's cover like a serial killer. It felt good to connect to writing again. Filling an empty page had always been my own form of therapy, except now I was the subject. After a few sessions, I could feel myself growing calmer and stronger. It was almost too good to be true. Would it be this easy to fix my mother?

"Is this all it takes? A self-help journal, some cry sessions, and one day I'll wake up feeling normal?" I asked the kind-eyed man sitting across from me.

"That's a loaded question. I'm not sure how you want me to answer it."

"Lie to me."

I thought therapy would not only help me, but more important provide me with a convincing argument to take back to my mother, persuading Ma of her need for treatment. I would find a way to fix her before she was too far gone.

But soon I would realize I was too late.

"You need to come home," Erica frantically said the second I picked up the phone. "Ma overdosed."

DIARY OF AN UNFIT MIND

THINGS I SHOULD BE MORE EMBARRASSED ABOUT

Shame is the one thing that prevents us from walking through a supermarket stark-ass nude when we feel like we're having a really good ab day. It is what stops us from telling even our closest confidant of that sex dream we had about Hilary from *Love It or List It*. And though shame can protect us from extreme embarrassment, it can be detrimentally inhibitive. Personally, I lost all my shame the second I had to participate in a limbo contest on international television. And since then there is not a damn thing that has the power to embarrass me. I am in charge of my own shame. In the interest of full disclosure and proving myself right, here is a complete list of things I should probably be more embarrassed about, or at the very least have the good sense to never tell anyone.

1. Chopsticks are beyond my comprehension. No matter how hard I try to master them, I always end up looking like an arthritic victim of an arm-wrestling accident.

2. Swimming will surely be the death of me. I can't swim because during my formative years the only pool available to me was a public one our local newspaper proudly described as "back in business now that police have recovered all hypodermic needles."

3. I was the first in line at my local theater to see *Pokémon: The First Movie* on opening night. While wearing an unlicensed knockoff Pikachu T-shirt. I was also first in line to see *Yu-Gi-Oh!: The Movie*, while wearing a "blue eyes white dragon" glow-in-the-dark T-shirt. Because I'm a grade-A gangster.

4. I believe technology has a vendetta against me. It's mostly just the automatic stuff, e.g., auto-flush toilets, motion sensor faucets, sliding doors at the supermarket entrance. I am convinced that they purposefully refuse to acknowledge my existence and that they receive a perverse pleasure out of making me feel like an idiot and/or Bruce Willis in *The Sixth Sense*.

5. I believe bugs have a vendetta against me. If there is a mosquito floating around a large group, it will only bite me. And it will bite me thirty times. Every bee instinctively senses my fear and chases me indoors. On separate occasions, a fly, a ladybug, and a moth have kamikaze'd into my open mouth.

6. I always cry during the "Something There" musical montage in *Beauty and the Beast*. The Beast doesn't know how to use a goddamn spoon, so he just shoves his face into the bowl of whatever mystery porridge they were eating, and then everyone makes him feel really uncomfortable about it. Damn. I teared up just typing that. In fact, watching anyone eat while hungry generally makes me want to burst into tears. There's just something both adorable and pitiable about really shoveling it in. Side note, Belle has some pretty intense Stockholm syndrome, no?

7. I once had very real feelings for the fictional video-game character Solid Snake. And *Buffy's* Angel. And Seto Kaiba. And Spike Spiegel. And Vegeta. I'm talking intense and confusing feelings of romantic devotion. I was sure that behind the dark, brooding angst, curmudgeon demeanor, and tortured pasts these gravelly voiced antiheroes were capable of at least an ounce of love and . . . oh crap. My marriage suddenly makes complete sense.

8. I burn all my food. On purpose. Burgers. Bacon. Cheese. Hell, I even burn my eggs. Every douchebag who thinks they're being incredibly original by screaming "blasphemy" from their ivory douche tower when I order my steak well done needs to take it down a few notches. Rare meat makes me feel like I'm chomping into a human forearm.

9. I am incapable of eating alone at a restaurant. I don't understand how anyone can do that without crying into their beet salad. They are clearly stronger people than I am. There is no amount of pretending to be busy on my phone that could save me in that situation. And forget going to a movie alone. If I ever tried to purchase a ticket to a movie all by my lonesome, I'm sure I would spontaneously combust into flames.

10. I fear escalators. I eagerly await the day I can step onto an escalator without quietly whispering to myself, "Careful . . . careful."

11. I keep cereal boxes in the refrigerator. I keep bags of chips in there too. I'm not a monster. I grew up in such shitty apartment buildings, if any opened bag or box of food was left out overnight, it would undoubtedly be pillaged by a swarm of cockroaches. And when you're six, it is very easy to mistake a floating roach for a raisin. Understandably, I was scarred for life.

12. I peed the bed when I was eight. The pee traveled so far while I slept it actually touched the nape of my neck. When I woke up, I simply tiptoed into the bathroom, washed my clothes in the sink, put the wrung-out-but-still-soaking-wet clothes onto my body, and crawled back into bed. I'd like to take this moment to apologize to my sister for letting her sleep in a puddle of my urine, as well as blaming it on her in the morning.

The Mendez children. Erica is quietly considering squeezing my ribs until I pop.

Adorably evil.

Flashing the horns on Easter Sunday.

A crab who hates forced family functions (*from left to right:* me, Erica, Janet, Robbie, and Robert).

Caterpillar-browed captain of my 7th grade Academic Bowl's winning team.

Celebrating my 18th birthday like an official adult.

Signing autographs for my first trading cards.

I was the referee for one of the greatest title matches in wrestling history.
Mike Mastrandrea

The fitting for my Kane mask. Skipping around the ring dressed as a tiny demon was one of my all-time favorite moments.

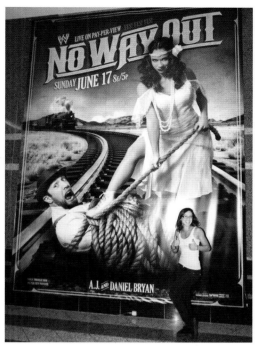

In front of my first pay-per-view poster, busting out one of the two poses I know.

An official Mattel prototype of me as Kane. The outfit I wore in this segment was an homage to the Queen of Crazy, Harley Quinn.

Opening *Raw* the night after my heel turn. Fun fact: I almost fell off the ladder during rehearsals.

My finishing move, a submission called The Black Widow.
Mike Mastrandrea

Ugly crying after winning the championship.
Mike Mastrandrea

In the locker room, moments after beating the holy hell out of each other.

My controversial "Pipebomb-shell" promo, in which I tore everyone new holes, resulted in almost a year of title defenses against every single female on the roster . . .
Mike Mastrandrea

A final bow. *Mike Mastrandrea*

. . . And culminated in defending the title against the entire roster at one time during my first WrestleMania match.

Jonathan Bachman/AP Images for WWE

Just an ordinary day at the office.

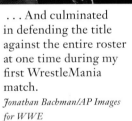

Seriously, guys, a completely ordinary day.

Eve trying to convince me it's not my fault that she's retiring.

When I was on a show at MSG, I found the exact seats my father and I had sat in years earlier.

Heterosexual life partners in Paris.

I climbed Lion's Head Mountain in South Africa and then asked to piggyback down.

Erica fixing my hair before my wedding. She's excited I am about to be someone else's problem.
Cathy and David Photography

Erica, Dad, and me. He flew more than twelve hours to give away his favorite daughter.
Cathy and David Photography

These are my special occasion chucks because they're covered in glitter.
Cathy and David Photography

Nerds.
Cathy and David Photography

Erasing my Google
search history.
Cathy and David Photography

KEEP OFF

I hope one day to find a love as
strong as Phil and Larry's.
Esther Lin Photography

Me and all my friends.
Cathy and David Photography

CHAPTER 7

THE ROBIN HOOD OF THE EXPRESS CHECKOUT LANE

When Grandpa got sick, Dad had traveled back to Puerto Rico to help care for him. He was concerned about leaving Ma alone in New Jersey for a few weeks, but I had promised I would do my best to help out. Unfortunately, a short time later I received a call from him letting me know Grandpa had passed. Dad, never one to let his guard down, was uncharacteristically emotional. I had never heard my father's voice crack with grief. It was unsettling. I didn't know how I could help, but I offered it anyway.

"Actually, if you could break the news to your mom, I'd really appreciate it. I've got a lot of other things to worry about," he asked while fighting tears.

"Of course. I can do that."

Coffee makes everything better. So I had stopped at the Dunkin' Donuts a block from home before seeing Ma. The employees knew all the Mendez clan by name, since Dad had befriended them upon moving into the neighborhood. They were kind enough to let him open a tab of sorts to get coffee and baked goods on credit and never made him feel uncomfortable or rushed into paying it back. Dad had to swallow his pride while asking a lot of different owners of local bodegas for credit over the years, and so it was refreshing there was one store in town that treated him with respect, kindness, and generosity.

I bought my mother a blueberry muffin and a French vanilla coffee and made my way to her front door. I had expected her to take the news badly, since Grandpa had opened his home to us and because she empathized with Dad's loss. What I did not expect was for her to wail like a dying animal and hit the floor. The sounds that came out of her were not from this world. She lay shaking facedown on the floor, and using all my strength, I could not budge her from that spot.

Yes, I expected her to be sad. We all were. But she did not have a close relationship with her husband's dad. I tried to rationalize her behavior by telling myself that everyone grieves in different ways, but something still felt dangerously off.

A week later, a psychiatric hospital found Erica's phone number in Ma's belongings and let her know our mother was involuntarily admitted. Having to deal with the stress of being home alone while my father was still in Puerto Rico, Janet took an almost deadly combination of pills to try to ease her mind. Realizing she was in trouble, she called 911 and reported her accidental overdose. But the hospital considered the overdose a suicide attempt. Her bizarre and aggressive behavior while being treated led them to believe she had suffered a complete mental breakdown and they admitted her against her will to their psychiatric unit.

After a month, Ma not only came home with dozens of crayon drawings she made during therapy sessions and a story about a nurse stealing her Twizzlers (which if true, means that nurse deserves to be swiftly kicked in the crotch), but also a much-needed diagnosis. Janet had bipolar disorder. And as discovered through weekly therapy, she had been suffering from its effects for most of her life.

Without any of us knowing, she had recently visited a doctor who misdiagnosed her with depression. Antidepressants can have adverse effects on someone with bipolar disorder, and the doctors at the hospital blamed this for her suicide attempt.

I thought it was sadly ironic how my mother and I had both secretly sought out treatment at almost the exact same time. We had both initially been diagnosed with depression. Now that I learned she was misdiagnosed, I wondered if it was possible I had been as well. But her bipolar disorder seemed so severe, so consuming, I brushed the thought off. There was no way I was as sick as the woman I was now helping fill out disability paperwork.

Ma had to enter a government-funded disability program to be able to afford proper medication. Because of her disability status, Ma was no longer considered capable of paying the student loan she had taken out to help send me to NYU.

I could no longer afford to go to school. And honestly, my head was not in the right space to continue anyway. I couldn't focus on anything. I started missing assignments and skipping whole classes. And even though at the end of the semester I had straight As, my series of unfortunate events led to my leaving NYU.

I was heartbroken. I felt like a failure. All I had wanted was to escape the grip of my small town and create my own future for myself, and yet I let circumstances take me down. In the months that followed, I considered every wrong move I had made, playing out countless possible scenarios that could have ended things differently for me. After flying so close to the sun, I was now a cashier at Pathmark Supermarket and living with my parents. The almost mighty had fallen very, very far.

When you have a job that requires you to serve other people, many parts of that job will, unequivocally, suck a top hat full of dicks. Whether you are a janitor at a day care, a cashier at a supermarket, a secretary, a waiter, or a valet driver—the best part of someone's day is going to be shitting atop you. So try and wear a hat, a raincoat, and asshole repellent.

You can tell a lot about individuals by how they treat the people they believe are beneath them—people who cannot help them get promoted, who cannot report their actions to human resources, who don't have their level of education or a fraction of their bank account. It is scary to realize what some- one is capable of when no one is watching. When no one will hold them accountable for their actions. Basically, it's the exact same attitude people have when using Twitter, but in real life.

When you have a job on the lowest tier, when you are meant to be subservient and at the beck and call of someone else, most people will not care about how you are being treated. No one will notice. Working in the service industry means, more often than not, people will look right through you. Sure, you may feel indignant when your barista forgets to say "thank you" and spells your name wrong on a paper cup, but that is only thirty seconds of your day. Consider how many assholes this barista has had to deal with in the last five hours. How many people have not returned his "thank you"? How many douchebags have spoken to him rudely or questioned his intel- ligence? "Did you hear me say 2 percent milk? That milk must be 2 percent. If it's not 2 percent, I will drop dead right here on your counter and there's a long line behind me, buddy." It's human nature to want to feel in control. But many people never get that satisfaction. And so when they are in the pres- ence of those they regard as mere commoners who ring up their coffee order or bag their groceries, they will excise their control to make them feel better about their shitty existence.

My father is literally the only person I have ever known who actively tries to engage any and all humans who surround him. I have watched him ask stock boys how their day is going and giggled at how truly shocked and unaccustomed they were to having someone acknowledge their presence. Everyone is equal in his eyes. Because as he once eloquently explained, "Life is like a wheel. Some days you're on top and some days you're on the bottom. What's the fucking difference?" And that's the mentality I have tried to employ throughout my life and career—friends, strangers, interns, lighting crew, writers, bosses, what's the fucking difference?

It was an attitude I wish more people had when I was a janitor, a cashier, and eventually a secretary. The smallest act of someone smiling at me, saying "thank you," or even just making eye contact helped remind me I was an actual human being and not a robot designed to nonjudgmentally swipe customers' lambskin condoms and smile while being yelled at for expired coupons.

I tried to make the most of being a cashier. Even though I was making minimum wage, I tried to help pay the rent, and I often spent my meager checks bringing home discounted food from Pathmark.

I couldn't afford to go to therapy anymore, and I was too afraid to try the antidepressants hidden in my underwear drawer, so I spent some time researching homeopathic methods to overcoming depression. I tried everything from St. John's wort, to B_{12} pills, to fish oil. And maybe those are all kooky placebos, but it felt good to try to take control. Putting the effort in and being proactive was in itself therapeutic. I would feel like I was onto something when my panic attacks and anxiety would eventually subside for long periods of time, but the heightened nerves were only replaced by inexplicably deadened ones. It seemed my brain's only options were to run sprints or to shut down completely. I wasn't sure which was better.

The whole world seemed to be drenched in gray, like a foggy mist hung in the air, and everything had a little less life. Nothing pushed me out of bed in the morning. Instead I felt as if my body were eight hundred pounds and I had to peel myself off the sheets. Things I once found excitement and entertainment in barely sparked my interest. My sketchbooks collected dust, while my gaming consoles were only used to get me through the repetitive sleepless nights. I lost count of how many times I got off a shift at 6 p.m., went home to eat the Pathmark find of a 99-cent Banquet microwave dinner, and just played *Metal Gear Solid: Snake Eater* until my next shift at 10 a.m. Even food lost its taste, as if every meal was just made out of dry, plain oatmeal.

I wanted to worry about these changes, but I didn't have the energy. It was as if my brain knew something was wrong but my heart was just too numb to give a shit. The only solace that gave me was I no longer felt sad about leaving school. I no longer cried about it every night. I just felt . . . nothing.

But I did learn some very valuable life lessons while bagging groceries. Because a grocery store is basically just a microcosm of human behavior.

If you carelessly knock over items on a shelf, you probably have a very messy home. If you don't notice you have dropped unwrapped tomatoes on the floor, you probably take your wealth and ability to fill a fridge with food for granted. If you enter a "10 Items or Less" express checkout lane with a fully stocked cart, you are probably inconsiderate and selfishly put your own needs before others'. And if you are the type of person who doesn't return your shopping cart to the proper place, but instead leave it in the middle of a parking lot for a teenager to clean up after you, you probably have a mother who cries every night because she gave birth to a monster.

The hardest part about working around food in a low-income neighborhood was witnessing how hard it can be for some people to feed their families. I was unlucky enough to ring up several people whose credit cards got denied or "Family First" food stamp cards hit their limit. Watching someone burn with embarrassment as they have to leave bags of groceries behind, and then having to restock dinosaur-shaped nuggets that were clearly meant to feed a little kid, really ate away at me.

I remembered walking the aisles of ShopRite when I was about five years old, holding my mother's hand. Erica stayed back, sleeping in the car with Dad, because she had a nasty cold. We walked through the store briskly and were on our way out without having made a purchase, when a security guard grabbed my mother's arm. He pulled her hand out of her coat pocket to reveal a stolen bottle of children's Tylenol. I guess the security guard had seen her swipe something but didn't realize what it was. "I'm sorry. My baby is sick in the car," she pleaded with him. He was clearly stricken with a crisis of conscience. "You shouldn't shop here again," he said as he replaced the bottle into her pocket and hurried her out the door. I never forgot that small act of illegal kindness.

Was it wrong to give something away, just because it wasn't yours? Would anyone truly get hurt by stealing from a rich corporation to give to the poor? As a fully formed adult I can sit here and tell you that breaking the law in any way is a deeply stupid move that can have disastrous consequences. But as an eighteen-year-old with nothing to lose (note to self: research statute of limitations) I gave literally zero fucks about what was right or wrong.

Young mothers would approach my register and hesitantly place their baby formula and cereals on the belt. "Can you let me know when it gets close to fifty dollars? I don't have more than that left on my card," they would say, referring to their limited, government-funded EBT card. It is basically a debit card that holds someone's food stamp allowance. The items you can purchase with it are restricted to essentials like dairy, vegetables, and bread, and it cannot be used to purchase non-food items like soap, vitamins, medicine, or even hot foods from the supermarket food bar. These are considered "luxury items" not "necessities." According to the government, diapers are considered a luxury and thus cannot be bought using food stamps.

I would watch as these ladies accidentally had baby wipes, diapers, or children's Tylenol in their cart and a thousand different emotions would flood through me. And so I did what I thought was right.

Each register had a camera fixed on it from above to make sure no one stole money out of the cash till. I would begin the transaction, swiping milk and other approved items, and then I would pause the computer on my register. I would go through the motions of scanning products, but the frozen register wouldn't ring up an item or seven. With a few presses of a button, the register would turn back on, their total would miraculously come to thirty dollars, and the young women would breathe a sigh of relief. And that made me feel . . . something. In my new world of deadening monotony, having a rush of good intentions and a feeling of pride and accomplishment—like I had actually done something useful with my day—became a source of addiction.

I had helped these customers in what little ways I could, and I tried to make what is normally the shameful process of brandishing food stamps a comfortable, normal experience. A few ladies actually filled out comment cards, thanking me for treating them with respect and not making them feel as small as other cashiers had done. I felt like the ghetto's very own Robin Hood, but with substantially looser-fitting pants.

When I was awarded a name badge upgrade for my "excellent service," I felt a little guilty. My comment cards, and apparent exceptional grocery-bagging skills, had earned me a faux gold name tag with the phrase *100% Performance* emblazoned underneath my name. Sure, I had earned the "award" by breaking the rules, but as a depressed college dropout, I ravenously devoured the crumbs of affirmation.

Admittedly, my "good deeds" began to get a little out of hand. A sweet elderly couple came into the store once a week, and my heart exploded each time they gingerly inched their walking frames up to a register and pulled out a tiny change purse and a wad of expired coupons. As I watched a fellow cashier tell them their coupon for prepackaged cheese slices was no longer usable, I swallowed a knot in my throat when they walked away empty-handed, because they simply couldn't afford it without the discount. When they came into my line the next week, they again had expired coupons.

I couldn't bear to deny them a simple necessity—a small half gallon of milk. And so I input a code to override the expired coupon message on my register's screen and swiped the coupon's bar code as if it were not a year old. The next week, the precious couple was back in my line again. As I tricked the register into accepting their expired coupons, I noticed they had two gallons of water on the shelf underneath their cart. It was hard to spot with the conveyor belt between us, and I could tell that was by design. Since they couldn't afford to buy cheese two weeks before, I assumed they were desperate enough to steal the cheap gallons. I felt so awful for them and gladly looked the other way as they pushed the cart hiding two stolen jugs of water out of the store.

When they came back to my register the next week, I started to get a little pissed. There were, yet again, two jugs of water skillfully hidden on the cart's lower shelf. But now, joining the paraphernalia was a box of Brillo pads. I could understand stealing water, but no old guy was going to fall over dead because he couldn't scrub stubborn eggs off a pan. But I couldn't bring myself to call them out. And as they handed me two-year-old coupons for a cart full of food, I surrendered into being their dependable partner in crime.

Maybe these adorable seniors were just too fragile minded to realize what they were doing. Maybe they really were desperate to save as much money as they could. When I watched them pull the cart into line at Customer Service to return all their items, including the stolen ones, for full price, I realized they were actually just crooked motherfuckers.

As Customer Service checked their receipts, they realized I had approved a dozen coupons I shouldn't have. The phone at my register rang and I picked it up to hear a shrill "Close your register and come to Customer Service right now." My store manager—my boss—had been manning the counter that day and was about to make me pay. I hung my head and walked past the old crones fighting with her about not getting their money back and sullenly walked into her office.

"I don't want to see you back in my store. You just got this girl fired. Are you proud of yourselves?" she yelled as they reluctantly pushed the cart out of the store.

"I don't give a fuck!" the once adorable old lady yelled from her filthy thug mouth on the way out. *I thought we were partners in crime, lady!* Turns out I was just an easy mark for these criminal masterminds. I wouldn't have been surprised to see them pull off their old people masks in the parking lot, jump into a running convertible, and speed away while flipping me off.

"I could, and probably should, fire you right now," the store manager began. "I don't know why you would think it's okay to approve expired coupons and cost my store money. But I'm just going to take that money out of your check. If it happens again, you're out of here."

"Okay . . . I'm . . . sorry," I managed to squeak out.

"That doesn't sound like a thank-you," she said as I stood up to leave the room. Now, the woman had every right to can me right there. And I appreciated that she hadn't. But the way she phrased that sentence just rubbed me wrong. As if I was supposed to grovel at the chance to continue making minimum wage. As if I was supposed to be happy that week's hundred-dollar paycheck would now be reduced to fifty. Sure, I owed the store that money and was lucky I wasn't being dragged into shopping mall jail, but she was trying to make me feel even smaller than wearing a blue smock and scrubbing butcher meat blood off a belt ten times a day already did. Now she wanted me to swallow my pride and thank her? Fuck. That. Noise. This was not the life I was supposed to be living.

A year ago I was a student at a prestigious school, living on my own, and trying to turn art into an actual career. I refused to grovel for fifty dollars. I was worth so much more.

"No, thank you," I calmly responded as I unpinned my name badge, tucked it into my pants pocket, and handed the manager my smock. As I walked out of the building I realized I hadn't actually said the words *I quit*. To this day I wonder if they're still waiting for me to show up to my afternoon shift.

No matter. I was done throwing myself a pity party and living in shades of gray.

I made it home in a daze. I think my brain was trying to panic about being jobless, but my body was too tired to notice. As I hopped into a steaming shower, my mind began to drift off. The scalding hot water felt painfully good against my skin. I sank down to sit cross-legged on the floor of the tub and closed my eyes beneath the heavy water. I felt my mind drift away from my body.

I looked at the sad little creature beneath me. She had failed at school, failed at work, even failed at being a daughter. And now she was no one. Just a small girl, in a bathtub, talking to herself.

And then I made a decision. *Stand the fuck up. Cry out whatever tears you have left and let them rinse away down the drain. Today was a wash. Yet another failure to add to the list.* Today I would allow myself to cry about it but force myself to realize there was nothing I could do to change the past. Whatever pain and depression I was feeling could have today, but it could not have tomorrow.

Sounds about right.

DIARY OF AN UNFIT MIND

MY IRRATIONALLY LONG LIST OF IRRATIONAL FEELINGS

Things That Make Me Irrationally Scared

- Revolving doors
- The first step on a moving walkway
- The last step off an escalator
- Food that is close to the "Sell By" date
- Cats sitting higher than the height of my face on a staircase I am walking up
- Cats
- When I am walking at a brisk pace toward an automatic door and it still hasn't opened
- Spiders/lint that could be confused for a spider from far away
- The oil popping while cooking
- Being chased . . . even as a joke, I will drop into the fetal position, cover my eyes, and curse at you
- My teeth scraping on a wooden Popsicle stick
- Accidentally incurring the wrath of a shaman
- Flipping a sunny-side-up egg

Things That Make Me Irrationally Angry

- Children doing choreography
- Sitting in a seat someone has just sat in and it's still warm
- Children with inexplicably sticky hands
- Strangers who ask "Where do I know you from?" and expect you to start guessing
- The B-52s' song "Love Shack"

- People who quote other people while doing an impression of that person
- Women who use the phrase "my man"
- Men in V-necks
- Men in sandals
- Backhand compliments (e.g., "I love how you don't care what you look like without makeup.")
- Red nail polish
- How no one from *It's Always Sunny in Philadelphia* has won an Emmy yet
- Old people in movies using slang like "Get jiggy with it." It's not funny. It's never funny.
- When people use sad face emojis while texting about tragic events
- Toe socks

Things That Make Me Irrationally Happy
- Coffee
- When Lori and Barbara are on the *Shark Tank* panel at the same time
- When old people kiss on the Kiss Cam
- When someone refuses to kiss on the Kiss Cam and the Kiss Cam awkwardly stays on them for too long
- The sound of dogs drinking water
- The sound of a wooden dresser drawer opening and/or closing
- Right angles
- The tears of my enemies
- That corn chip smell dogs get when they're sleepy
- Destiel FanFics
- Overweight pigeons
- Watching someone pull a door they are supposed to push and then get superconfused

- Megan Fox
- When chefs cut themselves on *Chopped*
- More coffee
- Children cursing
- When dogs audibly fart and scare themselves

CHAPTER 8

BORN AGAIN

I am not very good at doing anything halfway. There is something about the middle ground that makes me want to jackhammer it into a steep hill and then watch things violently roll down it. People tend to find too much comfort in half measures. They want everyone to like them and so they never say anything too offensive. They never pick a side in an argument so they don't lose a future ally. They don't allow themselves to love completely so they avoid getting hurt. They never take too strong a stand on what they believe in for fear of standing alone.

But for me, there is excitement in extremes. When I love, I love with every ounce of my twisted soul. And when friendships or relationships go south, I tend to set them on fire just to make sure they're really dead. Because as the wise, young scholar Dylan McKay once said, "May the bridges I burn light my way."

If I have to apply to college, I'm going to put all my eggs into one basket and try to get into one of the most prestigious art schools in the country. If I'm going to work at a supermarket, you bet your sweet ass I'm going to be awarded with a gold name tag within a month. And when I decide to get off my ass and make something of my life, there is not a damn thing that is going to stop me.

I had tried the traditional route touted in after-school specials and preached by practical adults. Go to school, live off your parents, get a nine-to-five job, don't make too many waves, and politely wait for death. Living off my parents wasn't going to be an option like it was for the majority of the kids I encountered at college. I helped pay the bills since I was fifteen. I tried to go to school and get myself out of my small town, but somehow ended up right where I started. If insanity really was doing the same thing over and over again and expecting a different result, I was going to have to change things up.

I tried making my academic dreams come true and that was a bust, so now it was time to dust myself off and explore that other childhood fantasy. While most people would love to be the wild thing they dreamed of as a wide-eyed child, actually jumping in with both feet to make it happen seems like an absurd indulgence. There is no safety in that. There are no guarantees like there would be, say, working your way up the Pathmark corporate ladder. But at eighteen, I had nothing to lose. And so I made up my mind.

When I was twelve years old, I promised myself I would become a real-life superhero. I would be strong and powerful, brave and independent. This scrawny, five-foot-two, one-hundred-pound asthmatic nerd with knotted hair and acne was going to join the supermodels and bodybuilders before her, and somehow—some way—become a professional wrestler.

So first things first. I needed money. While at the time most women in professional wrestling were scouted from modeling jobs, that most certainly was not going to be my way in. I've always been fine with my looks, but that's not because

I think I'm conventionally attractive. I know I'm nowhere near a model. On my best day, with the assistance of highly skilled professionals I'm a television 6, which equals a solid Jersey 8. And that doesn't mean I'm insecure or a fisher of compliments. I'm just comfortable with my appearance in the same way a dog is comfortable licking his crotch in the center of a crowded room. It is what it is, and if you're uncomfortable looking at me, that's your own damn problem.

I think that's mostly because I've never put much stock in my appearance. The majority of my life was spent in sweats with my dirty hair pulled back to accentuate my troubled skin. I just didn't care. And the act of not caring what anyone thought made me feel incredibly free. Being comfortable with myself meant not needing the approval of others to build my confidence. That's not something any caring adult taught me. No one gently guided me into womanhood by helping me see my inner beauty. I just innately knew my value. I knew it because the world seemed to be denying it and that just made me want to prove it even more. My value was not in my looks but in my mind. I knew I was smart, funny, creative, and tough. What I brought to the world was going to be something of my mind's creation, not my body's.

But I also knew the pro-wrestling industry had a high standard of beauty, which I just couldn't measure up to. I figured I could just fake my way through that particular requirement somewhere down the line. But to get my foot in the door and to one day make an indelible mark, I was going to have to bring something else—something undeniable—to the table. What really mattered, and what was truly lacking in the landscape, was skill.

There was a glorious golden age for women in wrestling over a decade back, when the roster had plenty of talented, well-rounded athletes, who were just as physically imposing as their male counterparts. But over time the major companies had repackaged the concept of a female wrestler. Now the majority were amazing to look at but not so amazing inside of the ring. So the only examples I had of female successes were jacked-up Amazonian goddess–like weightlifters or drop-dead gorgeous, voluptuous sexpots. On a scale of 1 to 10, I was a negative 14 for both categories. I couldn't change that. But what I could control was how good a wrestler and performer I would become. I knew what my currency could be. And it wasn't going to be found in any of the trails made before me. I was going to have to create my own path.

And for that I needed professional training. But for professional training, I needed a lot of money. So the day after my Pathmark walkout, I opened a newspaper and called, literally, every Wanted ad. Even if I had none of the skills they were looking for, I called every office building, every store in a thirty-mile radius. Eventually, a small prepaid calling card company two towns over invited me to interview for a secretary position. With virtually no experience, I got the part-time job. After two days, I talked my way into making the position full-time. I went from making around $100 a week to about $300, and at the time I genuinely thought I had entered the highest of tax brackets. Though I wanted to swim atop a bed covered in my hard-earned fistful of bills, instead I opened my first bank account. I had a game plan and a debit card. I was on my way to becoming a full-fledged adult.

Wrestling schools around the world can often be heartless scams meant to take money from clueless wannabes with lofty dreams. I wasn't sure if the school I found in an empty warehouse on a sketchy Jersey street was one of those, but I knew for sure that was how they saw me—an all-too-small, incapa-

The entrance to my first wrestling training school
on a street where it was easy to get shanked in
broad daylight.

ble wannabe who was trying to enter a world she wasn't tough
enough for. I know this because the owner of the school came
out and told me so. "You know this hurts, right? You're a little
girl and you could get really injured. But if you want to pay the
tuition, you're in."

Anyone who knows me knows that the best way to ensure
I do something is to tell me that I can't. That's how I learned
that dolls will surely melt in a microwave and domesticating
a squirrel can be dangerous. And so my first few paychecks
went to putting a down payment on wrestling school. The

owner, though doubtful of my ability to actually survive the training, was kind enough to let me pay in installments. Every two weeks a portion of my check would go to putting myself through wrestling training, a fact that my mother wasn't all too happy about. Upon seeing me come home covered in welts and bruises after my first two days of training, she let me know exactly how she felt.

"We have bills to pay here and you're wasting money letting guys beat you up. Have you thought that maybe you're too fragile for this?"

I moved out soon after. In choosing to start over, I had to reevaluate my relationship with my mother. For so long I had put her needs before my own. I had been the kind of kid to get slapped and thank her for the lesson. I had worried about her mental state while completely ignoring my own. I knew so much of her behavior was due to her disorder, but I couldn't be sure how much. Had her bipolar caused her to hurt and doubt me? Had it been in control when she put her pain before my father's and ended up in the hospital the week of Grandpa's death? Was she secretly happy I was back under her control even if it meant going nowhere in life? I couldn't help but resent the situation. I didn't know what was appropriate to feel. Can you be mad at someone for being sick? All I knew was that I needed space. I didn't want to resent my mother. It was bipolar disorder that became my greatest enemy, not her, I hoped. I would do my best to provide her with the help she needed, but what I needed was distance. I gave myself what I needed despite her wishes.

Erica needed a roommate, and I was making enough money to (at least try to) pay half of the rent. Having to still help my parents with their bills and pay for training meant that we were stretched a little thin. Sure, we didn't have cable, I slept on a couch in the living room, and we ate plain rice for every meal, but hell, we were surviving on our own. After a lot of trial and error, Ma had found a particular regimen of medicine that controlled her disorder and wild mood swings, and for the first time I felt like it was okay to put my needs first. But after a week of training, I began to worry that she had been right about my chances for success.

LIFE

Every wrestler inevitably gets asked the question "Is wrestling real?" by some rude stranger, who is convinced they are being original, in a quiet, gravely serious tone of voice one might use when asking a CIA operative about the magic-bullet theory. They ready themselves for the inside scoop they have neither earned nor are prepared to handle. I always giggle at this. For one, this question comes off just as intrusive and indelicate as walking up to a woman and asking if she waxes her mustache. They know there is a level of magic and work that gives them a pleasing end result, but for some reason they can't help but want to have their bubble popped. And they never actually desire the painful truth.

Wrestling requires a suspension of disbelief like any other scripted television show. It is planned and choreographed. It is a dance between two people skilled enough to appear like they are killing each other, while taking every precaution to keep the other safe. The outcome of every match is predetermined. The wrestlers who "win" or are prominent figures are the wrestlers a company has faith in to make it the most money through ticket sales, ratings, and merchandise.

It is an entertainment business like any other, but with the caveat of sometimes breaking bones. Just because something is planned doesn't mean the physicality hurts any less. If someone tells me they are going to punch me in the mouth, does that make the punch hurt any less just because I know it's coming? I'd argue it takes bigger balls to know that pain is coming your way and not run in the other direction. When done right, pro wrestling can and should be a work of art.

It combines the toughness and resiliency of stunt work with the improvisational skills of *Saturday Night Live.* There are no second takes. When performing in front of a live crowd, surrounded on all sides, there is no room for error, and sleight of hand must be perfectly imperceptible. Punches connect, falls hurt (no, the ring is not a bouncy, padded trampoline—it is made of metal, wood, and an inch of foam padding), and sometimes you need to improvise. A good wrestler doesn't need every move rehearsed but reacts to the emotions and needs of the crowd and adjusts accordingly, slyly letting the opponent know the changes without anyone in the crowd hearing the conversation.

These skills are both perfected over time and innate in true performers. And that is exactly what wrestlers are: tough-ass performers. There has been and will probably always be an aura of traveling circus around the business, as many people find it to be the sideshow act of the entertainment industry. But it was an industry I took great pride in entering. I felt like a freak and an outcast, so naturally I would want to run away with the circus. And to this day, when anyone asks me if wrestling is real, I let them know that dislocating both my knee-caps, dislocating my elbow, breaking my foot, getting over seven concussions, displacing my hips, sciatica, shooting my tooth through my face, and the arthritis in my cervical spine certainly felt real.

But ten years ago, my bony little body had never experienced such pain and wasn't used to physical exertion. I hadn't so much as done one sit-up in my entire life. Clearly, I was not a natural athlete. I was clumsy and awkward, often just fall-

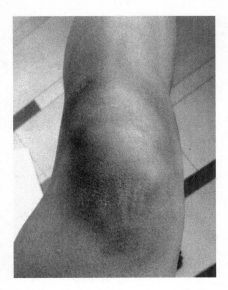

That time my knee exploded and I just hid it underneath a kneepad and wrestled on a three-day tour of Mexico.

ing over during a strong gust of wind. Learning how to take my first bumps was a rude awakening. In wrestling, a bump is a way to fall flatly onto your back while keeping your spine, hips, and head safe. With proper technique, wrestlers learn how to distribute the impact of a bump evenly across the top of their back, so the fall looks devastating but they don't actually break their neck.

During a match, a wrestler takes dozens of bumps. It is a basic, fundamental move you need to learn before moving on to anything else. The first bump I took felt like how I assume a gunshot to the spinal cord must feel like. It knocked all the wind out of me in one sharp, blinding blow. It was so painful my body could not entirely process it and so it became white noise reverberating through my bones until it circled all the way back to painful.

After assuring myself I had not crapped my pants, I did two hundred more in a row. I only remember this number because one of my trainers counted out loud while laughing. That was

Day One. Day Two was the exact same thing, except upon arriving home after my second training day, I spent forty-five minutes hugging the toilet and projectile vomiting. My body was not handling physical activity so well. Eventually the vomiting turned into dehydration, which was then followed by uncontrollable chills, which naturally led to full-blown pneumonia. As I spent the next few days laid up in bed, I wondered what the hell I had done to myself.

I basically paid someone to beat me up and make me sick for a week. Could I really handle this? Was I actually strong enough to be a wrestler?

But I went back the week after. And the week after that. I got my first concussion and first broken bone within six months of training—the concussion when a three-hundred-pound man accidentally slammed my head directly into the mat, and the broken foot when another guy threw me over his head into a backflip.

I was the only girl training at the school, but you wouldn't know it by how the guys treated me. My classmates were accepting and encouraging, and just saw me as one of the boys. They were specifically instructed not to take it easy on me. Not only did they avoid babying me, but they took it upon themselves to see exactly how much damage I could absorb without exploding into dust. We would run through training drills and practice matches together. Sure, everyone was three times as big as I was, but I still had to try to lift their entire bodies to suplex each and every one of them, just the same.

It was an amazing experience. Actually being inside of a ring, though smaller and cheaper than a professional TV setup, was mind-blowing. The first time I tried to enter the sacred squared circle, I was told some people like to wipe their shoes on the edge of the mat before stepping through the ropes. It was a sign of respect to the ring. While staring at the puddles of sweat on the canvas the ninety-five-degree building refused to allow to dry up, and the smatters of blood covering almost every other inch, I laughed at the idea that my shoes would somehow make the mat dirtier.

But the small gesture, to show the sixteen-by-sixteen area I had long dreamed of entering that I would respect and cherish it, struck a chord in me. It was a long road to get to the simple moment of stepping between the ropes, and so for the next ten years, I would wipe my shoes each time I entered a wrestling ring.

Inside of those ropes, I felt invincible. I could get knocked down a million times but get up a million and one. I could fly off the top rope, suspended in air like a tried-and-true superhero in spandex. I was actually (finally) encouraged to take my aggression out through physical violence. Here, inside of these crudely taped together cable wires posing as ring ropes, I could fight back. Here, violence was an art form.

Over time my injuries became battle scars. I was proud of them. The bruises, cuts, concussions, and casts were all tangible proof I could truly be strong. I'm not sure if the exercise affected my serotonin levels, or if the physical activity provided me with steady endorphins, but for the first time in years I actually felt in control of my shaky brain. Even though I lay on a hand-me-down couch in a living room, I finally began to sleep soundly every night.

DEATH

Everything was falling into place. Which, I should have realized, is also how the first people to die in horror movies feel. I had a bank account and an apartment and was studying my craft. My mother seemed to have finally hit her stride in treatment and medication. There was a time, at her sickest, when I would answer her phone calls and realize she was already in the middle of an expletive-filled nonsensical sentence. But now, we were actually able to communicate. Phone calls were civil and sometimes even shockingly pleasant.

Erica and I had avoided visiting our parents' apartment for a little over a month. When we moved out, we thought weaning them off their reliance on us would be exactly the tough love they needed. They had spent years using us as crutches, but ultimately they were adults. And we believed adults would be able to stand on their own feet. The first month on our own, we were too strapped for cash to be able to help them with bills. And we felt like shit about it. We thought we would be able to live on our own and take care of them, but it was harder than we naively expected. And so we tried to stuff our guilt down by simply avoiding being in the same room. It was the coward's way out, and I tried to find a way to ease my guilty mind.

After cashing a check that was larger than usual due to putting in some overtime hours, I decided to call Ma and ask if she needed anything for her fridge. They lived only a bus stop away from our new place, so I didn't have to lug the bag of groceries far. When I approached their building, a woman standing in its threshold greeted me. It took me almost five whole seconds to recognize my own mother.

My heart stopped. The woman before me was rail thin. Her cheeks were sunken in, emphasizing the sharpness of the bones above them. Her eyes seemed as if they had been sucked into the depth of the sockets. The warm smile she greeted me with was almost too big for her now withered face. On her brittle frame was a size 2 tank top I had left behind. It engulfed the diminutive woman, who only a short time before was a healthy size 8. In just over a month, my mother had wasted away. We embraced, and the feel of her hard bones drained the life from me.

The apartment I once called "home for now" felt foreign. Smaller somehow. Dirtier. Every surface was covered in dust. The glued-on plastic tile flooring stuck to my sneakers with each step. The scent of dog pee that permeated every room led me to believe Mugsy and Kagome had been relieving themselves indoors. The yellow-stained mop propped against the kitchen wall was a clear indicator that their messes were being hastily cleaned up, causing the sticky floors. When I opened the refrigerator to put away the groceries I had brought with me, it was empty. In just over a month, everything had gone to hell.

How could they implode so fast? My mind raced to try and understand what had happened. There were plenty of years when we were younger when the fridge was bare and cash was tight, but for the past few years it had felt like things were improving. Before Ma's breakdown she was working full-time, and Dad had inherited a few thousand dollars after Grandpa's passing. I believed they would be capable of supporting themselves. But they somehow had no money for food, and Ma had become a shell of herself because of it. Dad was also alarmingly thinner than he had been the last time I saw him. Not only were they not eating, they seemed to lack the desire to clean and look after themselves. I worried they were both in the grips of a depressive state after having to live on their own essentially for the first time in their adulthood.

I felt like I had entered a bizarro world and saw a glimpse of what my parents' lives would look like without us. But I was only a bus stop away, and it had only been a few weeks. The realization that the tough love and push toward independence had swiftly broken them crashed down on me like a thousand-pound weight. What had I done? I felt like an ungrateful brat who had abandoned her parents after years of shared struggles. I was worried only about paying my bills and feeding myself and had let them wither away in the process. I handed the rest of my paycheck to Ma and searched my mind for a way to undo my mistake.

Robbie had been staying in Puerto Rico since our grandfather first became ill. Struggling with his PTSD, he had an episode there in which he believed his life was in danger and reactively flew to the States overnight. As he recovered in the apartment with Robert and Janet, he saw the condition they were living in and we all decided it would be best for them to start over in Puerto Rico. Admittedly, I was relieved. It would be easier to only have to pay my parents' phone and grocery bills, now that they lived rent free in Robert's family home. But I still felt like I failed them. Again, I was given a responsibility and I ended up a massive failure. It sent me into a tailspin.

My neurosis took over. Sleep eluded me once more. The dark cloud reclaimed its spot hovering over my head. I wondered if I should reenter therapy. It had been a while since I had gone, and maybe all I needed was to talk to someone about the heavy shame I was feeling.

And then I remembered the prescription I had been given almost a year earlier. I searched for the plastic container and found it hidden within a dresser drawer. It was almost as if I was too afraid to get rid of it but unable to look it in the proverbial eye. For months I argued with myself about the need for antidepressants. A part of me was unwilling to let go of my training, the constant message preached to me that mental health was something a strong person could control on their own. My pride had stopped me from accepting the help of medicine. But this sadness felt deeper, more intrinsic than before. Like its seeds were planted in the valves of my heart and its branches extended through my veins. I convinced myself my only options were to try the medication or be crushed beneath the wicked weight hanging over me.

I took one. The next day I took another. And after a few weeks I began to feel stranger than usual. Convincing myself this uneasy feeling was just the meds kicking in, I continued to take a pill every day, for months, refilling the prescription a few times over. I expected my body to have some sort of side effects to the introduction of a foreign substance to my system; my doctor had warned me that there was a transitional period to every medicine. But still, I was blindsided when one day I woke up completely and utterly shattered.

Upon opening my eyes, I realized my face was covered in tears, having apparently cried in my sleep throughout the night. I tried to eat breakfast but it had no taste, and so I returned to my room, closed the shades, and crawled back into bed. After Erica had left for work, I called in sick to my own job.

Sobs uncontrollably escaped my body. *Why am I crying?* I wondered without worrying. I could feel something was wrong, but for some reason that did not scare me. I felt strangely objective and removed from myself. As if I were watching this blubbering mess hiding from the world under a TJ Maxx discounted quilt. I grabbed the orange bottle from my dresser drawer and took a pill earlier than usual. An hour later I woke up in tears again, but this time with a throbbing headache. Forcing myself out of the bed, I stumbled into the kitchen to find some Advil. Instead, I found a bottle of prescription painkillers I had received after breaking my foot, but remembered I had been too scared to take even one before. The side effects of such a potent pill intimidated me. If my body was in pain, I would find a way to tough through it. I could control that. Physical pain had never bothered me. I had taught myself to endure it, to numb myself from it. But this felt different. This consuming migraine didn't feel like a pain coming from my body; it came from deep within my soul. Maybe I would need to try a painkiller for the first time to combat it.

And that's the last thing I remembered for a while.

The next time I opened my eyes, Erica was speeding through red lights while I violently puked out the window of her car. I watched as a haze of chunks and bile splashed against the car door, until my eyes began to roll to the back of my skull. My vision blurred. My heart raced so fast and hard I could feel it pulse in my arms, behind my eyes, in my throat.

What the fuck was happening? What did I do to myself?

The next few days were a blur of vomit, lab tests, and panic. When I finally felt my brain settle with recognition of my surroundings, I shot up in the bed. I was not home. I was in a cold room on a hard hospital bed. One of my arms was attached to a bulky IV. The other was painfully extended with plastic tubes shooting out the center of it. Thick, black track marks replaced every single blue vein on the inside of my arms.

Like a movie montage, the events surrounding my stupidity began to flash in front of my eyes. I had fucked up monumentally. In a deep depressive state, I had overdosed on antidepressants and painkillers. I had almost died trying to make an inner pain fade away.

So was this a suicide attempt? Was it a cry for attention? The doctors labeled it an accidental overdose and didn't force me into a psychiatric ward like they had done to my mother. But was it an accident? Here is the truth. I have searched within myself for years for the answer and have come up with only this. In the weakest moment of my life, without emotion and without thinking, I tried to make the pain stop. It felt like a mechanical and rational decision. *There is pain. I cannot handle it. This might help. This might help more.* I never told myself I wanted to die, but I never told myself I didn't. I just didn't care. Searching for a solution in that instant, I made an idiotic series of mistakes. I believe I should've been analyzed in a psych unit. It should have been treated like a suicide attempt. Because something was deeply wrong with my brain, and I could not handle it alone.

When Erica came to pick me up, she was warm and a bit nervous. It was as if she didn't know how to treat me. She didn't want to come off as judgmental, but she was also hurt. This poor girl had picked our mother up from the hospital a year earlier, and this was eerily reminiscent.

"I hope you know . . ." she said, breaking the awkward silence, "you're going to have to clean my car."

REBIRTH

As we drove home from my shameful hospital visit, a realization hit me like lightning. It was all too similar. It was not a coincidence I was following my mother's footsteps. She was diagnosed with depression. And so was I. She overdosed. And so did I. But what doctors realized in her case was that she had been misdiagnosed to begin with. She was not depressed. She had been mistakenly diagnosed during a depressive cycle of her bipolar disorder. The antidepressants had the worst possible reaction they could have. I knew then and there that was what had happened to me. I knew in my heart I was bipolar.

For a long time I believed I was prone to depression when circumstances overwhelmed me. And so I thought, if I stayed happy enough, I could fight back the darkness. Essentially I was trying to put a Band-Aid on a festering wound. I thought if my erratic behavior had subsided for this long, it certainly meant it was gone for good. I excused my odd behavior as momentary depression. There were weeks I was incredibly, ridiculously happy. Getting to experience being inside of a wrestling ring had given me a strength and confidence I had never known. Having a full-time job, living as a proper adult, made me feel like I was on the path to success. So why couldn't I sleep at night?

Nights I did manage to get some rest, I would wake up feeling off—heavy and dazed, as if I were shrouded in a dense fog. I began calling these my "dark days." Days in which I would mope around, dragging my feet. My appetite would diminish, and even if I tried to eat, I would taste nothing. Within these days, often midsentence, I would break down into tears—for absolutely no reason. But I wrote off all of it as moments of weakness. I didn't respect the possibility of inheriting my mother's mental illness.

The hardest thing in the world is to accept that something is wrong with you, face the uphill road to recovery ahead, and realize that none of it makes you less than human. I had been so scared to end up as sick as my mother, I had refused to notice the warning signs. I wanted to think that I had little bouts of depression caused by the heavy situations in my life, but that was not the truth. The truth was, I was bipolar. And I had been for several years. The only difference between me and my mother was that I was catching the culprit early on. I had a chance to end up differently. And I would never take that chance for granted. The day I got home from the hospital, I cut the plastic hospital band off my wrist and replaced it with three thin black bracelets. One representing the life I had lived and the mistakes I had made, one representing the death I had escaped, and the last representing my second chance at life—my rebirth. I have worn them every day since.

What comes next can be demoralizing for a lot of patients. I would eventually confirm my diagnosis with a professional. After that momentous occasion, finding the right medication

I still wear these almost every day.

and dosage can be a pain in the ass. Sometimes a treatment can take so long to produce any sort of result, you give up before you can get its full benefits. Oftentimes medication meant to soothe the extreme emotions ends up dulling all of them. I spent a few months feeling like a robot in a cloud of smoke. But if you stick through the highs and lows of trying to control your highs and lows, there is a light at the end of the tunnel.

My disorder is not something that can be cured, but its severity can certainly be controlled. The process takes guts. It takes a brave person to accept they need help and go get it. It takes an even braver person to not feel shame in the process. I understand psychiatry and therapy can be intimidating to a lot of people. After I found the right treatment, and took the time to attend consistent therapy over the years, I felt so silly for waiting so long to finally find peace.

If you are sick, you get medicine from a doctor. When people can see an injury or hear a cough, they take notice. That ailment is tangible. It is real. But when an illness cannot be seen, when it is felt, however deeply, people tend to ignore it.

My family did not believe in mental illness. They thought it was a creation of pansies who couldn't tough it out when life got rough. And then it screwed us without even having the courtesy to buy us dinner first. My mother had a breakdown, I suffered for years, and even Robbie was extrasusceptible to PTSD, having a chemical imbalance already in his genetic makeup. We were forced to face how very real mental illness was only after it had had its way with us.

What I wish for anyone reading this who feels even the slightest worry that something could be wrong inside of them is that you find the strength to talk to someone about it. Get advice from someone who has experience. Talk to a friend who you know will support you. Or really sac up and go to therapy and bare your soul. You might just find exactly what you are looking for. As I've gotten older I've become less toler-ant of closed minds that think psychotherapy and psychology are tantamount to weakness. Being proactive takes a lot more strength than hiding.

I know a lot of secure women and men who go to therapy. They don't see it as an admission of a flaw. They see it as a luxury, serving their minds the way a massage spoils the body. Some of the happiest couples I know go to couples therapy weekly. And that's why they are the happiest couples I know. Because they take the time to check in with their emotions be-fore a problem arises. And if modern medicine isn't your deal, then try homeopathic methods. Try meditation, anything. Just taking the time to put your mental health first, acknowl-edging that it deserves respect and care, and accepting help when you need it, can save your life. You are worth saving. And you are not alone.

DIARY OF AN UNFIT MIND

SURVIVING SISTERHOOD

Growing up next to another set of blossoming ovaries will un-doubtedly create some friction in your life. My sister and I have had a love story more tumultuous than Sam and Jason on *General Hospital*. She has been my surrogate mother, my best friend, and my worst enemy. We have made each other laugh almost as much as we have made each other bleed. We are complete opposites, and yet, the perfect match. There is no relationship that has hurt me or healed me more.

So here is my guide to surviving sisterhood. Boyfriends and girlfriends will come and go. Friends will try their best. But there is no bond more sacred than the one between two sisters who have been cursed with the same chubby nose.

1. Do your best to avoid fighting about:
- How long it is still age appropriate to play with Barbies. A two-year age difference is enough to ensure one sister will spend half an hour setting up an elaborate Barbie playdate, complete with makeshift Ricki Lake talk-show set, only to have the other sister bounce within five minutes to walk around the mall with her stupid, stupid friends.
- Clothes. My sister and I shared a handful of clothes for over a decade. When we eventually got our own jobs and could buy our own stuff, the blood feud began. Your sister is going to want to borrow something you own. That plain black T-shirt will then suddenly transform into something so ap-pealing you will protect it like Gollum in *Lord of the Rings*. Just share it. It's not worth losing wads of hair over. Unless it still has the tags on. You might as well be asking for a kidney.

- Boys. There was a boy in high school who, when dumped by my sister, tried to move in on me, in a pretty twisted attempt at revenge. That is how stupid boys can be. In general, it's a good rule to just avoid fighting about guys altogether throughout life—with friends, other women, etc. Most guys are not worth fighting over. Trust me. The good ones will fight for you. The rest can kindly fuck off.

- Money. I always felt bad that my mother and her sisters were divided over money and promised myself that Erica and I would be different. And for the most part we have done a stellar job of not letting money come between us. Unless you count that one time I didn't pay my half of the rent six months in a row. Or that other time when she secretly drained my bank account to buy shoes.

2. Stay on her good side, because you never know when you'll need her:

- To pay your half of the rent for the many years you are kind of a mess.

- To not secretly drain your bank account to buy shoes during the years she's kind of a mess.

- To loan you her bra in the middle of a school day because you forgot to wear one, because your boobs are nonexistent, but you have to change in front of the other girls in gym class, and they actually have boobs, and those boobs are inside of bras.

- To let you know it is time to start plucking your eyebrows.

- To let you know you have grossly overplucked and can't pull off the chola look.

- To read your shitty screenplays.

- To secretly buy you tampons.

- To describe in horrifying helpful detail how to use those tampons.

3. Remember, at the end of the day, only a sister would:

- Shave your legs for you when you are a crying, hairy nine-year-old who is too terrified to hold the blade for the first time.
- Buy Johnson and Johnson's No More Tangles detangling spray and comb the knots out of your hair when you are a lazy, disgustingly unkempt fourteen-year-old.
- Let you sneakily borrow her makeup when your mom thinks it'll just make you look like a "cheap painted whore."
- Work overtime to make sure you get at least one Christmas present.
- Help plot bloody revenge on a boy who breaks your heart.
- Take turns writing only "You are one year closer to death" in each other's birthday cards. Every year.
- Have a massive blowout of a fight and act like nothing happened the next day.
- Forgive you every time you are kind of a dick.
- Blindly believe you are capable of anything.
- Encourage you to chase even the wildest of dreams.

Thank you for being my sister, Eri. You're kind of okay. Shut up, don't make it weird.

CHAPTER 9

I WANT TO BELIEVE

itting rock bottom set me free. I felt like I had been given a clean slate, a second chance at life, and I sure as hell was going to make the most of it. When you are at your lowest, there really is nowhere else to go but up. My foundation was cracked. The whole building needed to be torn down and reconstructed. Every day felt like knocking down walls and gathering bricks. But brick by tedious brick, I would rebuild and become someone better. After taking the time to heal and learning about proper treatment, I was refocused and ready to continue the upward trajectory.

Wrestling school was my primary focus. I trained for about a year before actually getting paid to wrestle. There are small promotions all over the country, and the world for that matter, that run wrestling shows in high school gyms, bingo halls, state fairs—basically any place you can build a ring and gather a crowd. Together these promotions make up the "independent circuit," pretty much any wrestling that is not a part of the bigger promotions on television. The rings are more of the makeshift variety, the crowds can sometimes consist of less than ten people, the pay is practically nothing, and the wrestlers can be dangerously undertrained. But getting any opportunity to live out the childhood fantasy of performing in front of a crowd made me unbelievably happy.

Unfortunately, women on the circuit are not as plentiful as men. It was difficult to find companies that had any possible opponents for me to work with. The owner of my own training school didn't like the idea of having such a tiny, inexperienced woman wrestle on his events. "You're just so small, and these other girls are so much bigger than you. I'm scared you're going to be too fragile to handle it."

There was that goddamn word again. I had proven my grit for a year now, and I was still being judged by my size. I knew he was concerned for my safety, but doubt coming from my own training grounds was demoralizing. I wasn't going to learn from people who were better than I was without getting the chance to enter a ring with them, so I looked to other promotions for work.

A few companies gave me great opportunities to gain some experience and make a few bucks. And I mean a literal few. The most I ever made in one night was forty dollars after wrestling four different matches in a tournament. One time a promoter let me know the show didn't sell enough tickets to actually pay any of the wrestlers at the end of the night, but he was kind enough to offer one free snack from his concession stand. Essentially, I was paid in french fries. Dream big, kids.

It wasn't much of a profitable career, but I still felt like I was doing something worthwhile and important. I started to make a small name for myself on the independent circuit (eventually, in early 2009, I became a tag team champion in a badass all-women promotion). When one of the company's shows took place in a twenty-degree movie theater, with a ring that had tire-sized holes in it, only two working ropes, in front of a crowd of four men who just spent the evening touching themselves underneath their winter coats, I still went to bed with an accomplished smile on my face. Not because I was accidental spank material, but because I felt like I was doing "IT." I was actually becoming a wrestler, though the "professional" part was still a bit debatable. I had set a goal, and each day I was getting closer to achieving it.

In 2008, one of the wrestlers from my training school mentioned the WWE was holding open tryouts. At first this sounded like a glorious opportunity to get a contract with the biggest wrestling company in existence. The WWE had multiple shows on television and was known all over the world. I was excited until some of the other guys made it seem like a big scam.

"You have to pay two thousand dollars and get your own flight and hotel. I heard it was just a way to rip off suckers and pay for a new ring for their developmental team," one of the guys said, scoffing at the idea.

But I wasn't quick to write it off. Sure, the WWE was certainly going to make a lot of money off any indy wrestler with two grand to spare, but it was still an opportunity.

The tryout was a full-blown, three-day camp at the WWE's developmental facility in Tampa, Florida. This facility served as the company's minor leagues. New signees would move to Tampa and train at the school until they were promoted to a main roster spot on one of the company's network shows.

WWE writers, producers, and agents would attend the tryout camp and watch the prospects train and put on matches. Whether or not it was just a cash play, there were going to be very real eyes with very real authority watching. Even if it was just a sliver, there was a chance. The problem was, I was working my butt off to barely make rent every month and didn't have that kind of extra cash lying around. If I did, I would've surely been using it to "make it rain" on my sister while she tried to sleep. There was absolutely no way I was going to be able to afford two flights, four nights in a hotel, and two grand to enter the camp. But rumor was the tryout camp would be made into an annual occurrence. I was determined that the next time the opportunity came around, I would make sure I was ready for it.

I decided I would need a new, better-paying job. Making six dollars an hour fetching coffee for pervy misogynists at the calling card company for the last year had helped me pay for wrestling school, but I needed to start doing better than living paycheck to paycheck. I also felt like the calling card company had run its course of survivability. Having under twenty-five employees, it was legal for the bosses to smoke indoors. And smoke in my chubby-cheeked asthmatic face they did.

When I had broken my foot, I was still not excused from carrying boxes up and down stairs into storage or fetching coffee whenever my boss snapped. And he literally snapped his fingers to get my attention. When I would bring the coffee behind his desk, more often than not I would catch a quick glimpse of porn on his computer as he rushed to minimize its window. I envisioned throwing the scalding coffee all over him while I snapped a thousand times in his now deformed face.

I tried to deal with the grossness I could not shower off me at the end of the day, but the day he snapped his fingers and smugly called me "baby" I told him I would be moving on. Though I wasn't qualified for much, I borrowed my sister's clothes, typed up a malnourished résumé using a really big font, and went on interview after interview. After a few weeks of searching, I was offered a job . . . as a secretary. But this time I would have a sick view of the Hudson River from my desk, be treated with respect, and make enough money to afford cable, so it was a total upgrade.

My new gig was at a beautiful day spa directly on the river in Hoboken, New Jersey. The manager liked my personality despite my lack of experience and hired me to man the front desk. If I wasn't thanking callers in a tranquil hippie spa voice, I was staring out onto the water while listening to a nature sounds CD on loop. I was making enough money to not feel guilty about buying a morning coffee to drink at my desk with a view, engulfed in the scent of lavender oil diffusers.

Not taking into account the semiregular callers inquiring about "happy endings," this was the life. I would work five days a week, full-time, at the spa. On weekends I would travel around the tristate area taking wrestling gigs. I finally bought my first cell phone and went on my first date. There are those who would argue that's late in life, but for me, they were both things I felt only came with maturity. I was in no rush to throw extra bills or responsibilities onto my plate. But I finally started to feel like I was getting my shit together.

When the second WWE tryout camp was announced for May of 2009, I knew I couldn't miss out on it. Though I had saved up an impressive amount of money for someone who reused paper towels at least three times before throwing them away, I still hadn't met the amount I needed to pay for the whole trip. And so I cut every corner I could think of. Each trip to the grocery store was twice as long as I carefully sought out the cheapest chicken breasts, even if it was only by five cents. And forget name brand anything. The Mendez girls would enjoy meals of "Compare to Kraft!" macaroni spirals. I began cutting meals altogether. Knowing what was at stake, I decided it was worth it to skip the beloved morning coffee I was just getting used to spoiling myself with. Eventually I calculated how much I could save if I skipped lunch too. I had some moderately cheesy macaroni spirals or white rice waiting for me at home. I could survive a workday without food.

Luckily, the spa always had a cracker and fruit plate out for guests to nibble on in the waiting room. So when a phone wasn't ringing and no one was around to catch me, I would tiptoe into the tranquilly decorated haven and stuff as many crackers and grapes as I could fit into a napkin without making too much of an obvious dent in the display. I would make several trips throughout the day, basically living off the lightest of finger food. One day I almost blew my cover by eating too many crackers while only one guest had checked in. "Wow, Mrs. Anders must've been really hungry before her Brazilian. Half of the fruit plate is gone," one of the aestheticians suspiciously noted.

In three months of skimping on food to afford the tryout, I lost fifteen pounds, weighing in at a scant ninety-six pounds. I looked sick and dangerously thin, like if someone blinked fast enough, the wind their lashes created could thrust me across the room. But I had done it. I had saved enough money to apply to the tryout, pay the admission fee if I were accepted, and travel to the majestic faraway land that neighbored Donald Duck.

Erica and I were struggling to get by now that a healthy portion of my checks was being squirreled away on a pipe dream. She was generous enough to let me come up short on rent so I could afford the tryout, but we were sorely lacking in simple essentials like food and bus fare. My spending over two thousand dollars on a mere chance was painful for her to sit back and watch. But she had enough faith in my determination to not stand in my way.

A ray of glimmering hope came in the form of an e-mail from a Hotmail account. Yes, that was once a thing. A small wrestling company offered me the opportunity to make some serious cash, and, no, it was not to support a foreign prince in a pyramid scheme. A legitimate up-and-coming wrestling company offered me four thousand dollars to take part in a two-day shoot for its television pilot. That was more money than I had ever seen, and it was being extended to me like a lifeguard's hand the several times I almost drowned in a public pool. It could pay our rent for the next few months and stock our fridge and provide endless amusement when I inevitably covered my bed in it to make snow angels.

I was beside myself with joy . . . until I read the proposed date of the shoot. The pilot taping would overlap with the try-out camp I had prepared a year for. So here was my choice: shoot a television pilot, be flown first class and put up in a fancy hotel, on top of being handed more money than I had ever known could exist in one place—or pay my last dime for a sliver of a chance I would see a return on that investment.

It was as if a siren call was trying to lure me into the prom-ise of riches. It took every ounce of Erica's strength to not slap me upside the head and order me to go earn the rent money I owed her. But we both knew I had to see this thing through.

For a year I had given my all to make this tryout possi-ble. It was an investment—though a painful one—in myself. Though it hurt me to walk away from guaranteed money, I chose to take the chance.

When I arrived in Tampa, I took one step off the plane and my hair grew three sizes, like the Grinch's heart. Humidity was not my friend. The temperature and atmosphere, though wreaking havoc on my already frizzy hair and oily skin, gave me a sense of nostalgia. Florida reminded me a lot of Puerto Rico, except there were more paved roads and slightly fewer machete-wielding grandmothers.

Immediately I was struck by the difference in attitudes of the locals. When I walked into a Walgreens an employee greeted me with "How's it going? Let me know if I can help you with anything," and I had to bite my tongue from yelling "You wanna start something?" in response. It took me a minute to realize people in the South actually greeted strangers, as opposed to prolonged eye contact starting a fistfight where I came from. I wasn't sure if she was really helpful or if I just looked really suspicious, but her alarming warmth actually turned out to be genuine. I would have to get used to this development if I succeeded in getting hired.

If I got a contract, I would have to move here. I would leave cold winters behind for a solid year-round eighty degrees. I salivated at the idea. The palm trees and warm air reminded me of our time on the farm, the only time in my childhood I felt truly safe. Maybe that was a sign this tryout would go my way.

The first day of the camp, over seventy applicants filled the small warehouse converted into a small wrestling arena. Three rows of metal chairs surrounded the ring used for the developmental roster's local shows. Behind the curtain at the top of the wrestlers' entranceway were two more rings meant for daily practices. There was too much for my excited brain to absorb. First I noticed how large the ring was compared with the indy ones I was used to. These were twenty by twenty, and would require an extra four bounds from my tiny Chihuahua gait while running the ropes. Next my eyes fixed on the story-high fabric posters covering the entirety of the walls around the main ring. They were posters promoting pay-per-view specials and had the faces of every famous wrestler plastered on them. I made a mental note that I would have to make sure I made it onto one of these one day.

Only three other women were among the candidates: a tall blond foreign model; a dancer with a body so sexy if I had it I would never leave the house because I would be too busy staring at my naked body in a full-length mirror; and a fellow indy wrestler with five more years of experience than I had. *Welp. I'm boned*, I thought. The candidates were split into three groups, one in each ring, and made to run basic drills together. After an hour, I felt a tap on my leg. Turning around, I met eyes with Tom Prichard, a trainer at the school and a former wrestler in the tag teams the Heavenly Bodies and the Bodydonnas.

"They want you to cut a promo in the main room," he said as he motioned for me to follow him.

"Cutting a promo" is wrestling terminology for performing a monologue. I quickly tried to figure out what was happening. The main room, housing the main show ring, was currently filled with all the candidates with over five years' experience as well as agents, producers, and writers for the main roster program. I figured the less experienced wrestlers wouldn't have to worry about facing these intimidating decision makers for at least another two days. My event schedule had listed Promo Day at the end of the week. I was nowhere near ready, during hour one of day one. But I didn't exactly have a choice now.

When I entered the room, I immediately spotted the head of Talent Relations, Ty Bailey, along with a few main roster wrestlers. I walked into the center of the ring. Alone. With a microphone in my hand. And completely froze up. *Why don't I have anything prepared? Everyone is staring at me and I'm holding this microphone like I'm about to jerk it off. Say something. Anything!* And then, as if guided by some sort of fairy godmother magic, words seamlessly escaped my mouth.

There are two types of characters in wrestling: a "babyface," aka the good guy, and a "heel," aka the bad guy. For two years I had practiced as and played the role of the babyface on the independent circuit, but for some reason known only to my frayed nerves, I cut a heel promo. I insulted everyone watching me and talked myself up like a conceited villain. It was nice to find out that my fight-or-flight instinct was to be a total dick. Whatever nonsense that came out of my mouth was ridiculous and off the cuff, but I delivered it with an unfaltering bravado. *Fake it till you make it,* I thought, shrugging, but apparently the performance was good enough to get the attention of the people whose opinions mattered.

For the next two days I was filled with a confidence I had rarely felt within. Something about being noticed early on made me approach every camp challenge and task head-on. I had several matches, performed a few more promos, and was critiqued daily on how to improve. And then one of the wrestlers from the main roster watched a match of mine and gave me his two cents on what I needed to work on.

"You're really skinny. I feel like someone could just break you in half." Then, directing his comments toward the crowded room of contestants listening, "You guys have to be prepared to look the part. Not like some wannabe off the street."

This comment devastated me. A wrestler talented enough to be on the main roster took one look at my body and let me know it wasn't up to snuff. I knew I had lost weight skimping on meals, but I was tired of being reminded how I was too small to be strong. My bubble of confidence was being tested.

At the end of the week, all the hopefuls were gathered in the building's main room. We had heard rumors that someone might actually be announced as a contract winner that day in front of the whole group in some sort of ceremony. Sitting in rows facing the main ring, it felt as if we were at the Oscars and everyone was nominated for the same award. Tensions were high. Nails were bitten. I crossed my legs in my chair and stared at the floor. I heard rumblings that besides the one main contract winner, a few people might be offered contracts in the weeks to come. I had my hopes set on one of those. I knew that there was no way that out of seventy burly men and three more attractive and skilled women my name would be called that day. I was at peace with that realization and excited to see which of the guys would get the chance of a lifetime.

Ty Bailey stood in front of the shaking sea of muscles and self-tanner and thanked everyone for participating. He made some sort of moving speech, but all I heard was white noise until I saw everyone turn and look at me. As if his words traveled on a delay through sound waves, it took me what felt like an entire minute to actually hear the words "Congratulations, April Mendez!"

My fingernails clawed at my cheeks as I shot up from the chair. My legs were still crossed so I almost face-planted, which would have been entirely consistent with my luck before that moment. Ty handed me a card that had something written on it, I shook his hand, and then just collapsed onto the floor in a messy crying heap. Imagine Halle Berry winning the Oscar but with a heavier nose drip and looking substantially less endearing. I looked at the card in my hand and realized it was a business card on which Ty had scribbled, "Contract with WWE." It was hilariously unofficial, but only enhanced the absurdity of the moment. My competitors were genuinely warm and congratulatory, and I received seventy bear hugs in a row. It felt like the closing montage of every cheesy sports movie in existence. But it was actually the beginning of an even more absurd, trying, beautiful journey.

A legally binding document.

The first person I called was Robbie.

"Hey, remember that thing I promised when I was twelve?"

DIARY OF AN UNFIT MIND

A LETTER TO MY FUTURE DAUGHTER

If you are reading this, congratulations; you can read! I am proud to have apparently done at least one thing right in your life. (I once left my iPhone in the fridge for an entire night and in the morning checked for my alarm on a Dorito, so forgive me for appreciating I have gotten you this far.) As I write this, I am twenty-nine with abs of steel and an ass that I have—on multiple occasions—dared people to bounce a quarter off. If for some reason you have ruined any of this, I need you to know that I do not forgive you.

I never really imagined myself as a mother. While my sister cherished her baby dolls, I created various, ID-Channel-worthy reenactments in which they were kidnapped. Somewhere along the line I must have become slightly more tender. The fact that you exist at all must be a testament to my newfound maturity, my embraced womanhood, my courage in accepting that life's greatest accomplishment is creating a lasting legacy in the form of a loving family, or I forgot to take my pill that day. Either way, I might as well give you the guidance you need to become a strong, confident woman who never takes a duckface selfie. May your journey through life be easier than mine, but not so easy you become an ungrateful dick. Here are some tips I hope will help.

1. Tame that mane. You are half Puerto Rican, which means that you have a great chance of inheriting my gloriously thick, shiny head of hair. Coupled with this enviable gift are strong, defined eyebrows. Women around the world spend exorbitant amounts of money to create the illusion of what you have been naturally given. But don't get cocky. For it is not just a gift, but also a curse. Did you think your dark tresses would just contain themselves to your shiny mane? No. This hair has been passed down from generation to generation because it is powerful. And it is determined to take over your entire body. So to avoid ever being confused with a small bear cub, I want you to investigate body hair bleach at a very early age. Don't even bother waxing. This hair cannot be killed. Only pacified. You should, however, tweeze your eyebrows early and often, as you will find that throughout the day you will inexplicably respawn a unibrow. This ability is both useful when the hair on your head is long enough to fall in a rich cascade to the small of your back within seven days of cutting it to your jawline, and horrifying when by lunchtime your eyebrows are seemingly the first step in a full-body transformation into a werewolf.

2. Your skin hates you. While you watch whatever is on MTV in your generation—I'm assuming something about pregnant teenage wolves getting scammed through Facebook—you will see commercials that would lead you to believe that acne is something you can conquer while singing pop songs into a shampoo bottle as you shower. This is a lie. Unfortunately, being born into a family rife with hormonal "eccentricities" means that acne is not something you will be able to throw a delightfully scented wash at and call it a day. That would be like sharpening a chopstick and bringing it to a gunfight. Acne is packing an Uzi. You come from a lineage of troubled skin, I assume because one of your ancestors killed acne's wife and acne is still avenging her. Please demand I take you to a highly skilled dermatologist the second you feel puberty knocking on the door. Which brings us to number 3 . . .

3. You're not dying, you just got your period. My mother firmly believed that if she did not educate my sister and me about our bodies, we would simply never hit puberty. It is because of this blissful ignorance that at the age of thirteen I stormed into the school nurse's office shouting, "I think I've been shot!" Upon further inspection, I realized that a tiny, silent assassin had not made her way into my Ninja Turtle briefs, but I did just start my first period. So let's plan that somewhere between the ages of nine and thirteen, you and I will thoroughly discuss the war your maturing female body will wage on you. My mother believed tampon use was a virginity litmus test, as its insertion clearly meant a hymen was no longer guarding the perimeter. And birth control pills were basically a license to fuck (note to self: *License to Fuck*, possible title of next book). That methodology is nonsense. It is okay to embrace maturity if it means sparing yourself inconvenience and pain. You are going on the pill the second that first egg drops a beat. Not only will it help clear your skin, make your cycle shortened and predictable, and soothe the fetal-position-in-bed-all-day cramping that is hereditary in your family, it will also help prevent you from forcing me to raise a grandchild. I firmly believe every woman should have complete control over her body as well as the comforting knowledge of when it is safe to wear white pants.

4. Be a kid and like it. While I will help you understand the natural evolution of womanhood by putting you on the pill, sharing my makeup, teaching you to shave, and buying you one sensible thong, I demand you embrace your girlhood while you are in it. When I was fourteen, I spent my lunch breaks challenging friends to spirited games of *Duel Monsters* or arguing why Vegeta was clearly the superior Saiyan. Now, I assume, most teenage girls spend this time posting their boobs to Instagram. Be the girl who plays tag with the boys and not the one supplying handies behind the bleachers. Be the girl who can confidently wear asexual sweatpants and Chuck Taylors, and not the preteen in clothes so short and tight a passerby would have no trouble describing her fallopian tubes to a police sketch artist. Don't rush to be an adult. Just enjoy being a kid for as long as you can. Because once you are not a kid, you have to open a bank account, buy prophylactics without blushing, and get approved for your own cell-phone plan.

5. Never fit in. Your mother can be googled alongside the phrase "ass shots," so understand you are never truly going to "fit in" among your classmates. But who the hell cares? The desire to fit in is basically resigning oneself to the comfort of inferiority. It may feel safe to be a face among the crowd, to have someone else dictate your style and attitude, but it takes guts to stand out. Be your own leader. Set your own standards of what is cool and beautiful. Make people follow YOU.

6. Have some selfie respect. My darling daughter, if you would ever like to take a selfie, please wait until after I am dead. Ninety percent of selfies posted online are silent screams for the world to give the affirmation withholding parents never did. We get it, ladies; Daddy didn't hug you enough and with each "let me cum on dem titties" tweet a forty-year-old living in his mother's basement sends you, that hole in your heart is slowly filled. But despite my general disdain for an act so oxymoronically vain and insecure at the exact same time, I will admit that there are rare occasions when it is perfectly acceptable to take a selfie:

- While standing in front of a national monument.
- When using your phone's camera to check if your makeup is holding up and your hand slips and accidentally takes a picture.
- As a polite time-saver after you get the permission of a celebrity who is clearly in a rush.
- When at dinner with a friend, but there are no strangers around who look trustworthy enough to hold your phone without trying to steal it. (Helpful Hint: Just ask the waiter.)
- If you are really trying to sneak a pic of someone behind you and don't want to make it obvious you're a creep.
- If a dog is sleeping adorably atop you and you don't want to wake it up.
- When taking a pic of you and your significant other kissing. Those are actually adorable. (Helpful Hint: These are only cute when showing them to your friends or as a five-by-seven photo taped to a dresser's mirror. Posting these pictures on social media is an awkward invasion of your

relationship's intimacy. I feel like people with fulfilling, genuinely happy relationships don't have to keep reminding the world. You'd save time by just tweeting, "I pray every second this penis doesn't leave me. #blessed")

- When you've had your makeup professionally done and you want to try to re-create it yourself later, but will inevitably fail and just make yourself look like a hooker who had a really profitable day.

- If you are Mindy Kaling or Anna Kendrick, who can do no wrong.

- When showing off a delectable dessert. (Helpful Hint: Completely social media approved. Everyone wants to see the pure joy on the face of a person who is about to eat a donut the size of his or her torso.)

- When you want to show your guy your freshly salon-styled hair or superflattering outfit to help fester his insecurity about how hot you look when he is not around.

- If someone else is holding the phone. The shame is now theirs.

- If you can 100 percent guarantee the intention of your selfie is not a desperate cry for strangers to help make you feel pretty, but truly an act of harmless arrogance. Anyone so self-confident, so genuinely proud of her own image she feels the overwhelming desire to share it, deserves to take a selfie. If she is eighteen or older. No one likes Instagram jailbait.

7. Always bring a sweater. Self-explanatory. It would also be a good idea to make sure the following are either on your person or only a short, panicked sprint away: tampons, travel-sized deodorant, gum, an inhaler as you are sure to inherit my asthma, a fully charged Nintendo 3DS (there will never not be a new Pokémon), and a condom.

8. Eww, gross. My mom just said "condom." Yeah, I know. You don't want to associate the word *sex* with the person who cuts the crust off your PB&J. But guess what, your parents are god-damn bunny rabbits. How do you think you were accidentally created in the first place? Nevertheless, I promise to educate you about safe sex the second you unroll your first poster of [insert your version of Angel from *Buffy the Vampire Slayer*]. I want sex to be something you and I can openly talk about. I want you to be smart and knowledgeable of your lady labyrinth and not just assume babies are made when a bird and a bee love each other very, very much. (Note to self: "Lady Labyrinth," possible name of all-girl rock band.) I would also appreciate if you try to be a virgin until you get your Ph.D. But just in case, it is my job to teach you to respect your body, to make only the choices you feel comfortable with, to help you understand that 92.3 percent of guys will give a detailed play-by-play of how far he gets with you to his garbage-man if he's willing to listen, and to provide you with condoms behind your father's back.

9. Unconditional. No matter how much you fuck up or how badly you behave, I promise to always be your best friend and confi-dante. I will accept you for who you are and provide you with a safe, loving home for as long as I live.

10. On one condition. If you ever own a single piece of *Breakfast at Tiffany's* or Marilyn Monroe basic ass paraphernalia, I rescind number 9.

I realize there is a chance my future offspring may be a boy. Here is the list of essential information you, my dear son, should know.
1. Morning boners are perfectly normal.
2. Try not to be an asshole.
3. Be good to women. They deal with way more shit than you do.

CHAPTER 10

HELLO, SUNSHINE

No one ever tells you what happens after "happily ever after." The book gets shut or the credits roll, and we're just supposed to assume that when the hero of the story gets exactly what they want, the story is over. But when you finally cross the finish line, slay the dragon, marry the prince, reach the pot of gold at the end of the rainbow—when you actually get ahold of whatever the hell it is you've been chasing like mad—there is only one thought that will cross your mind: *What now?*

I folded the aqua-blue quilt twice over so it would hopefully be thick enough to prevent my ass from falling asleep this time. After placing it on the freshly steamed carpet, I plopped myself cross-legged atop it.

In my new apartment in the Sunshine State, this quilt dutifully served as my only piece of furniture for quite some time. It was my living room couch when I used my laptop to watch *It's Always Sunny in Philadelphia* DVDs, it was my office chair every time I stole my neighbor's Wi-Fi to check my e-mail, and, when I wrapped myself in it like a human burrito, it was my bed.

I was training at Florida Championship Wrestling (FCW) as a member of the WWE's developmental talent roster. And even though the expensive transition of living on my own in another state meant I would have to get by without a car or furniture that wasn't made of faux down feathers for a while, I was perfectly content.

I was adamant about saving as much of my weekly checks as I could. I knew money to be a fleeting thing, and if I could survive just fine without a proper mattress, then I wasn't going to overextend my wallet chain to get one. Even if there were only Hot Pockets and Little Debbie's Honey Buns in my refrigerator, at least it wasn't empty. In fact, it almost felt like a grandiose splurge when I sprang for the Pizza Rolls too. (Nutrition was a lost concept to me at this point.) I had survived on less before. Knowing I had finally entered a real career—my dream career—made me feel like this was just a part of earning my stripes.

As I sat on the lumpy quilt, I opened a spiral notebook across my lap and uncapped my pen as if I were unsheathing a sword. Pen and paper were my weapons before my body ever learned to be, and it was comforting to return to the white and blue lines to plan my next moves. For a decade I had a singular mission: to make it to the WWE. To become a professional wrestler. I had done that. I had accomplished what had at times seemed unattainable, but what was I going to do now? I couldn't rest on my laurels and be satisfied with simply "making it." When you finally live out your biggest dream, the next step must always be: Dream bigger.

On a blank sheet of paper I wrote "My Ten-Year Life Plan" in giant letters. Visualization is important to me. I believe that imagining yourself, in agonizing detail, in whatever dream life you want, is the first step in getting there. Writing the words was a way for me to stare at my desires and be held accountable for bringing them into the world. Here is what was hastily scribbled on the page in hopes of willing the words into fruition.

MY TEN-YEAR LIFE PLAN
1. *Make it to the main roster.*
2. *Win the championship.*
3. *Have an action figure made in my likeness,
   but with exaggerated body measurements.*
4. *Be in a video game.*
5. *Be on a pay-per-view poster.*
6. *Find a haircut that hides my fivehead.*
7. *Have my own merchandise.*
8. *Have a match at WrestleMania.*
9. *Write an autobiography.*
10. *Adopt more dogs.*

It was a lofty list, but it was also nonnegotiable. (Except maybe for the haircut as long as stylists were incapable of magic.) I knew what dreams I wanted to chase next, and even if they seemed impossible to reach, that only made me want them more. My dreams were the hot girl in high school, and I was going to convince them to go to prom with me, and then maybe get them pregnant so they were stuck with me forever. The realist in me (the tiny voice I regularly beat into submission) knew that this was not going to be easy.

I had scored a contract, and though that felt like the end of a long road, I knew it was only the beginning. Ahead of me was a high hill to climb. I would have to train hard and perfect my craft in order to be noticed among the fifty other developmental talents, some already having waited years for a promotion that had yet to come.

The developmental roster, though spending most of every day collaborating and depending on one another while training and performing on shows, were in direct competition. If the writers and producers needed a new character for one of the two main roster television shows, *Raw* or *SmackDown*, they would pick whoever they thought was the most polished and prepared for superstardom. But sometimes, a promotion would be given to a wrestler who wasn't entirely ready for the road, but had the look higher-ups were interested in. Essentially, it was a crapshoot. All we could do to control our own destiny was to make ourselves the best wrestlers and performers we could be, and be prepared when the opportunity presented itself. Though there is always the option of kicking in opportunity's door like it owes you rent money.

It almost felt like we were doctors on call. Horror stories floated around the training facility of wrestlers getting phone calls at midnight and being asked to pack a bag and jump on the first flight at six o'clock that morning. In a whirlwind experience they would travel to whatever city the show was taping in, as the main roster traveled to five different cities across the country each week.

They would perform in the ring for agents and had a shot at debuting on television that night. Everyone wanted that call, but at the same time feared it, should the worst-case scenario happen. No one wanted to get in front of agents and be turned down, depressingly sent back to FCW to train for who knows how much longer. Some of the wrestlers had experienced the rejection several times, totaling anywhere from two to five years within the developmental system. Suddenly I realized why everyone in FCW seemed tired, dejected, and not nearly as naively bright eyed as I had entered.

I had worked hard at training in New Jersey, but once I started the rigorous schedule at FCW I realized what I once thought was hard work was almost laughable in comparison. FCW was not a place you could pop in for two hours, have a practice match, and call it a day. We had to eat, breathe, sleep, and bleed training. And I bled a lot.

I was now known as AJ Lee. In developmental we had to

choose our own character names, but couldn't use our real ones because the company wanted to own the copyright. I pitched "AJ" since it was my family's nickname for me and "Lee" after Wendee Lee, a voice actress in my favorite anime, *Cowboy Bebop*. Initially, "AJ" was turned down because the company felt it was "too tomboyish." But when legal rejected the rest of my pitched names and there was only an hour to submit a name to print in our FCW magazine, I got to sneak the name "AJ" in before anyone noticed.

I chose an apartment only a few blocks away from the warehouse we trained in, and each morning I would drag my giant suitcase full of extra clothes, kneepads, elbow pads, and towels down the road in the blazing Florida sun. I would be drenched in sweat before I even got in the ring, which made people really look forward to rolling around with me. A typical day of training started around 8 a.m. The roster would be split into groups and made to run training drills together. Since there were only a handful of women on the roster, we were integrated into drills with the guys.

After a few hours, we would be paired off with either a guy or girl to have a practice match on the fly. For performances on shows, there would normally be a game plan for the match, but in training it was essential to learn how to adjust in a moment's notice and communicate without letting the audience know. We would then practice promos and study old matches. Three evenings a week we would travel around Florida and put on ticketed shows. If there wasn't a show that evening, we would be allowed to go home around 5 p.m. But trying to expedite the training process and get to the main roster, I started staying until 8 p.m. to squeeze in extra practice.

Two new signees, Zivile, a fitness competitor who had won the Arnold Classic, and Trinity, a dancer with insane natural athletic ability, would eventually join me after hours. Our little crew of rookies was looked after by Tom Prichard, Norman Smiley, or Billy Kidman, former wrestlers and now trainers with the patience of saints and an apparent death wish. They would let us keep the lights on in the building for as late as we liked and were brave enough to let us use their bodies as crash test dummies. We beat the everlasting gobstopper of shit out of them during hours they were not even getting paid to work. A great teacher is selfless. And they just wanted to see their students, who had enough fire to spend an entire day in a humid warehouse, succeed.

I would drag my suitcase home, wash my annihilated workout gear, eat dinner on my quilt, ice my entire body, and fall asleep watching DVDs. In the morning I would peel myself off the floor and do it all again. Day in and day out, every second not sleeping or eating was spent either in the ring or watching tape, trying to perfect every facet of the art form. So deep within the grind, I began to literally dream of performing in the ring. The nightmare was always the same. I was pushed through a curtain in front of an audience of thousands, but I didn't have time to put on any of my wrestling gear. So I would be forced to wrestle in whatever my cruel subconscious decided to torture me with: a sundress, pajamas, laundry-day underwear. There was rarely a moment my mind was on anything else.

Inevitably, there were growing pains. And I mean that quite literally. Through a new rigorous weight-lifting regime and healthy diet now made possible through a growing bank account, I gained ten pounds of muscle. My body quickly transformed from a stick figure to a stick figure with teeny tiny guns. Naturally, I invested in several tank tops. But just to make sure I wasn't getting too confident about my body, it began to fail on me as often as it could. I suffered two more concussions, a dislocated elbow, two dislocated kneecaps, herniated discs in my thoracic spine, and a charming hole in my face.

During an intergender tag team match, I dove out of the ring and onto an awaiting Zivile who was standing, arms outstretched, on the ground below. She was so concerned about my safety in landing, she wrapped her arms tightly around my waist, and the snuggle made my mouth connect with her forehead. Pulling away I noticed a gash on her dome and freaked when I realized my tooth had somehow scarred her face. I freaked even further when I realized that my determined snaggletooth had actually punctured through my own face to get to hers. The bottom half of my face was quickly drenched with the warm blood I couldn't help but dribble out. For the rest of the fifteen-minute match I poked my tongue through the hole above my lip to freak out the children sitting in the front row. After the show, Zivile drove me to the emergency room, where I spent the night waiting to get my face stitched. I got a cab directly from the ER to the airport to fly out for my first shows with the main roster. Every time I look in the mirror and see that little scar above my lip, I remember carefully chewing my airport dinner/breakfast burrito on one side of my mouth and then falling asleep across three chairs at my gate while still clutching the wrapper.

The days began to bleed into one another. Before I knew it, months had passed and I was no longer the rookie on the female roster. So many women had come and gone through the system that somehow I was the female wrestler with the most experience. It was a strange adjustment. I was used to looking to others for guidance, and seemingly overnight I was given the responsibility of the locker room leader. As a sort of "passing of the torch," in early 2010, I won the title of "Queen of FCW" in a taping of our local cable show. Up until that point it was the greatest match of my career and came with the distinguished perk of having to balance a small plastic crown on my giant lollipop head during every show.

The group of girls I spent my days with in developmental were smart, tough, and eager to learn. Watching them blossom into full-fledged performers made me beam with a momma's pride. Not only was I growing as a wrestler by leaps and bounds, I was helping shape the future of the main roster's women. It was a hell of an honor. My trainers began to put so much faith in me as a leader that for the next five years almost every woman who had a tryout with the company had her tryout match with me. Agents would even ask my opinion of the potential of the girls in the ring and their personalities in the locker room. As much as I loved being trusted with that responsibility, I was essentially putting my body on the line in situations where I would never see most of these women again. A lot of wonderful experienced indy wrestlers came through tryouts, but a ton of ladies who were getting into the ring for the first time got to learn the ropes using my 110 pounds of bony might.

Along the way I realized that I was being treated like a "utility man." In wrestling, that is a person who is well rounded enough to be counted on to make their opponent look good and help them learn. I was Old Reliable. And though that was flattering, that meant I would probably never get out of FCW. I would be used as the person to help more exciting and more beautiful women graduate to superstardom. I don't think anyone looked at me and saw a potential star. A year and a half had passed. I had been brought on the road a few times but was always sent back down. I bought some glue and glitter to decorate my pity party hat.

I would never let depression grab ahold of me the way it had before, but being bipolar means experiencing emotions to an extraordinary degree. So when I began to feel down, to lose faith in myself, it hit me hard. Living alone for the first time while doubting my own potential made for an isolating experience. Living in a new state, working at a new job, not knowing if I would ever make it up our corporate ladder, made me feel very small and very alone.

Some people seek out relationships to avoid seclusion, but I liked being single. I had a lot of practice and considered myself a professional. What I did miss, oddly enough, was having someone to look after. I wanted to take my mind off the 24/7 pressure without getting gonorrhea. I was stressed and in need of someone to talk to. Preferably someone who did not talk back. I thought of Mugsy. It often felt like the only time I knew what unconditional love could mean was when his fat ass curled up in my lap and made me sing him to sleep. Mugsy was now in Puerto Rico with my parents, but maybe it was time for a new rescue pup. I felt prepared for it. I had finally rescued myself, so why not share the wealth? Ultimately, I wanted to feel useful, like I was doing more in the world than waiting for someone else to decide my fate. And so I began chiseling away at my ten-year plan.

I found myself scrolling through the website of my local Humane Society. I lit up when I saw that a litter of pit bull puppies had just entered the shelter. Pit bulls were my absolute favorite breed, and I secretly hoped I could find one that had a head as large as Mugsy's. And so I visited my local shelter, the Humane Society of Tampa Bay, to check out these pups.

Upon arriving, I filled out an application to visit with the litter of pits and impatiently hung out in the waiting room. As I looked around I noticed all seven visitors were waiting on meeting the adorable pups. After my initial competitive instinct to beat everyone in the competition for these dogs' hearts subsided, I felt tremendous guilt. This building was full of older dogs, lying on the cold floor of a cage as every visitor passed them by to play with the shiny new puppies. I figured it couldn't hurt to at least stroll through the rows of cages and see if any other little guys would catch my eye.

My barometer for human decency is to see if someone can make eye contact with a shelter animal and not immediately turn into goo. Within seconds I was bawling as I looked at the innocent, hopeful eyes, wondering if I was going to be the person to bring them somewhere warm and safe. And then I noticed the one dog that wasn't rushing toward the gate of his cage.

A small, blond Chihuahua wearing a bright blue turtleneck lay shaking in a ball inside of his food bowl. Sure, dogs look adorable when dressed in clothes or as inanimate objects like when a wiener dog wears buns, but morally I am against this. No, lady, your dog does not "love" wearing that dumbass tutu. It's not a human baby. It's better than a baby because you do not have to teach it the English language or how to hold a sippy cup. And it will never grow up and talk back.

Upon further inspection, however, I found out this Chihuahua had to be covered up, because the building was chilly. And he was balding. The paperwork attached to his cage labeled him as a "special adoption," requiring extra care from an attentive, committed owner who would be willing to administer his six different medications. Not only did he have kennel cough, a sick stomach that inhibited his eating and made him underweight, and a knee injury, but he had a skin disorder that caused his hair to fall out, presumably permanently. Basically, he was a winner.

The volunteers at the shelter told me he lay inside of his bowl because he felt safer being surrounded, and normally he was not very social. He mistrusted all humans, after surviving several harrowing ordeals. The Chihuahua exhibited strong signs of abuse and had been turned in to a kill shelter in another state when animal control found him limping in the street. The shelter discovered he was microchipped and contacted his registered owners to let them know they found their pup. But it became clear, when they refused to come pick him up, the owners were the ones who had hurt him and left him out on the street.

He spent a month in the kill shelter, and when it reached maximum capacity, he was put on the euthanization list. And that is when the world's truest superheroes, the animal shelter volunteers, stepped in. The government will provide funding for a shelter if it regularly euthanizes its animals, to help clear up the homeless pet population. If an organization wants to be a nonkill shelter, it must rely on donations and volunteers to operate. With limited resources they do their best to visit and assess the behavior of animals who are closest to being euthanized at government-funded facilities and then will transfer the best candidates for adoption to the safety of their shelter. They may stick around the shelter for months, but at least they have a shot at life.

This Chihuahua was one of the lucky few brought into the safety of the Humane Society of Tampa Bay. But no one was interested in taking home a sickly, bald Chihuahua. This poor little guy was unwanted, unloved, abused, and alone in the world. Having been homeless, incarcerated, and placed on death row, he clearly had enough street cred to make a rap album. He was a survivor.

I delicately reached through the bars of his cage and scratched at his rough head.

"Are you my tiny furry soul mate?" I asked while he lifted his head and gently inspected the hand petting him.

I got lost in his giant, watery eyes. He stood up in the bowl, and I was sure this was a sign that he had indeed chosen me too. And then he proceeded to puke all over my hand.

"I'll take that as a yes."

Strolling through a pet supply store with the newly christened

Nacho Cheese. Putting it out there.

Nacho Cheese Mendez was an eye-opening experience. Customers looked at the meek little man the same way people look at homeless people in the street, with a sad look of sympathy before quickly averting their eyes to avoid being rude. Or maybe they just thought I had stolen a half-eaten rat from the snake tanks.

I had removed Nacho's blue sweater, and though he was visibly relieved, the bald patches on his body were now exposed to uneasy passersby. One customer shopping with a beautiful, fluffy golden retriever puppy actually directed a pitying "Bless your heart" my way. An employee told me he thought Nacho's skin condition looked permanent and I should consider some cute outfits to cover him up. I clutched tighter onto my wonderful little freak and whispered to him, "I think you're perfect just the way you are."

Though pet store employees and even some veterinarians doubted Nacho could blossom into a healthy, beautiful flower, after months of medication and TLC, that's exactly what he did. He was my very own puppy chia pet, growing all his glorious, fluffy fur back and shaking off the harsh memories of his past. His indomitable spirit and tenacity were inspiring. If Nacho Cheese could overcome the odds, so could I.

————

And as if he knew I had a new companion to carry the torch of looking after me and providing an unwavering source of unconditional love, Mugsy began to let go. "I don't think he has long left," Dad warned me as I entered the farmhouse in Puerto Rico during Christmas vacation. I had two weeks off the nonstop schedule each year to visit family during the holidays. I would not be able to travel back to Puerto Rico for another twelve months.

I hesitantly entered the bedroom Mugsy spent most of his day inside. On a small mattress, he stayed lying on his side even as I approached. In my mind Mugsy was still the hulking brute of his youth, but he was an old man now. My eyes always had to adjust to the withering sight of him. Having once been a ball of vibrant energy, he now couldn't find the strength to lift his head. I watched his thinning tail lazily smack the soft surface as he wagged upon realizing who I was.

My little guy. My beautiful chunky monkey. He had been through so much as part of the Mendez clan. Though my father rescued him from a life of violence, he ended up on every harrowing journey we endured. When we lost our home, so did he. When we slept in a car, he was right there curled up in my lap. He shared a couch on a screened-in porch, and a mattress in a motel room. When I feared the danger of our neighborhoods, he was at my side to make me feel safe. He was never a dog. He was a member of the Mendez family. And I could see in his eyes, he would be gone soon.

Stroking his now rough fur, I knew he wouldn't make it to next Christmas. His breathing was labored as he noticed my lap and tried to prop himself up to sit on it. But he was too tired. And so I lay down beside him on the mattress, wrapped my arm around his warm belly, and sang to him for the last time. "You are my sunshine, my only sunshine . . ."

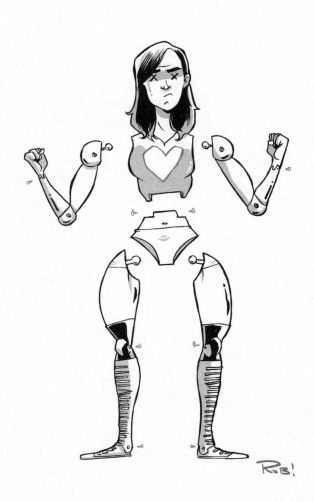

CHAPTER 11

NO ONE WANTS TO HAVE SEX WITH YOU

P urgatory is a place in Tampa, Florida. It had been almost two years since I first stepped foot in FCW, and though in some ways I was living a completely new life, it also felt like I was running in place.

On the one hand, things had never been better. Not counting the sciatica, the stitches in my mouth, or the need for brain medication to avoid punching strangers in the face, I was healthy. Finally educating myself about nutrition and making enough money to buy more than one avocado at Whole Foods, my out-of-shape stomach had tightened into what almost resembled an ab. I could finally afford to buy furniture, which was now covered in Nacho's newly grown, and surprisingly abundant, fur. And I had moved Erica to Florida to live with me after she had outgrown our small town in New Jersey and/ or burned an ex-boyfriend's house to the ground and needed to lie low for a while.

But on the other callused hand, progression through the wrestling ranks was painfully slow. For two years I had spent every waking hour training in one form or another. Occasionally I would see a glimmer of light when I'd get an invite to travel with the main roster. However, at the time, when a female wrestler went on the road for a trial period, it was only in a hosting capacity on untelevised events. While the guys got to have matches on the "house shows"—smaller arena shows where wrestlers and producers would try out ideas for the TV programming—the women would "host" a fan trivia question or dance contest.

Women had more opportunities in speaking/character/valet roles than in the ring during this era. So we hopefuls had to first demonstrate we could be bubbly and charming before we would get our chance. The host was only required to do two things: wear a dress, and speak to the audience without stammering. One out of two would have to do.

I didn't own any dresses at the time, so when I got my first phone call to travel on house shows, I rushed to the one store I depended on for all my clothing needs, Burlington Coat Factory. (This was years before I would start making Target clothes money.) All of the women on the roster consistently stunned in skintight designer dresses, but I knew that (a) I couldn't pull those off, (b) I didn't want to flash my vagina to an audience of thousands just yet, and (c) I could buy an Xbox and two games for the same price as one of those fancy dresses. After pillaging the bargain racks at Burlington, I finally found a dress that fit my prepubescent frame. Sure, it was a child's medium, but buying it would get me five dollars off a KitchenAid toaster and I couldn't resist such a deal. Pairing the dress with the kitten-heeled shoes one of the girls in FCW had sweetly bought for me at a thrift store, I really thought I cleaned up well. For about five minutes. When I walked backstage in a half-sequined, half-floral-patterned shift dress that resembled an art project a five-year-old would make out of curtains she inherited from her dead grandmother, I was met with perplexed eyes. A sexpot, I was not. One of the wrestlers walked up to me, put his hand on my shoulder, looked deep into my eyes, and said, "You look really good." He then busted out laughing when he thought he walked out of earshot. I had no clue how to style myself, let alone walk in even the smallest of heels, so when the time came for my inaugural walk through an official WWE curtain, I stumbled in front of the crowd looking like a baby deer on ice, who was somehow also drunk and pregnant. As I steadied myself, I realized an audience of thousands was quietly staring at me, awaiting something charming to fall from my trembling mouth.

I had never been in front of so many people, let alone had their undivided attention and a microphone in hand. It occurred to me that nothing was really stopping me from violently shouting "Douchebag balls!" into the mic besides a desire to not be fired, even though it would make a helluva story.

Customarily, the host would welcome the city by name before picking a child in the audience to answer her trivia question. A kid who answered right would get to sit ringside for the upcoming women's match, which for a long while had involved lots of hair pulling, prop balls, and at least two spanking spots. So it was important to pick a child young enough to hit puberty on the spot or at the very least return to the child's parents with a lot of uncomfortable questions.

As I opened my mouth to welcome the crowd, I suddenly forgot where we were. The crippling stage fright that came over me made it impossible to remember which city we were in. But I had already begun making unintelligible sounds into the live microphone and couldn't turn back now.

"Uuuuurrrgghh . . . heh . . . HELLOOOO . . . guuuuuuys?" I was off to a great start.

"How is everything going tonight?" A question as exciting and personable as *Some weather we're having, huh?* But at least I stopped making guttural noises.

"Who likes trivia?!" I asked like a second-grade substitute teacher.

When the child I called on was too young to form words, the second child I forced the microphone on answered incorrectly. *Well, shit, no one prepared me for what I was supposed to do if the damn kid got the question wrong!* Instead of saying anything . . . anything at all, into the mic, I just turned to the ring announcer, Tony Chimel, and nervously shook my head. He was kind enough to bail me out and let the kid sit ringside anyway. At least I assume so. I had already kicked my heels off and hauled ass behind the curtain before I could spontaneously combust.

Normally, our trainers at FCW would receive reports on our performances while traveling on the main shows, and I was sure my first would be the death of my career. It was tragic, but not for the reason I had anticipated. Sitting in the trainers' office in Tampa, Tom Prichard tried to gently break the news to me.

"This is not a big deal, but I wanted to give you a heads-up on something," he warned as I braced myself for the scathing review.

"I just want to say that I personally think you're one of our best female wrestlers here. It's just that sometimes that's not enough. Have you considered repackaging your appearance?"

Wait, what now? I had Hindenburged my first hosting gig, and the only feedback I was getting was about my looks?

"They didn't like your dress. They said it looked . . . a little conservative . . . matronly." He was visibly uncomfortable, so I tried to help ease his mind by yelling.

"Matronly? I swear it was from the kids' department at Burlington!" I wasn't helping.

"I just thought you should know. And personally, I'm not saying it's right, but it would probably be a good idea to start practicing makeup and all that other girl shit. I just don't want our bosses to walk in here and see all your dolled-up competition and look right over you because you're wearing a hoodie."

He was undoubtedly relaying the message of my superiors softer than they had intended, but it still stung worse than that time I fell into a red anthill on the farm in Puerto Rico. As a host on house shows, a woman's purpose was to look stunning and act fun and flirty so the audience would remain entertained in between matches, and I couldn't do either. I wasn't a good fit for the job. I was naturally unkempt, and even when I tried my hardest to doll up, I still looked homely. So it made sense when I wasn't invited back on the road the next week.

I was getting far on skill alone and had secretly hoped I could help change the minds of WWE executives into thinking that was enough. But to be fair, this was still a business. A business that had a successful formula when it came to their women, and I wasn't going to change that overnight. It takes time to start a rebellion.

This was my face and body when I got signed, but now the pressure was on for me to change. The question was no longer *What makes a good girl?* It was *What makes a girl good enough?* And whatever that was—body, hair, or looks—I, apparently, wasn't enough.

But when I got inside of that ring, people paid attention. They cheered for me because they related to me. They felt connected to me and shared my pain and didn't give a crap that my eyeliner wasn't straight or my body was that of an athletic preteen boy. I needed to make my bosses understand this. They needed to see it in action. But it was hard to grab their attention when I was a singular voice in a crowd. I wasn't going to have an army supporting my cause. I had to become a one-girl revolution.

A few weeks later, I was surprisingly brought back on the

road. The last time, I had tried to mimic what I had seen before me and essentially just came off as a shitty version of a hot chick. I was not going to outsexy the rest of the female roster. So I had to find whatever it was I did best and embrace that. And what I did best was wear sensible shoes. Luckily, success is when opportunity meets preparation.

The first night on the two-night house show loop, I asked a fan a trivia question, the kid got it right this time, and my work for the evening was done. I sat ringside with the fan for the women's match that followed my segment. It went gut-wrenchingly bad. I know how hard females in the industry work to be respected, and when a match does not go well, it hurts all of us. Mostly because the decision makers felt it was only proving their point: that a woman's time in the ring should be limited. On television the women's matches were a meager two to three minutes compared with fifteen to twenty-five for the guys. So watching the ladies crash and burn that evening made me feel genuinely sorry for them.

One of the "top guys," a phrase to describe main event wrestlers who are such attractions they sell the most merchandise, garner the highest TV ratings, and are essentially considered the reason fans buy tickets, was vocally disappointed with the match. And when I say vocally, I mean he threw a water bottle at the backstage monitor while the match was on the screen, breaking the expensive TV set, and yelled at the producers, "Get some fucking talented women wrestlers on this show, please!"

When I got backstage, the show's producer, Fit Finlay, immediately pulled me aside. "I hope you have your gear on you, because you're wrestling tomorrow night."

"What? Yes. Okay. Why?" I was a cornucopia of emotions.

"You can thank CM Punk for that one. He's got a hell of an arm." Fit laughed while walking off.

The next night I had my first official WWE match. And it was everything I had ever dreamed. Not only was I wrestling with the main roster for the first time, it was in a match for the women's title against the champion Layla. Layla was always helpful and welcoming and was generous enough to let me shine in the match. She played the "bad guy" heel role to perfection and knew letting the babyface have exciting moments only made her character seem even more dastardly when she shut them down with dirty-handed methods. I appreciated her generosity and willingness to let me have my moment, since it could potentially lead to a full-time spot on the roster.

The match went off without a hitch. It was fast paced, exciting, and far exceeded any match I had up until then. Even more overwhelming was the fact that the crowd was uncharacteristically loud for a women's match.

Every guy on the roster congratulated the two of us, even the douchenozzle who made fun of my dress a few weeks earlier shook my hand out of respect, and Fit pulled us into an office to let us know he would put the match on a DVD for us to remember this significant moment. He let me know he would put in a good word for me on the road and hoped he'd see me again soon.

It felt like a dream. Like a cheesy sports movie where a player gets called off the dugout and scores the game-winning hoop. I don't know sports. All I knew was that I had been waiting two years to get a shot at proving my mettle in the ring, I stumbled into an opportunity, and I made the most of it. I could feel the good juju vibrating in the air, and I hoped my call-up would be imminent.

And it was. A week later I was brought to the television tapings and my debut was written into the *SmackDown*'s first draft! First drafts change, you say? Nonsense! I was scheduled to debut alongside Vickie Guerrero and Dolph Ziggler, whose characters were phenomenal villains and something of an item. The plan was my character would lead Dolph astray and cause a rift between them. Upon hearing the news, I found a custodian's closet backstage and cried tears of joy inside of it for fifteen minutes. I also applied my makeup and got changed in the closet because I was too nervous to enter the female locker room.

An hour before showtime, I was still waiting to see a script or talk to a producer who could let me know what to expect. Ed Koskey, the show's head writer, was nice enough to break the news gently.

"So some stuff got shuffled around in the script and your debut is not going to happen tonight, but definitely next week, okay?" He tried to soften the blow, and keep my hopes up, but I was devastated. "Next week . . . I'll just wait till next week." I locked myself in my unofficial dressing room and opened a roll of toilet paper resting next to a dirty mop, proceeding to cry off my sloppily applied mascara.

Next week never came.

But a few months later FCW's female roster got a pleasant surprise. The SyFy network had aired two seasons of a competition-based show featuring the men of FCW. Each season a winner had been picked and given a spot on the roster. It was a new way to debut on the main shows. Season three had not been picked up by the network, but their contract with WWE required them to air a few more episodes of the show. So it was decided these four weeks of airtime would be given to the women of FCW. The rest of the competition would be aired on the company's website. It was a step down from the previous seasons, but we were all still pretty stoked to find out we would be filming alongside the main roster and traveling around the country.

I was happy to have a change of scenery from FCW, but

frankly a little disappointed. I had spent two years competing to earn a spot on the main roster, and a debut was tantalizingly dangled just out of reach. Now I would have to compete all over again for the opportunity that had just been written out of a *SmackDown* script. It was a frustrating step back, but at least I would have more opportunities to show my worth. At least we would get the chance to show what we could do in the ring, that we were capable and strong women, that we were here to take our rightful spot and be respected.

So inevitably the first contest on the show was a dance-off. There was also a chocolate-eating contest, a limbo contest, a present-unwrapping contest, and a sumo wrestling contest complete with blow-up fat suit. It's possible we weren't being taken entirely seriously. But when there was a sliver of a chance at proving myself, I took it. On WWE history contests, I smoked my competitors, displaying my knowledge and respect of the business. I had learned to handle the mic a lot better than I had as a host, as I finally felt like I had something worthwhile to say. My promos and attitude began to garner a following. The fans were ready for a change, and the five-foot-nothing nerd in Chuck Taylors instead of wrestling boots was giving them an option.

During the first season-three episode of *NXT*, a writer and producer actually went through all the other contestants' luggage to help find me something suitable to wear, after deeming what I had on not fancy enough for television. Layla, with the best of intentions, even helped me find heels and unsuccessfully tried to stuff my bra. And so for episode two, I hid from sight until a minute before showtime and emerged in what I had wanted to wear the first week: knee-high Chuck Taylor sneakers and a loose-fitting dress. I was scolded after the show, but it was too late. Fans had taken notice of what at the time was blasphemous style for a woman in the company.

Women in the WWE were meant to wear expensive, tight-fitting dresses and high heels. They were glamorous sex kittens. Alongside a group of smoking hot Barbies, I looked like lil' sis Skipper. But suddenly I noticed an influx of girls proudly sharing their pictures on Twitter of them honoring the style. Chucks with dresses, Chucks with I HEART NERDS shirts. I knew I had something there.

While everyone was concerned about being appealing to our male fan base, it seemed they were neglecting their fellow females. I realized that was who we as women should be targeting. They made up almost half our fan base but didn't have someone they could see themselves in. I would be their reflection on the TV screen (or computer monitor). I would get them to join an uprising. I would find a way to succeed by using the things I had been told would hold me back.

A few weeks into the thirteen-week competition, I was called into the office of a member of Talent Relations. In essence, this man was one of my bosses underneath only the owners of the company. So I assumed this was not going to be a chat about the weather.

I stared at my intertwined fingers fidgeting in my lap as I racked my brain trying to figure out who I pissed off. Was it one of the veteran guys whose hand I forgot to shake? Had the head office found out about that speeding ticket? Had somebody seen me eat five chocolate chip cookies in catering?

"Don't look so nervous, I promise you're not in trouble," he said, trying to quell my obvious unease. "I just wanted to talk to you about our Diva brand. How well do you think you're fitting into that brand?" "Diva" was the name of the federation's women, while "Superstar" was the term used for men. Battles have been waged over the discrepancy between the two.

"Well, honestly, I'm not trying to fit in. And I think that's working for me. You guys have told me I get the most fan votes every week, so I think that means they're connecting to the message I'm trying to send." The *NXT* competition held weekly eliminations in order to crown a winner. Who moved on in the competition was determined by fan votes and an "expert panel," aka the higher-ups in the company. I knew just winning the fans over was only half of the work, but I figured if my bosses could see the reaction I was getting, it would help them to see me favorably.

"And what message is that?" He was obviously not expecting that response, but he was willing to see where I was going with this.

"That wrestling matters. That there are a dozen gorgeous women here to choose from if you're looking to put someone on a poster, so why not focus on ring skills and personality. Half our audience is women. I think they want someone to represent them, someone they can get behind. Also they really like my shoes."

This was true. Not just the part about my Chucks being killer, but that I had begun to connect to the fans on a different level. Any chance I got the microphone in my hand I made sure to distinguish myself from the pack. I had a strategy. Not only did I think it was important to represent myself genuinely, but it just made smart business sense. I remembered that when I was a young girl watching the product, I wasn't into designer dresses and high heels. I watched pro wrestling because I was a tomboy. It reminded me of my video games, and the rough-and-tumble nature spoke to me more than any fashion magazine or teenybopper show about high school relationship drama. It made sense to me that women watching years later would probably still skew more toward the down-to-earth variety.

I assumed they were tired of their only options for heroines not being relatable. And while the male fans thoroughly enjoyed the voluptuous vixens in little clothing, I doubted they would emotionally invest in them and put the effort in to vote for them. Sort of like how not every woman gets taken home to Momma. To get the guys to actually care about a female contestant, they needed to be more than a one-dimensional plaything.

I had had mostly guy friends my whole life because we shared the same interests. And so that was my approach with the male fans. Let them know we both played video games and read comics and enjoyed a sensible sneaker. I wasn't trying to portray myself as some perfect unattainable specimen, which had been the formula laid out before us for years.

Often the makeup artists, having plenty of girls to prepare who were on the actual TV programs *Raw* and *SmackDown*, would be so overwhelmed they would have to prioritize their time. They would rush our makeup, only do half, or skip it altogether. As television rookies, being a part of the show while not looking the part made a lot of the girls insecure. So they would arrive at the arena early and put their impressive makeup skills to work, taking the initiative to prepare themselves for TV. It wasn't an easy task considering the level of perfection a professional makeup artist provided and how we were vying for a spot among a "brand." But I think part of the refusal to help us out was a test.

The *NXT* competitions before the all-female season had endured similar second-class-citizen treatments, in a sort of fraternity-hazing/stripe-earning kind of way. I'd like to assume that's why the dressing room provided for six women week after week was the bottom of a staircase covered in tarps, a handicap bathroom stall, or a room as small as a closet with no tables or chairs. Once, upon noticing a door inside of our "locker room," we opened it—only to realize the door led to an actual locker room and we were literally being housed inside a closet.

I didn't have the innate womanly abilities to paint my own face, and so I learned to embrace looking like hot garbage on TV. It was kind of freeing. If I looked crappy on TV, I didn't have to be worried about getting caught in an airport with no makeup on. I would look exactly the same—tired, puffy, and sort of like a hungry squirrel. If I set the bar real low, no one would be disappointed. (Which is also how I approach most relationships.) Without realizing it, I was training the audience, and myself, to be comfortable not measuring up physically with everyone else.

Instead of trying and failing to compete in that department, I embraced being the best version of myself. That started on a visual level but then went much deeper. When given a microphone, I let my freak flag fly. I talked about robot handshakes, playing Xbox, and eating pizza and displayed a vast knowledge of pro-wrestling history. I made jokes, snort laughed, handed out fist bumps, and acted like my true dorky self.

To understand how obscene that kind of behavior was for a woman at the time, one needs to only look at the vignettes used on the main programs to welcome audiences back from commercial break. A stunning blonde was naked in a bathtub, surrounded by candles and strategically placed bubbles, purring, "Welcome back to *SmackDown*." And often that was the only time a woman was seen on the show. Unless you count being used as a spare backup dancer for a famous musical guest. But one could argue that was progress in comparison to only a few years earlier when women competed in "Evening Gown" and "Bra and Panties" matches—bouts won by stripping a humiliated opponent to her underwear.

It wasn't only a risk to go against the grain so hard, it was a bit disrespectful to so outwardly combat the conventional system. I understood I was probably pissing off my bosses, but I felt for the women who were so amazingly talented but were relegated to roles that focused on their looks and utilized them as glorified props.

I wanted to start chipping away at that glass ceiling. I wanted to throw rocks at it little by little until I made a crack. If taking a risk and pissing people off meant having even the smallest of shots at changing the landscape for myself and every woman who came after me, then it was a risk worth taking.

And it worked. The fan response was overwhelming. Most important, the fans were tired of watching women's wrestling that didn't take itself seriously. They were itching for talented matches with exciting performances. They wanted to rally behind a female performer, not just catcall her. I felt embraced and accepted, like I was the audience's voice in the competition.

But not everyone was as hopeful as I was.

Back in Talent Relations: "Look, we know you can wrestle, and not many women can. We appreciate that, we just want you to understand that it's important to be the full package. Right now, you're the best wrestler in the competition. Our female fans want to dress like you. Our male fans want to hang out and play video games with you. But no one wants to have sex with you. Do you see how that's a problem for us? I don't know how they do things in FCW, but here we have a standard our women are proud to stand up to."

Well, fuck. How exactly does one respond to that? Should I wait until I get back to the privacy of the locker room/closet or should I just break down in tears right now? After all my hard work and actual, tangible success taking a different route, everything still came down to how fuckable I was. And apparently I wasn't very. In all fairness, I understood where he was coming from. At the end of the day, this business had a long-standing, proven formula for moderate success. Executives had accepted that their women could sell posters and calendars but would not spike the ratings.

Women's matches were often put in between two very important male matches, as a way to give the audience a break from action. While the women wrestled, the fans could relax, build up their energy for the next match that actually mattered, and take a bathroom break if needed. This was a real, accepted strategy when putting a show together. A fluffy women's match was meant to help the fans catch their breath.

When a show was running overtime and minutes needed to be cut, the sacrificial lamb was always the women's match. They did not receive high ratings, and thus it made sense to throw ten women into one thirty-second match. Literally, thirty fucking seconds. The mentality was *Hey, look at all these hot chicks; but don't worry, they won't bore you for too long.*

That was the landscape I was entering. That was the landscape I was determined to change. And as I listened to the rest of his well-meaning advice on considering going blond, I wondered, *Has any man ever been asked to step up his sex appeal in the name of job performance?*

I was kicked off the show that evening. I decided to flip off the system one last time before I went back to training at FCW for the foreseeable future. When a contestant was kicked off, he or she was allowed to say good-bye to the audience, and most took this moment to say a quick "thank you" or "you got it wrong." This was the send-off speech I came up with on the spot while choking on tears.

"I know I'm not a supermodel. I know I'm the girl that didn't go to prom and stayed home to play video games, but I think that's the girl you guys are ready to have as a 'Diva.' I think that it's time that a 'Diva' represents every single girl in the audience watching. A girl that every single guy would want to hang out with. I have wanted this my entire life and I have fought to get here. Every step I have taken has been for this moment, to be in this ring. There is not one thing that is going to stop me. I will be back and I'm going to accomplish all of my dreams. Thank you so much for every single second. You will see me again."

Back down at FCW, a new title had been created for the women's division, and this time it wasn't a sparkly crown. The women of developmental finally had an actual title belt to

Super psyched to hang out in our bathroom stall/ locker room for another year.

compete for. Sure, it was bright pink and had two mud flap ladies adorning it, but as long as it wasn't a piece of jewelry I considered it progress. When I became the first woman to have held both "The Queen of FCW" and "FCW Divas Champion" titles, I was proud to make history. But ultimately, I knew what holding a title in FCW meant. It meant I wasn't going anywhere anytime soon.

. . . *BUT EVERYONE EXPECTS SEX FROM YOU*

Growing up, surrounded by guy friends and idolizing my brother, it took me a while to realize I had a vagina. And it took me even longer to realize how much of a problem that was going to be. As kids, we don't necessarily see our limitations through gender. For the most part, we are just an asexual pair of jam-hands on an indestructible Gumby body. Sure, I once had a boy tell me I wasn't invited to play tag because "girls are slow," but I just showed him how fast I could sock him in the thigh and he relented.

As we get older, simply beating people up to prove our worth isn't going to achieve the same results. But, boy, have I wanted to try. Believe it or not, being told the majority of America did not want to penetrate me wasn't the meanest thing a guy has ever told me. But having it happen not only in the workplace, but also in the job of my dreams, held a different kind of weight. Suddenly, sexiness was not an option, it was a prerequisite. And as I continued to work with large groups of women, I realized I wasn't alone.

For women in every field and facet of life, there is some expectation of physical beauty. It is as if simply having a vagina has signed us to a lifetime contract with Sephora cosmetics. A period is a literal blood oath to join the never-ending quest for physical perfection. But why? Part of the answer is that for

generations upon generations men have been preconditioned
to put this pressure on women. Not all men, but enough for it
to be a problem in this modern age.

If you are one of the good ones to whom this does not apply,
high five, brother. May your manners and respectful treatment of women get you laid like a bandit. But there are a great
deal of other men who just believe it is a woman's duty to look
good. That is what society has raised them to believe. That we
are here for their viewing pleasure. And to deny them of this
means we have failed at being a woman. And, they think, if
you're not going to put the effort in to look attractive, at least
don't make the cardinal sin of being unappealing.

If a woman is not a giggling, lilting flower, a lot of guys
will just assume she's having her period or is a cold shrew—
instead of considering that maybe he's just not that funny. Just
because you are a man does not mean I have to giggle at your
jokes. I don't owe you anything just because I have a vagina.

And I owe no one a goddamn smile. If a woman makes
eye contact with a man and doesn't grin, chances are that guy
is going to call her a bitch in his head, or sometimes he will
just yell it at her loudly for displeasing him. Men, this is a real
thing that happens to your mothers, sisters, and girlfriends
when you are not around. Then there are the obnoxious bunch
that will just go ahead and make a demand of her face, while
using a voice that would imply he is gifting her with attention.
"Smile," guys will tell complete strangers, when they really
mean, *Why are you not trying to get me to sleep with you? You are
a woman, which means I have the right to be pleased by looking at
you.* Ask yourself how you would feel about a man approaching
your daughter this way.

I once read an interview with Megan Fox in which the interviewer felt the need to mention that he had been greeted
by Fox with a handshake and not a warm smile. He said it

put him off and made her seem cold and withholding. Would any interviewer complain about the same thing if a male actor greeted him with a handshake? He would probably applaud the man's manners.

Society expects their women to respond to men with warmth and immediate intimacy. To do anything but must mean the woman is an icy bitch, not simply professional and expecting to be treated as an equal.

Asking a woman to smile is either a creepy invasion of personal space or a rude assumption that a woman needs rescuing. We are not damsels in distress. I'm a self-rescuing princess, thank you very much. And even if I were actually in a foul mood, your tiny penis would do nothing but only further bum me out.

I assume the only men who can truly understand how annoying this is are the dancers in Las Vegas's *Thunder Down Under*. Because while every single female on the planet is born with a list of physical expectations stapled to her forehead, only a male stripper can truly understand what it feels like to be marginalized on his looks alone.

Men, on average, do not have to worry about this crap. They don't get pulled into an office and told to work on their sexiness for the sake of their job. They can be perfectly respected for their talent without any mention of their looks. And most of them certainly don't have to feel unsafe walking down a street. They don't get accosted by female drivers who think honking a horn is a polite compliment.

I once tweeted that I was offering free to low-cost castrations to any man who enjoyed honking his horn at a chick as a form of mating call. I was blown away by how many guys went on the offensive, reprimanding me for being so ungrateful for the attention. I don't want these men to reproduce, so my offer still stands.

"He just wanted to let you know you are beautiful, you bitch." So he wanted to compliment me through the use of a startlingly loud noise and then speed off? Using this logic, the next time my guy does the dishes I will quietly lurk behind him, scream directly into his eardrum, and then run away into the night.

No woman likes this, guys. In fact, the second a driver slows to catcall us or honk his horn, we reach for our pepper spray, understandably assuming you are a sexual predator and you intend to stuff us in your trunk.

And sure, there might be men reading this who think, *Hey, trying to compliment a lady does not make us sexual harassers!* Except that it kind of does. Because the actual definition of sexual harassment is this: unwelcome sexual advances, a request for sexual favors, and other verbal or physical harassment of a sexual nature. So, yes, seeing an attractive woman and requesting she open her mouth for you in an ass-backward attempt at being flirty and making a woman feel even the slightest bit like she might be in danger can be a form of sexual harassment.

It's important to realize the severity of these actions because it's a slippery slope from unwanted advances to becoming a red dot on your local sex offender registry. *Bitch, why are you taking this shit so seriously?* you might ask while telling your wife to stop staring at you for yelling at a book and to get back in the kitchen. Well, sir, because I have seen the worst of these kinds of situations. And it all comes down to assumptions and expectations.

It is assumed that as women, we want men to find us attractive. And when we do not appreciate a "compliment," some men feel like this is a slap in the face. They assume a "compliment" was what we wanted. Please note the difference between my guy telling me I look beautiful and a stranger telling me, "You got a nice fat ass on you." They assume being extremely forward is flattering and not intrusive. And some men give a bad name to all when they expect the access and opportunity to approach a woman however they see fit.

A typical workweek in wrestling included five days of traveling. It started with two flights into a town, a show in that town, three to four hours of driving to the next town when that show ended around 10 p.m., and repeating this five days in a row until taking two flights back home. As a woman, occasionally traveling alone, it was important to be aware of my surroundings. When I stopped at a gas station one morning before a show, a man filling up next to me refused to peel his eyes from my ass.

I watched as he overflowed his tank with gas and cursed as his shoes got covered in the foul-smelling liquid. That's how inappropriately long and intense he locked onto what my momma gave me. While I finished paying, I noticed him watching me in his car. He had no further business at the gas station but was not driving away. While I drove to a restaurant to grab some food to take to the arena, I noticed he followed close behind the entire way and simply parked outside, just waiting for me to come out.

As I entered the store, I let an employee know I thought I was being followed and a kind girl and guy walked me back out to my car. When we walked out and I saw him roll his window down, despite my having company, I thought the worst of his intentions. He shouted at me, "Hey! Has anyone ever told you you're beautiful?" Ignoring him, I got back into my car and drove to the arena, noticing he was still on my tail. As I drove through a security checkpoint I watched his car bust a U-turn in defeat.

What exactly was this guy's game plan? Was he going to follow me in his car all day showering me with compliments, hoping that one day we would laugh to our children about how

Daddy stalked Mommy until she loved him? Or was his plan something more sinister? Luckily, I didn't have to find out.

On a scale of 1 through Mayor of Creep Town, this incident barely registered against the type of experiences I've had and the women I've worked with have had. I can guarantee you they all have anywhere from five to twenty stories just like that. So I've learned to keep my guard up. If a guy gives me any reason to worry, as a well-traveled and street-smart woman, I'm going to assume the worst. Because sometimes a guy may start by staring at your ass at the gas station, but then that situation may escalate.

As a woman in a sport that can sometimes have small outfits and salacious story lines, there was an odd expectation of access. Sort of like how guys want to take pictures with their arms wrapped around a group of Hooters waitresses. *These are women who are meant to be looked at*, they think, *so naturally that must mean I have an all-access pass to them.*

I have had men follow me in dark airport parking lots to try and get a picture. I don't assume the picture part and reach for pepper spray or my keys to defend myself from the guy FOLLOWING ME IN A DARK PARKING LOT. Then they act like I'm the weird one. I've had a father bring his son up to me for a picture and held his small child in one arm as we posed for the photo. He then wrapped his other arm around my waist and squeezed my ass as his friend, jumping to my other side, wrapped his arm around my shoulders and tried to slide his hand down my shirt. These two grown men planned a sexual assault on a woman using a child.

Instinctively I elbowed back at both men and watched as our badass security woman, Muriel Howell, took both men by the back of the neck to airport security.

I have had two men follow my car from one state to another, check into my same hotel, and request the room next door to me. And they were actually given it! When I opened my door in the morning, they popped out and asked for autographs. They could've easily just pushed me into my room and attacked me. But that kind of carelessness from a hotel's staff doesn't surprise me; I had one man call my room five times asking if I could meet him for drinks in the hotel bar. When I called the front desk to speak to a manager, turns out it was the manager who had been calling in the first place.

And sometimes these hotel interactions aren't so innocent. One female wrestler actually had a maintenance worker use a master key to open her room door while she was asleep at 3 a.m. Luckily she had the door bolted, but for a terrifying second she locked eyes with a man who cracked a door open with the cruelest of intentions.

So understandably, I feel a little on the offense. How far separated is a guy who can objectify a woman online or while in a moving car because he can anonymously get away with it from a guy who would break into a woman's hotel room because no one would find out? For women who have to endure all levels of sexual harassment every day, the lines begin to blur.

But I believe there are plenty of guys who are smart and polite enough to act appropriately with a woman; it's just really hard to hear them over these obnoxious car horns. So, nice guys, speak up. Get louder. Whether you see it or not, there are women all around you who would really appreciate being able to pump their gas without feeling in danger.

And misogynists, please shut the fuck up. Treat women the way you would want someone to treat your daughter, sister, mother, or wife—or scratch that—treat women how you want to be treated. Step up. Be kinder. Be smarter. Be better. Or just smile real pretty for me, so I can punch you in the teeth.

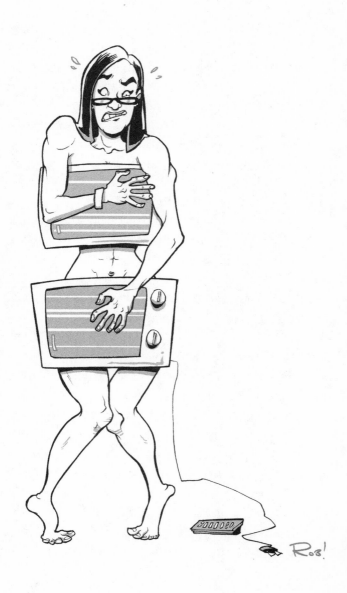

CHAPTER 12

EXTRA WHIP

don't believe in anything but myself. I don't believe in fate. I don't believe in destiny, soul mates, or really anything that suggests that I am not the final word in the path I take. It's one of the many reasons I avoid drugs and alcohol. Not only do I respect the power of my brain at full capacity, I relish being in complete control. But there have been moments so coincidental, so fortuitously miraculous, they have made me wonder.

When wrestlers had spent a certain amount of time in FCW and could not gain anything more out of the system, the company executives would bring them on the road and choose from one of two options. Either they would let them advance to the main roster in case an extra body was needed, or they would determine their investment was going nowhere and fire them. When after six more months in FCW had passed and I was invited on the road, I was sure this was my swan song.

But as luck would have it, the wrestlers I would be working with that weekend on house shows were a group of collaborative, talented women: Celeste; the current champion, Beth Phoenix; and Layla, whom I already knew I could depend on in the ring. Celeste (known as Kaitlyn in the ring) and I had become fast friends when I handled her tryout match and she was thrust onto *NXT* season 3, two weeks after getting hired. She had proven herself to be a hard worker and was full of personality and potential. When we realized we were the only women on the roster with the same asinine, deeply inappropriate sense of humor, and strikingly similar upbringings that had made us hardened sarcastic monsters, we quickly became heterosexual life partners.

The four of us worked together seamlessly. I let them all know this may be my last chance at being employed and so we pulled no punches. At the time, women were not known for taking risks in the ring, so when we put on a tag match that was full of dangerous acrobatic "high spots" for myself and Layla, and feats of strength for Kaitlyn and Beth, the producers took notice. I even got an e-mail from the Talent Relations department congratulating me on the positive reports. I truly believe that match saved my job.

Not only that, in May 2011, about two weeks later, I finally debuted on WWE television. To make the moment even more cry-worthy, I got to debut in a tag team with Celeste. When the announcers approached us before the show and asked if we had a team name, we jokingly told them it was the Chickbusters. Taking us seriously, they actually called us that on television. The match was on the company's B show, *Smack-Down*. We each got one move of offense in, subsequently lost the match, and were warned it might be cut from the taped show's airing because the event had run overtime—but none of that stopped my heart from soaring. I had finally wrestled in a WWE ring. I had finally debuted on the main roster.

For a few months I continued my role as a utility man. *NXT* had become its own noncompetition show, and alongside two other shows, called *Main Event* and *Superstars*, the three programs were taped before *Raw* and *SmackDown*. For many weeks I would serve double or triple duty, wrestling on

NXT, Superstars, and *SmackDown,* usually getting my butt handed to me and playing the role that suited me best: the underdog. After this went on for some time, I had what is called a "squash match" against Beth on one of the main shows. In a squash, one person (me) gets relentlessly pummeled for the entirety of the match. It is meant to demonstrate how imposing and unbeatable a wrestler (not me) is. Without realizing I could hear their conversation, Beth, who was the champion at the time, pulled aside the new head of Talent Relations and put in a good word for me. "That was just her third match in one night, and they were all great matches. I hope I'm not the only one that noticed that."

Maybe this was just a passing moment in her day. Maybe she was the type of person who was just unabashedly kind, but I would never forget it. She didn't have to stick her neck out for me. She could've insecurely seen another woman as competition. Instead Beth was open-minded and self-assured. Herself, Layla, and other former champions Michelle McCool and Eve Torres would go out of their way to make me feel welcome in the locker room. It was a comforting change from resigning myself to the maintenance closet. These women saw the big picture. We were in this challenging, grueling, nerve-racking world together. And the way to survive that would be to create a supportive environment. Supporting a fellow female doesn't detract from a woman's strength, it only makes the pack stronger. It makes us all better. I promised myself I would pay their acts of kindness forward.

In every match I tried to do just that. I knew I had to make myself stand out and perform well, but that didn't have to be at my opponent's expense. We could have better matches when we worked as a unit. I had learned that firsthand. And it wasn't going unnoticed.

Because I had put on a solid collection of matches, I was

thrown a proverbial bone in the form of a small undercard story line. The "main event" story line was reserved for the top guys; following that was the "midcard," and beneath that the "undercard." These were the more disposable matches and stories that were the first to get trimmed for time constraints, and they almost always included the women's matches. But getting even the tiniest of opportunities to participate in backstage skits and segments and showcase my personality was mind-blowing.

I was paired with Daniel Bryan, a wrestler who was also undersized, atypical for the sport, kind of geeky, but a champion for the fans who saw themselves in him. We were two underdogs who weren't expected to amount to much in the world of giants. One writer, the creator of our pairing, Kevin Eck, lovingly referred to us as his "revenge of the nerds" story line. Though not much was expected of either of us, due to our inability to fit a mold, we started to fall into opportunities.

Several roster injuries and contract negotiations led our little duo into picking up the slack. Though we started as an "undercard" story, we would end up thrust into the spotlight.

THIS IS NOT A LOVE STORY

Now, I know that being a person who has unironically worn pigtails in her mid- to late twenties might lead people to believe I am someone who is comfortable sharing her orifices. But in actuality, I am a notorious prude and proud of it. Having been trained to avoid embracing my sexuality by an overbearing, often unhinged mother, my puritanical nature began as more of an assigned duty than a choice.

But if there was a healthy message to forcibly extract from my mother's extreme method of parenting, it was to not take my value for granted. It was to treat my mind and body with the respect they deserved and demand the world follow suit. Or maybe she just didn't want a slutty kid making her a grandma at thirty. Nevertheless, I spent my young adult life treading lightly toward intimacy. A kiss was not a throwaway moment to me. It was to be respected, appreciated. It had to mean something. I loathed the idea of sharing my body trivially.

Most of my coworkers assumed I reproduced asexually, like a plant. The majority of the female roster—in their finest professional wear of skintight minidresses, crop tops, and sky-high heels, leading one to believe the enforced dress code was "high-end escort who caters exclusively to politicians"—was a stark contrast to my Virgin Queen style. With my work-wear of a cardigan sweater, dark framed glasses, twenty-dollar jeans, and shin-high combat boots, my aesthetic was clearly "smooth like a Barbie down there" or at the very least "late-in-life lesbian."

But it returned the result of enforced personal space I was looking for. Unfortunately, there is a bit of misguided expec-tation that comes along with joining a male-dominated busi-ness. If you're not going to put out in your first few months on the job, at the very least, a lot of men expect you to stroke their ego and flirt. Giggling at unfunny jokes, having boob-to-chest contact on hugs, and laughing off blatant workplace sexual harassment are considered prerequisites of women in the minds of many ignorant men. Knowing this going in, I made an extra effort to make it clear no one had even a remote chance of getting into my jean shorts. I can't help but feel a distinguished pride in being a certified boner killer.

Quickly adjusting to my boundaries, the guys were pretty cool, embracing me as a type of little sister rather than po-tential one-night stand. I was the girl they could talk to about whether Hugh Jackman would make a suitable Solid Snake.

I was the one they felt safe asking to do recon, sniffing out if they had a chance to hook up with one of the "hot ones." They would ask me if whoever I was dating was being good to me, and if there was any guy I wanted them to beat up.

One wrestler, "The World's Strongest Man," Mark Henry, actually lifted a local crew guy off his feet and pinned him against a wall after he caught him ogling me as I stretched backstage. I swooned. Another one of the guys, after witnessing a male fan propose to me at an autograph signing, shared, "I sometimes forget that guys think you're pretty."

But I enjoy being one of the guys. I've always been more comfortable in the company of like-minded dudes who don't make me worry about what my hair looks like. I made a choice to avoid dating until much later in life because I relished the lack of drama caused by relationships. Life was trying enough already. I was a determined kid who grew into a focused adult, and I didn't want anything to distract me. For what purpose? For love? It wasn't something I entirely believed in.

Putting it lightly, I was not a hopeless romantic. In fact, I hate love stories—romcoms being a particular bane of my existence. Listening to friends complain or gush about who they are dating makes me want to go full Sylvia Plath on a kitchen appliance. When it came to romance, I was less a giggling schoolgirl and more a jaded divorcée in grade school. My general approach to dating was always *Meh. No thanks.*

While my sister, Erica, made scrapbooks of her dream wedding growing up, cutting out pictures of poufy wedding dresses and listing romantic honeymoon locales, I doubted if I even believed in marriage. I had written it off in kindergarten somewhere around the time Billy Cook decided leaving his dirty tissues in my cubby and successfully rubbing his chicken-pocked arm on mine meant, *Now you're mine and we have to get married!* When we played The Game of Life and a tile required me to stop and pop a blue peg husband in the plastic car, I would often just spin the wheel again, ignoring the rules. Though occasionally I would concede—only if we all agreed my blue peg could be David Boreanaz.

Looking at the heartache my parents had caused each other, I didn't think I wanted any part of what I knew marriage to be. And so for as long as I can remember I loudly declared that I would never get married. I couldn't understand receiving that kind of unconditional love from someone who did not walk on all fours. I had been taught love and tenderness was dependent on my behavior and on what I could provide. I just didn't trust in the idea that anyone would love me forever. That sounded like a hell of a long time. If I didn't know what to make of my own mother's love, if it came and went with the tide, how would I ever trust a stranger's?

I had been so scared of physical contact by the insane parenting approach of my mother that I knew I wouldn't be able to handle dating while living at home. I would've had to hide a relationship and constantly worry about her finding out and drowning me in a bathtub. And besides that, I loved school. All I wanted to do was focus on it and get into a good college and then worry about having a life. Guys in school knew not to try anything, because (a) they wouldn't get very far and (b) they had heard I had a tendency to crack skulls. Basically, I was every dad's dream daughter.

Though, in high school, I did have a major crush that my best friend, Sophie, would patiently listen to me talk about every day for a year. When, at the end of that year, that guy was found by police having sex with another guy in a porta-potty in a public park, I figured it was a sign I was meant to be alone.

Technically, my first kiss was at nineteen. I say "technically" because when I was fourteen, my gay friend Chad asked to borrow some ChapStick, and when I took too long finding the tube, he just pressed his lips against mine. I was genuinely terrified somehow my mother would be able to tell just by looking at me.

When I was nineteen, I went on my first official date. A cute guy walked into my workplace and I asked him out. But at the end of the night, when he dropped me off at my front door and leaned in, I jumped back, shouted, "Ummm, no thank you," and ran into my apartment. I was clearly a natural at romance. I wanted my first (official) kiss to mean something more. I had waited this long and I wasn't going to waste it on a guy who hadn't asked me a single question the whole night. My first kiss ended up being with a longtime friend who would spend hours, amounting to months, asking me about myself, being genuinely interested in the answers, and simply enjoying my company. He even wrote me a poem once. And not even he could get in my pants.

When I was told by a superior that no one wanted to have sex with me, ironically enough, no one had. Though not even my closest friends knew it, I was a virgin well into my twenties. Because I had a varied dating history—that included a white guy, a black guy, and a girl—friends assumed I was a bit experimental. But I wasn't wild; I just didn't have a specific taste. I didn't know what I was looking for, but I knew no one had made me feel safe enough to get my V-card punched.

My first year on the main roster I started dating another wrestler. Greg was my first real adult relationship and my first love. He was my first everything. He was kind, called me beautiful every day, made me birthday gifts by hand, and was close to my family. I felt safe and loved and did not regret it. Waiting until I was mature enough to handle the emotional baggage that comes with sex was worth it.

I wish that all girls could fight the peer pressure to grow

up fast and sleep around young, because odds are guys that age just aren't worth giving that precious piece of yourself to them. It's only been about ten years since I was in high school, but the canvas of childhood has changed completely. The mainstream media of my generation idolized Britney Spears, a proud virgin who was considered a scandalous blasphemer for baring her midriff. My favorite young adult television shows, like *Buffy the Vampire Slayer*, *Dawson's Creek*, and *Gilmore Girls* (WB 4eva), would devote entire seasons to the trepidation leading up to and the consequences after their main characters lost their virginity. Somewhere along the line, through the advent of social media and the popularization of reality TV ditzes, the pop culture compendium targeted toward those not old enough to have a learner's permit has become increasingly, uncomfortably mature and overtly sexualized. Kids now enjoy TV shows where every main character shares an HPV strain before the first commercial break.

Soon I would be traveling the world and rocketing toward the limelight. My career became my main focus, and being young and incapable of focusing on two things at once, I started to let my relationship fall to the wayside. I was finally succeeding in the job of my dreams, and to get where I wanted to go, I had to give it my undivided attention. Even though I was being a shitty partner, it still knocked me on my ass when I got dumped.

I made a ton of mistakes in the years after. And by mistakes I mean one of the guys I dated actually wore leather bracelets. If you judge me for one thing in this book, I won't argue if it's that. I almost got wrapped up with another wrestler. While he aggressively courted me, I ignorantly giggled, enjoying the affirming attention. What I didn't realize was that he was secretly dating another woman in the company, and she would understandably hate me forever. Since he had way more stroke than I did, I worried that he would try to have me fired after I told him to back off. But he ended up taking it like a champ, and we just awkwardly passed each other in the halls from there on out. After that I spent almost a year dating someone who ended up sleeping with one of my best friends. He was then very surprised that it bothered me. *Wait, were we supposed to be exclusive this whole time?* They weren't all winners.

What I should've done while trying to recover from romantic trials and tribulations was lock myself in a room with my dog and cry into a tub of mint chocolate chip ice cream. When trying to reenter the dating world, I wish I had had a strong female role model to cry to and to help remind me I was worth more. But like most things, I was just going to have to learn that the hard way. I guess as humans our judgment isn't entirely trustworthy during and after heartbreak. But luckily for me, after getting dumped for the first time, live television made for great free therapy.

When Bryan ended up winning the World Heavyweight Championship in December of 2011, his character was turned into a villain. And thus, growing cocky and power hungry, he began to mistreat his dutiful lady. When he dumped me on-screen for inadvertently costing him his championship, I laughed at the ironic timing. I was sure my run in the story line was over, but it was amazing while it lasted.

Two underdogs had won the hearts of the crowd, dominated ratings, and made an impact no one expected. People really cared about what was going to happen to these characters next. And so the suits in charge were forced to take notice. Though they didn't understand our appeal, I was pleasantly surprised and impressed when they began thinking of ideas to bring us back together and further the story line. It was a bold move to use two characters who didn't abide by the proven formulas in such a prominent way. The writers and decision makers took a brave risk with us. And we would prove that we were worth it.

It was easy to play the heartbroken mess with an unrequited love when I spent each night crying into my hair over being dumped. What astonished me was how therapeutic it was to show my raw emotions on-screen under the guise of performance. I twisted my real-life heartache into the broken character, and it was thrilling to blur the line between the two. I knew exactly how hurt and pathetic the character on-screen should be feeling. And being so accidentally open about it made the healing process fly by.

Not swallowing my pain like a bag of razors but instead allowing myself to be vulnerable and work through it actually made me feel better. Who would've thought taking a healthy approach, however alternatively, would help? Using my personal life as fuel, I was accidentally oversharing myself with the audience. I was a raw, honest, bleeding heart and was being cheered for it instead of mocked.

This was fascinating to me. In life we try our hardest to save face, to seem tough and unfazed, and to never let our exes know they affected us. But in the world of make-believe and escapism, people want to vicariously express themselves through you. They want to see someone expose all the emotions they are too proud to share. They want assurance that there are others out there who feel their pain, and so when a character on TV openly shares this experience and vulnerability, they connect to it. Watching me cause havoc, stalk my ex, fuck up his life, and act out in rage was like therapy for everyone watching who had ever been dumped.

What I learned was that the key to success was going to be showing my genuine emotion, being open and honest. When you can accept and be proud of your flaws, they will become your greatest strengths.

Then I was faced with a moral dilemma. It blew my mind that only months after being told no one wanted to take me behind the school and get me pregnant, I was given this opportunity to enter a main event story line. To seem ungrateful in any way would be shooting myself in the foot. But when I found out what was planned for the character next, I couldn't help but speak up.

Some writers had pitched my character would become "the crazy ex-girlfriend." At first that sounded intriguing, as I was having fun being the "vengeful ex-girlfriend," until I found out what that entailed. The plan was for my "crazy" to be a point of levity in the show. A series of goofy skits in which this nutter revenge-kissed a leprechaun and danced with dinosaurs from outer space. I am not exaggerating—that was an actual plan.

We were going to make a joke out of mental illness. Sure, WWE wasn't an after-school special, but after everything I had gone through with not only my mother but myself, mocking an affliction that deeply affected me was not something I was interested in.

There are those who stand by their code, and those who just talk about it real loud. So many people think they are capable of making just and moral decisions in life, but when actually confronted with an opportunity to gain something out of bending their beliefs, they fold. That is not who I am. I knew speaking against these plans might be the end of my career. Not only was I a newbie on the roster, but I was a woman. Everyone assumed I should just be grateful to be used in something other than a thirty-second ten-woman tag match.

But did being grateful mean compromising what I believed in? Not only from a moral standpoint but also from a business one? Being relatable and true to myself was quickly turning me into a fan favorite. I didn't want to ruin that by doing something disingenuous, something I couldn't put my heart behind.

I've agreed to do countless, ridiculous things on-screen. I've worn fat suits, muscle suits, comically large boobs, and comically small cowboy hats. I've danced, done limbo competitions, ridden a mechanical bull, thrown temper tantrums, and had the sky rain poop on me. I am down for almost anything. If I think something is funny, I don't have a problem looking like an ass. There are few things more fun than making a fool of yourself and not giving a damn. But this pitch was unlike those things. I didn't think it was funny, and I thought it would hurt my mother's feelings. And so I said no.

Two months into my first and only real story line, I turned my bosses down. As a rule of thumb, I'll never say no to something without suggesting an alternative option; it's just a smart thing to do if you want to healthily collaborate with people. So I pitched we take things a darker route. I suggested instead of making the character a caricature of a mentally ill person, why not explore how dangerous that illness could make her. I wanted her to truly be broken, vulnerable, clingy, and downright unsettling. If simply being heartbroken on camera had garnered so much support, embracing the even more extreme flaws humans keep hidden away inside of themselves would be the ultimate catharsis for the audience.

Instead I was taken off television for two months as punishment.

But after those two months, my old friend—Convenient Circumstance—showed up again. Bryan was going to be wrestling for another heavyweight title and the writers wanted to throw a red herring into the mix. Suddenly using my idea worked in the grand scheme the writers were putting together. My character was reintroduced, integrating my wishes to play her dark and unpredictable. So now I had an opportunity. If I didn't want her to be a joke, then what did I want her to be?

Embracing the side effects of a broken relationship had initially been the catalyst for my connection to the audience. So I knew I had to continue exploring the depths of emotion within me. If I wanted to play "crazy" more truthfully, I only needed to look in a mirror.

I knew what kind of darkness could exist inside of me. Years of living unmedicated had shown me the altered reality my eyes were capable of seeing. I knew exactly how twisted and torn my thoughts could become. Those feelings, though at bay, were only a short trip away. But facing them wasn't easy. I had spent so long ignoring my bipolar disorder, I was still used to being in denial about it, and sometimes untrained in controlling it. Would reaching deep down and pulling it to the surface only serve in helping it to consume me? Or would it be the perfect way to hide in plain sight?

I had asked to be the face of proper "crazy," and now it was my responsibility to do it right. I got in touch with the deep, dark corners of my mind I had tried to never look at for too long. Even in people who don't have bipolar disorder, there are warped desires and perverse instincts they fight to keep hidden. Having bipolar disorder means those instincts jump to the surface without worry of repercussions. I decided that was exactly who I needed to be on-screen—an amalgamation of rash, selfish, frightening behavior.

I picked the worst qualities I knew I was capable of and my character proudly shouted them from the rooftops. When an ex hurt my feelings, I took it out on the friend trying to console me. If a girl looked at me wrong, I swung until she bled. I stalked my ex's every move from the shadows and played every childish game to make him jealous. I knew how to play these appalling actions because somewhere inside of me they existed.

When my character had to have several emotional breakdowns, I could feel my heart beat with trepidation. Giving in to crying fits and losing myself in animalistic screaming was the most raw and truthful I could be about my disorder while still under the guise of make-believe. "You're really good at playing crazy," Vince McMahon, the owner of the company, told me after I returned backstage from an in-ring temper tantrum. But to me, I wasn't playing crazy. I was discovering my superpower.

The writers wanted to make the audience wonder if our breakup had been a ruse designed to curry favor with Bryan's opponent, only to help him win the title. I was back in the game and I learned my lesson to never speak up again. Wait, no . . . that part didn't happen. I was snarkier than ever. Initially the plan was to tease this reconciliation for a month and ultimately have Bryan win the title, making us a heel couple. But as more players entered the story, it became too much fun for the writers to cut short.

The current holder of the title we were intended to steal was CM Punk. Covered in tattoos, with an irreverent attitude and a general distaste for authority and freshly laundered clothes, Punk, aka Phil, was the rebellious antihero the crowd went crazy for. A stark contrast to the all-American, fresh-faced, "drink your milk, kids" success stories that had preceded him. Another contender for the title was the masked giant and "Devil's Favorite Demon," Kane (real name, Glenn; it was a bit of a letdown learning these badass characters actually had the names of very white accountants). His character was a seven-foot burn victim who only found pleasure in bringing other people pain.

I had a poster of Kane over my bed when I was thirteen, so eventually having to straddle and make out with him on live television made for a bizarre experience, albeit a proud moment for my dad. My character stalked, harassed, and drove all three guys insane, in a soap-opera-worthy unrequited love square. Because even with three other losers hanging around, AJ Lee could not get laid. I would cost them matches and then flip on a dime and try to help them win some. It was never clear whose side I was on, or if my "charms" were possibly working.

It was ridiculous, soapy, brazen entertainment. It had been a long time since our programming had featured such a relationship-heavy, emotionally driven story line. It was groundbreaking and a brave step in a new direction. And that is why the fans jumped on board. They were excited to see something different.

They were intrigued to see a woman utilized for more than a bathroom-break match. The four of us were quite the motley crew of freaks and geeks not suitable for television, but something about it worked. We were like the Guardians of the Galaxy for the wrestling world, a bunch of castoffs who surprisingly worked well together. Antiheroes in an antilove story making bad decisions was a surprise hit for the ratings. What was supposed to be a one pay-per-view deal dominated a summer of television in 2012.

I got to wreak havoc, work with my childhood heroes, and introduce a new kind of woman in professional wrestling—a woman who when given the opportunity could captivate an audience with her words and performance, and not just her looks; a woman who could show range and layers of personality. The fans had spoken and wanted to see more of this kind of role for their heroines. They really dug crazy chicks.

Over the next year, I was the first woman in close to a decade to appear on a pay-per-view poster, naturally tying a man to a railroad track while a train barreled down on him. (The designers really got me.) I was voted the most influential female athlete on Twitter, beating out Serena Williams. I made it into my first of three video games and had not one but six action figures made in my likeness. I was the first woman to open and close the company's flagship television show. And I became one of only a handful of women in the company's history to wrestle in that show's main event. Not bad for someone so unfuckable.

MAD GIRL'S LOVE SONG

There is a locker room in Corpus Christi, Texas, that smells of my dirty shame. After the salacious opening segment of our show, I ran here to escape the prying eyes and suspicious questions of my coworkers. I couldn't shake what had just happened; the mixed emotions and racing thoughts rattled around my brain as I collected my padded bras and the plethora of unused clothing options that lay sprawled over a folding table. I sloppily chucked them back into my colossal, off-brand luggage, the one that on occasion I have felt the need to physically prove was large enough to fit my entire body. I couldn't quite figure out why I was packing so early in the show. But I needed to move, to keep busy, in order to prevent my brain from short-circuiting.

With stillness came a flood of images, a flipbook of the dirty deed just done in front of thousands of strangers. With the images came a jarring feeling in my gut, like a fist squeezing and then twisting my intestines. Mistakenly slowing down to fold a hooded sweatshirt was just the opportunity my racing mind needed to replay the moment. My gut squeezed.

Through a tornado of skull-emblazoned T-shirts and travel-sized soaps, I watched Celeste, my work wife, best friend on the road, and most trusted confidante, rush into the room. It was easy to play it cool with my other coworkers, but

Celeste had the uncanny ability to see through my bullshit. I desperately avoided eye contact while she steamrolled her way over to our corner of the room. She hovered, while I hunched over my bag pretending to be too preoccupied to talk.

"Soooooo . . . ," she began, somewhat annoyed.

"Yeah, what's up?" I feigned ignorance and asked.

"What the fuck was that?"

I stared at a bottle of prescription sulfate face wash.

"That takes some balls! I thought you guys were supposed to peck or something. I didn't realize there would be so much . . . tongue."

I fiddled with my Degree Clinical, For Men deodorant stick.

"Dude, what was that? Are you mad? Did you plan that?"

I tightened the cap of my ingrown hair serum roll-on and began to realize how many products it took to make me less disgusting and—oh crap, she was staring right at me.

"Oh my God. No, AJ! Eww, you liked it?"

Liked it? I was appalled by the question. How could I like something so intrusive, so unwarranted? I was just trying to do my job, and he chose to be rude and unprofessional and basically violate the unwritten rules of my mouth. This wasn't the first time I found myself morally strained by what was asked of me at work. This wasn't the first time I felt humiliated. This wasn't even the first time I found myself involuntarily dry heaving over a garbage can seconds before having to go live on air. But it was the first time it mattered. And I had no idea why.

Earlier that evening, I had arrived at the arena on a high. The night before I had starred in the main event of the show. In one of my character's darkest moments, she reacted to a lack of attention with a feigned attempt at self-harm.

At the close of the show, in front of thousands of fans,

I stood on the top rope of the ring, looking down onto a propped-up table eight feet below. My body language conveyed that I was about to throw myself through the table, like a suicidal cry for attention. It was some heavy stuff, and I was blown away by the balls of steel the writing staff displayed by going through with such a dark story. Of course, at the start of the day, the original version had me successfully crashing through the table—an idea I was so stoked about—but by showtime, in an attempt to be slightly more responsible to our PG audience, the plans had hastily changed.

When I climbed to the top rope and looked at certain devastation, CM Punk came to my rescue and stopped me from hurting myself. As he tried to talk me down, I grabbed the back of his head and punched him with my snaggletooth while forcing a kiss on him.

I then pulled away, revealed an adorably evil smile, and pushed him to the ground and through the table. It was deliciously twisted. The episode closed on my maniacal face enjoying the carnage I had wrought.

Punk was a mentor to me at work. My first day on the road, as I walked into catering, with the same insecurity and nerves of a new student walking into the school cafeteria, he had called me over. I had never met him, only heard stories of his being a mercurial curmudgeon, so naturally I was surprised. The simple act of inviting me to sit down at his table alleviated so much stress of finding somewhere to fit in on the road.

"Let me know if anyone fucks with you, kiddo."

"Kiddo" was an annoying moniker he gave me to remind me that I was about a decade younger than him. In turn, I gave him the nickname "Grandpa." While I competed on *NXT*, he provided sage advice and encouragement. He delivered color commentary for the show and always made sure to "put me over" or speak fondly of me, while he ruthlessly mocked the rest of the girls. I think he was indignant about the fact that while the other commentators audibly drooled over the rest of the contestants, they would only mention that I was diminutive and scrawny. His words were in support of different kinds of beauty and it let me know that he had my back.

When we started working together, our dynamic became that of a big brother and little sister. We had practically nothing in common besides a love of comic books and a belief that marriage was a ridiculous societal expectation, but we could talk for hours. We would seek advice from each other about the people we were in relationships with and share horrifying dating stories. Through these stories we learned each other's flaws, mistakes, and embarrassing pasts. But neither of us went running in the other direction. We apparently didn't scare so easy.

He would bring me Starbucks coffee every day at work and mock me for being a chubster who always wanted extra whipped cream. This would soon be how he listed me in his phone: "Extra Whip." Because as he explained, it represented how I was smart and feisty and also kind of a cow. He remained listed as "Grandpa" in mine.

When we realized that we both had a bipolar parent, it connected us even more strongly. If I needed someone to talk to when I was frustrated about still having to support my family while trying to save money for my future, Phil would meet me at a Denny's at 2 a.m. and listen. When I was frustrated with work, I would call him from my hotel and he would listen to me whine over the phone for hours.

Our ability to trust in each other made sense. We had both grown up in impoverished, chaotic homes and used wrestling to pull ourselves out. We had both spent the majority of our adult lives trying to undo the handiwork of our parents. We put our guards up around most people, having learned the hard way that not everyone could be trusted. We were both independent after earning everything for ourselves in life. Neither of us was prototypical, and though we were under-dogs, we came out on top.

As our friendship grew closer, we simultaneously began fighting a lot. The most trivial things would send us at each other's throats. "Why did you leave the building without say-ing good-bye to me?" he once furiously texted before ignoring me for a week. But no matter what random nonsense was caus-ing us to fight like cats and substantially older cats, if I needed a shoulder to cry on, the spat would be dropped and he would be there for me.

Having to smash my face against his on-screen was awk-ward as all hell. The first time, it really did feel like I was about to kiss my brother. But it was quick and simple, and before I knew it, I had thrown him through a table, so I felt fine.

The next day at work, I was feeling pretty confident about having closed the show the night before with such a dramatic, high-octane scene. I had already kissed a plethora of guys on-screen and figured that must've been the last. I was also really intrigued to see where the story would be headed. Running into one of the writers, I got the vibe I was about to be disap-pointed.

"Are we doing anything fun today?" I hopefully asked.

"Depends on your definition of fun," he hesitantly re-sponded.

"Oh, God. Do I have to kiss a guy again?"

"Not exactly," he said. A sense of relief began to sweep over me until "You'll be kissing two. One after the other."

Your move, Mono.

While waiting in Gorilla, the control room situated di-rectly outside the on-camera entrance to the ring, Phil could see my trepidation. The story called for me to break up a fight between Bryan and Phil, who had both previously ignored me. First I was to plant one on Bryan, and as Phil walked away, stop him by laying one on him. For those keeping score, I am somebody's daughter.

"You look like you're gonna throw up. I'm not that gross, kiddo." Phil was relishing how much I wanted to set myself ablaze.

"I'm fine; I'm always nervous before I go out there. But, yes. You are gross." *Is this what having a stroke feels like?*

"It'll be okay. Just make sure you rock my world."

"You're not funny and you're not a nice person." I desperately tried to turn my attention to someone else, anyone else. I successfully began a conversation with a writer, when Phil leaned in, interrupting.

"You never know, you could be the one."

I froze, suddenly out of comebacks.

The segment had gone off flawlessly. The Bryan smooch was out of the way and now I only needed to quickly smash my face on Phil's again, like we had been clearly instructed. Specifically, Phil was supposed to stand with his arms extended as if I were a sexual predator and he were screaming for help.

I held my breath as I ran after an exiting Phil. He scratched his head and began walking up the ramp, his back to me. Dismounting from the ring apron to the mat below, I was sure my knees would buckle beneath me. As he moved farther away, I reached out and grabbed his wrist. Using his arm as a pivot, I swung his body around, forcing us to be face-to-face. His character was frustrated and confused and began to ask me what it was I wanted his attention for. I lunged forward, pulling his face to my minuscule height, and placed my lips on his, shutting him up. And then something bad happened.

We're kissing! We're not supposed to be kissing! my brain screamed at my body.

I steadied myself by grabbing his neck and considered pulling away to save the integrity of the segment. *Just get out now, it'll be sort of what they wanted. OK, one . . . two . . . is that his fucking tongue?!*

There is an unwritten rule in on-screen kisses: no goddamn tongue. Tongue makes the moment too intimate, too real. For a moment I felt violated. Then I was infuriated. Then I was immediately very okay with it. Phil put his arm around my waist and pulled me tight to his body. I clawed at his shoulder.

Every single person in that building disappeared.

It was the best kiss of my entire life. What was supposed to be an unreciprocated peck was now bordering on smut, a hardcore make-out session, going twenty seconds overtime—live on air. We attempted to stop, and for a moment you can see us begin to pull apart, but hover just a second too long, before Phil adds one last tug of my lip. Years later, I let him know that was my favorite part.

When we pulled apart, I was certain my entire body was now equal parts human and equal parts a Jell-O-like substance. I felt the overwhelming urge to run as far and as fast as I could. I stared at Phil and his smart-ass "oops" smile for what felt like seven days, but was actually three seconds, and got the fuck out of there. I moved out of the shot so unexpectedly fast the director didn't even have a chance to get the shots he needed. And I ended up having to run back out onstage to let them get a shot of me smiling and patting myself on the back while inside I was setting myself on fire.

We left the editors scrambling, having to desperately cut to random shots of Daniel's face to avoid accidentally distributing a porno to our PG audience. Our hands roamed a bit too freely, and tongues were nauseatingly visible left and right. In fact, when the second airing came Friday night, there were significant camera-angle changes and cuts to attempt to scar fewer children.

"Oh my God. No, AJ! Eww, you liked it?" Celeste seemed revolted and amused all at once.

"No! Eww! Shut up!" I lied while she cackled and I recalled that weird moment behind the curtain.

You never know, you could be the one.

For the next two years, we went on dating other people, supporting those relationships while not realizing what we really wanted, being a mentor and student, and acting like brother and sister. I think we both saw a possible forever in the other and ran screaming in the opposite direction. But after living in denial, fighting all the time, my character proposing to his and then agreeing to marry someone else, and after two years of the world's most bizarre foreplay, one day Phil and I just said "fuck it," and we jumped headfirst into a serious relationship. There was so much history between us it was like starting a book in chapter 12. Understandably, those around us were shocked at how fast everything seemed to move after that. But for us, it felt like we had waited a lifetime to find our way to each other.

A few weeks into dating, he got my lips tattooed on him. One month in, he asked me what my dream wedding would be. A few months later, we were married. Our wedding took place under string lights at home, on a Friday the thirteenth. We were surrounded by candles, black roses, and ten family members. In my vows, I thanked Phil for having "an ass that won't quit" in front of a reverend and my father, and then we high-fived. And one day, if I forget to take my pill, we can tell our child that after our first kiss, Mommy put Daddy through a table.

And the rest of our story is just for us.

So how did I end up believing in marriage? I'm still not entirely sure I do. I certainly will never be one of those people who judgmentally preach to their single friends about settling down already. Because, honestly, marriage is not for everyone. It is not the prize your life should be building toward just because that's how fairy tales end. It pains me to witness how much stock some women put in marriage. As if they will only find happiness once someone puts a ring on their finger. As women, our life goal should not be to belong to somebody else. Marriage should be the cherry on top of our accomplishments, not the whole sundae. I had made a list of goals, and marriage was not on it. No man was going to complete me. I was a complete person all on my own.

When Robbie got married to his beautiful wife, Dayara, and had twin daughters, seeing the monumental change in him was inspiring. To witness him create the stable and healthy home he never had made me realize there were virtues in beginning your own family. Creating your own place in the world. When Erica, having wasted her time on numerous asshole boyfriends, married Ro, a gentle, caring, dedicated soul who also happened to be a chick, I realized that love can be unexpected. It will profoundly change you.

When my mother chose to not come to my wedding, I was reminded that sometimes love does not conquer all. I don't know why Janet refused the invitation. I offered to pay for the trip and hotel stay, as well as having paid for the small wedding and my dress myself, so I knew it wasn't the money. I understood she had grown fearful of flying, but she had often talked about having plans to fly back to the States. So what made those trips more feasible? More worthwhile? She told me

Dad could represent them both, and I accepted that as some part of her disorder getting the best of her and holding her back. I need to believe that. I love my mother and I forgive her. For everything. But we are still broken. There are so many "normal," traditional, arguably expected mother-daughter moments girls can take for granted, moments I never got to have. Moments, even as a grown woman, I still ache for like a child. I am jealous of every girl whose mother taught her about becoming a woman. I am jealous of every girl who got to cry to her mother when a boy broke her heart. I am painfully jealous of every girl who got to have her mother at her goddamn wedding. That is the moment I mourn the most. That is the moment that taught me that no love comes with guarantees.

When my father kissed my cheek and gave me away, I realized sometimes, if you're lucky, you get exactly the love you need.

What I had learned about love throughout my life was enough to make me question its resilience. But I had also learned that it could be worth the risk. And I had grown confident in my knack of leaping without looking.

I found the person who complemented me like no other. I met my match, my best friend, my dream guy. Like our customary traded coffee, he could be bright and sweet or dark and bitter, but always hot . . . and never far from my mouth. Getting married just felt like the right thing to do. There was no louder, more meaningful way to dedicate ourselves to partnership. Phil likes to tease that if I hadn't been so mean to him all the time back then, we would've been married two years earlier. But I don't think I was (always) mean; I think I was scared. Something in me knew he could be the one, and the promise of stability can be terrifying. Because with the comfort of stability comes the fear of losing it.

But ironically, the best relationships will make you more

independent. A good man will love you so much, he will remind you of how immensely worthy of love you are. A secure man will love you because you love yourself first. I knew I was ready for marriage because I was comfortable with being alone. I am self-assured enough to know I will not be broken or less than without a ring on my finger. But when you don't need someone, you get the privilege of choosing them. You get to choose each other every day. And what is more meaningful than that? With loyalty, understanding, and a little bit of work, we will make that choice until we are wrinkly and gray, him long before me. I have never believed in forever, but now I hope for it.

I guess what I'm trying to say is that marriage is not the only way to live happily ever after, but if you're lucky enough to find someone who stimulates your mind as successfully as your loins, lock that shit down.

Phil mercilessly mocked me for having to dress up like a girl for my TV story-line wedding. Sucker.

DIARY OF AN UNFIT MIND

HOW TO FIND LOVE

- Reject every guy who approaches you. Even if he was just going to ask for the time, reject him anyway. If he keeps trying, he must really like you.
- Remember that a partner will only respect you as much as you respect yourself.
- Don't go looking for it. If Fate is real, tempt her by declaring you are willing to die a virgin and live comfortably in your asexual sweat suits.
- Have a kick-ass career. It'll be hard to give a shit about the other side of the bed being empty when it's filled with stacks of cash, keeping you warm.

How to Keep Love
- Consistently knock your partner down a few notches. Not so far down they lose the confidence you first found attractive, but just far enough to remind them they will never do better than you.
- Openly talk about poop.
- In the Marry/Fuck/Kill game of life, be all three.
- Be okay losing it. You are the prize that must be won.

How to Know He's the One
- If he always holds your hand when you cross a street.
- If he brings you coffee in bed every morning, because he knows without it, you are a monster.
- If he leaves you sweet notes literally everywhere: under your pillow, in your books, in your luggage, sometimes between the bread of a sandwich.

- If he always opens the car door for you. Manners are sexy as hell.
- If he forgives you for that time you went jogging together and you pulled ahead and screamed, "Help! He's chasing me!"
- If he thinks you are the most beautiful with no makeup on and frizzy air-dried hair.
- If he adopts the dog you've been eyeing to help you recover from surgery. (And even though you worry what he brought home might actually be a chupacabra, or an old man that has been cursed by a gypsy, you raise him as your son anyway.)
- If he buys you a car, but it ends up being the biggest fight you ever have because you are irrationally defensive of your independence, so he reluctantly trades it in and forgives your ungrateful response.
- If you mention ice cream at 10 p.m., and he quietly sneaks out to buy you ice cream at 10:02.
- If he is not intimidated by the fact that Momma has her own bank account and pays her own bills.
- If he has always made you feel like the prettiest girl in the room, even when you were just friends. Even when you were mean to him.
- And most important, if he waits until you pause the video game to walk past the TV. That guy's a keeper.

CHAPTER 13

GIRL ON GIRL

I fear children. Mostly because I worry that they will fall into a pile of broken glass or set themselves on fire while in my charge. But also because they can be unpredictable. And the last thing I want is a pair of creepily tiny and inexplicably sticky hands moving haphazardly in my general direction. I am hesitant about having children the same way I used to be hesitant about getting married, so perhaps this too shall pass. But I'm not ready to share my action figures with anyone else just yet.

So unsurprisingly, when the WWE presented me with the opportunity to speak at a school assembly composed of over a hundred children under the age of twelve, I politely replied, "Fuck that noise." But after I realized the event was a part of a well-intentioned antibullying campaign meant to spread the message of tolerance and acceptance within schools, as well as completely mandatory, I jumped in with both feet.

Upon arriving at the middle school, I was brought into an empty classroom and handed a thick, extensive handbook filled with pages of integral information: hundreds of conversation starters, frequently asked questions, and a structured discussion outline. A course guide so detailed, carrying such an important message we were entrusted to convey to impressionable minds during their formative years, would take a rigorous amount of studying and preparation.

"Can you read this in twenty minutes and head out there?"

"I'm sorry, what now?" I hoped the event coordinator was making a terribly cruel joke.

"You'll be fine. Trust me, most of this stuff comes naturally. And if you need us to take over the conversation, just give us a signal and my team will take care of any code red." She laughed.

For a while, it seemed as if I might actually be pulling off the impossible. I had wrangled the kids' attention and they were actually pretty responsive. They even laughed at my jokes, presumably because those jokes were finally being heard by a demographic of equal maturity. I thought while I had them smiling it would be a good time to start a Q&A session. Kids love when they have to stand up and be vulnerable among their peers. I spotted a sweet little girl wearing a thick pair of glasses in the crowd. She couldn't have been older than ten and was preciously tiny.

Sitting quietly, fiddling with the hem of her dress, she seemed a delicate introvert, almost sad. Perhaps the assembly was striking a nerve. Maybe she was a victim of bullying or knew someone who was. I thought, *I will help this girl find her strength. I will give her support in front of her whole school and give her a chance to finally speak up. I'm so great at this!*

"Tell me, how would you help a friend who is a victim of bullying?" I asked the gentle wallflower, as an event participant handed her a live microphone. As three different cameras circled the girl hoping to get footage for a promotional reel about the company's charitable efforts, she nervously pushed at her glasses. "Well . . . Bitches be trifflin'!"

Code red. CODE RED.

The microphone, for some reason, had not been pulled away, and so the tiny mobster continued, "Sometimes you just gotta slap a bitch if you want to shut her up."

My eyes bounced around the room searching for an event coordinator to save me. *Didn't they say I just had to signal for them to swoop in? Wait . . . did we even designate a signal? I feel like hyperventilating should be a pretty strong signal. How could this be happening with all my extensive training?*

Help never came and/or I blacked out, but somehow we stumbled through the rest of the assembly. Ultimately, I doubt the correct response to that comment was in the handbook.

But what really worried me was the instinctual response of a mere ten-year-old girl when asked about her confrontations with her peers. That was a hard B she responded with. At the tender age of ten she had learned to use a word so full of hate and spite. She had learned to view her fellow female race as enemies. And conflict between them was to be solved with aggression and violence.

After getting into so many scuffles in school, I finally saw how terrifying adults must have found me. But I was more worried about the word *bitch* being on the tip of a child's tongue. It was an attitude so deeply entrenched in our culture, so ingrained in the lessons passed down, a child had learned to use it as a weapon.

If society disagrees with a woman's opinion, finds her anything but pleasant, or views her as a threat, the go-to response is to call her a bitch. There are so many men who will instinctively hurl this insult at women, but I've already discussed men's violent behavior toward women. What is truly painful to witness is when women use this word to attack other women.

We already have so many obstacles to overcome just trying to be seen and treated as equal to men that it seems laughable that women would further try to tear one another down, instead of unite to make the uphill climb a little bit easier. It seems we are getting in our way.

Throughout my career I have had women try to sabotage, manipulate, and trash-talk me. But I've just never had the will to respond in kind. I went to a wonderful high school full of warm, supportive, and encouraging men and women, so maybe I just missed the years in which childish behavior is prevalent. But it was in high school that I realized how important it was to come together in order to become stronger.

My public school was in an underprivileged town, full of kids who were desperate to make a better life for themselves. And in our united struggle, we knew not to make life harder for anyone else, but to try to raise us all up. The football team played ticketed games to help raise money for the Drama Club. Cheerleaders, artists, and Honor Society presidents were all members of the "Key Club," a group designed to organize charitable functions, grow our school library, and mentor younger grades. My own Peer Mediation group gave up their meager allowances to help me go to college. It was there I learned the very cheesy but very truthful idea that standing united yields stronger results than trying to tear one another down.

As not just women, but women in a competitive field, facing generalizations, discrimination, and misogyny from a thousand different angles, the only way to survive and succeed would be to work together. And from what I've noticed in wrestling, the women who could not come to grips with that notion essentially shot themselves in the foot.

One of the reasons I was constantly utilized on-screen, always in a main event angle and working with the best in the industry, was simply because I was easy to work with. I did not perpetuate girl-on-girl violence. I was not the kind of girl who was going to cry when I had to lose or the kind of girl who was going to barge into a boss's office and demand I not work with a particular competitor. I would not rat out anyone's bad behavior. But these were prevalent tactics of the less successful.

That's not to say I didn't confront a woman if there was a problem. I fully admit that I can be brutally honest and that it doesn't rub everyone the right way. But I never tweeted about my confrontations, talked about them in interviews, or whispered about them to my friends. A real woman has the strength of character to face conflict head-on, carry herself politely throughout it, and to move on when she's said all she has to say.

I am comfortable telling women how I feel, but a lot of women are not comfortable being confronted. I think the only way men will stop making cartoon cat noises when women disagree is if women can learn to embrace conflict, instead of talking harshly about another female the instant she has left a room. Overall, I prefer talking shit to someone's face. We don't need to yell and scream and insult each other. We simply need to have the guts to say "I don't like you" or "I don't like this thing you did," let it go, and continue being fair, civil, and collaborative.

I don't think it is a coincidence that the most success I have ever had has been when I and another woman decided to do everything in our power to support each other. It was our mission to make each other look good.

My friendship with fellow female wrestler Kaitlyn, real name Celeste, has been well documented on camera. On paper, we should not have been friends. I was the wrestling purist. She was a fitness model the company begged to sign on. I spent two years in FCW before making it to TV, while she spent exactly two weeks. The canceled story line I was supposed to have on my *SmackDown* debut was given to her for *NXT*. A show she went on to win. She got to travel the world while I died a slow death in FCW. Though we seemed like complete opposites and destined enemies, we were startlingly alike in personality and became almost obnoxiously attached at the hip. Often literally, as Celeste would carry me through the halls of each arena while I straddled her like a clingy child. We traveled hundreds of miles a week together, roomed together, laughed at inside jokes annoyingly loud while coworkers blankly stared at us, and often washed each other's hair in the locker room sink. No one could believe that when we eventually got married, it wasn't to each other.

She, too, would experience a different kind of pressure at work. Celeste was jacked like the forbidden love child of

A TV segment involved cosplaying as Celeste who
I assumed was cosplaying as Sonya Blade.

Wonder Woman and She-Ra. Higher-ups were concerned her muscles would be too intimidating and relegated her position on TV until she could slim down. On a live show, she took part in a multiwoman battle royal. The goal of a battle royal was to knock each opponent out of the ring until one person was standing inside of it. That woman would be given a shot at the championship. Celeste, a beast, hit our friend and intended winner of the match, Eve Torres, so hard she accidentally knocked her out of the ring and won the match. Oh, Convenient Circumstance, we meet again.

While a bunch of pissed-off people gathered backstage, I ran into Celeste's arms like she had just come back from Vietnam, and we laughed so hard people started to give us dirty looks. Eve ended up laughing it off as well. Maybe because she was a rational human or maybe because she had a lot of other things going for her, like having a genius IQ or always looking so beautiful I am convinced cartoon birds from a Disney movie help her get dressed in the morning. Either way, she was cool with the accidental story-line change.

When Celeste was actually awarded the championship, I cried like a proud momma. I was honored to be her opponent in her tryout, fierce competition in her first televised match on *NXT*, and the first person to hug her once that title was wrapped around her waist. No one deserved that moment more.

But her moment would be bittersweet. At the time, even being the champion wasn't a guarantee for television segments. The role of a female competitor was still being limited to one-minute to three-minute matches with a little story built around them to captivate the audience in the least.

I was fortunate enough to still be embroiled in story lines that were prominent, because they heavily featured men. I got to leave Daniel Bryan at the altar and then, just moments later, be chosen by Vince McMahon to run the *Raw* show as general manager. The original plan for the wedding segment was for psychiatric orderlies to drag me away after a ring was on my finger, and though I was initially bummed I didn't get to channel my inner Harley Quinn, I loved getting the opportunity to be a five-foot-two boss of giants. Though I be but little . . .

After that I got to be a part of another romance story line with the company's top star, John Cena, who had been a mentor and supporter from my first days on the road. I then had my long-awaited bad guy turn with fellow heels Dolph Ziggler and Big E Langston. Dolph and I got to play our very own version of Mickey and Mallory, and the three of us produced both hilarious and controversial TV segments. The opportunities were plentiful and appreciated. The company execs found not only that they could count on me to deliver in performance, but also that I had become a top attraction with the crowd. The next logical move was to put me in the title chase.

I could not have written my dream scenario any better. I was getting to work with my best friend in wrestling. And because so little attention was being paid to the women's division, we were accidentally given a lot of creative control. Writers who were considered lower-tier were assigned to work with us, and they were so cool and open-minded, it became more of a collaboration. I felt like I was finally using the creative writing muscles I had long abandoned. Being able to use the power of my mind reminded me of a strength and value I had forgotten about. Though, occasionally, giving us free rein on dialogue produced ridiculous results like this backstage segment:

AJ: (Walking past Kaitlyn) Oh God, please don't hit me! Oh, sorry. I thought you were going to savagely attack me from behind, like you did at Extreme Rules (a pay-per-view). My bad.

KAITLYN: Oh, that's funny, because the way I remember it, you are the one always savagely attacking me, so, yeah, it felt kind of good to get my revenge. And speaking of savages . . . I'd like my Savage Garden CD back.

AJ: Your Savage Garden CD? That was a gift, I'm pretty sure, so . . .

KAITLYN: No. I believe I left it in your car during an eight-HOUR road trip to Dinosaur World. Which, by the way, HUGE letdown.

AJ: You said that you liked that trip.

KAITLYN: Well, I faked it.

AJ: Oh, well, speaking of things that we never liked, your grandma is THE WORST.

KAITLYN: She hemmed all your pants . . . Okay, you know what? Tenth grade, your first crush: Bobby Dutch. I DID make out with him.

AJ: You knew I was in love with him! Hmm, okay, you wanna play it like that? Remember when you laughed so hard you had to change your pants at that party? Well, I told everyone!

KAITLYN: I NEVER READ YOUR SCREENPLAY!

AJ: (stunned gasp) I worked so hard on that buddy cop drama—starring US!

KAITLYN: Cops by day, dancers by night? It'll never work!

AJ: You never believed in me!

KAITLYN: I can't believe I wasted eight years of my life on you!

AJ: You were a terrible best friend, okay? I want those years back.

KAITLYN: You will never get them back!

AJ: I should bite your face right now!

So there's that. We shot it in one take and our director stared at us blankly. "I . . . don't think we can use . . . any of that."

"They didn't give us a script. They said to improvise, so . . ."

And surprisingly, it became the company website's highest-viewed video. People enjoyed our absurdity. They liked seeing girls show different sides of themselves, even if those sides told really asinine jokes.

Celeste and I were always on the same page, and our senses of humor and personalities gelled so naturally, because of our existing friendship. We wanted the other to come out looking good. In speaking segments, we made sure we both had solid lines, and in physical altercations, we accentuated each other's strengths.

She was the dominating, tough force of nature, and I was the scrappy, feisty scoundrel who was probably hiding a shank. The chemistry between us in these interactions intrigued the audience and the producers more than expected. This led to the decision to extend our story line by an entire two months. One of our assigned writers, Tom Casiello, was so open-minded and collaborative, believing the best stories came from actors who were on board, comfortable, and confident, he would check in with us multiple times throughout the week and gave us free rein to formulate how the story would play out.

We were even trusted with writing my career's most important promo, in front of a live audience, in which Celeste and I finally came to blows. It was our last meeting before the title would be on the line. She let me call her trailer trash and I let her slap the taste out of my mouth. Well, she probably could've done that without me letting her, but I was nice enough to clench my teeth to make sure it didn't break my jaw.

During our story line I was finally given merchandise. Only three women in the history of the company had their name attached to merchandise sold at shows and on the online store, and the last was a decade before I arrived. The market-

GIRL ON GIRL 255

ing department let me know a year earlier, as I tried to pitch for my own merchandise, that "women don't sell."

When they had considered giving a girl a hat as merchandise a few years earlier, the other women on the roster complained so much, they scrapped the idea. Since then they hadn't wanted the trouble and didn't think it was worth the backlash. Because "women don't sell." It was widely thought that not only did women not sell, but they couldn't get ratings either. My main event story lines had begun to change a lot of people's minds, but they weren't sure if the bulk of the credit rested on the shoulders of my male counterparts. And frankly neither was I.

When Celeste and I embarked on a journey alone, I wasn't sure if I would be proven wrong. Had I just been carried all this time or was I indeed a ratings pull on my own? I had petitioned the marketing department several times, showing them how many fans on social media, at shows, and at signings were mimicking and cosplaying my outfits. I purposely chose an outfit for my character that was the same in and out of the ring. This would make it more recognizable. I made sure it could be easily re-created by fans and lend itself to cosplay. I wanted fans to feel connected to my style. They could walk around a mall and buy my exact outfit for thirty dollars. They would cut up plain T-shirts, buy my Target jean shorts, rock a sweet pair of knee-high Chucks, and do great justice to my messy, boyish style. I felt instead of girls just cutting up their own T-shirts to look like mine, why not sell a sponsored product with my name on it so we could all make money. I fought with them over and over again, and then something magical happened.

During our story line, Celeste and I were the highest-rated segment on the show an unprecedented six times. Our writer was even promoted to a main event story line in an attempt to continue pulling in high numbers, but for the men. Our bosses even added themselves to our story line in front of the camera and creatively.

I was the first woman to be given merchandise in a decade. They produced several different T-shirts, hats, knee-high socks, and posters. I was the only female on a WWE-themed Monopoly board (though my property was worth the least, I was still psyched and ignored the perfectly sad allegory). I was on wrapping paper, birthday cards, and dinnerware. I wasn't sure if it was weirder being made into a garden gnome or a gingerbread man Christmas tree ornament, but I was grateful for it all. My merchandise remained in the highest seller's list, beating out several, more prominently featured men every year I was in the company.

I remembered talking to the merchandise department when I was just a rookie on *NXT.* Joe Hickey and his crew were funny and inviting, though when I told them they would for sure produce at least one merchandise item for me one day, they all laughed in unison. At the time, it just wasn't feasible for a woman. A member of Talent Relations was there and joked, "Just one piece of merch? How about five?," as he playfully or condescendingly punched my arm and laughed off my foolish dream. Three years later, they made about a hundred.

We were successful in changing minds, and I could not have done that without Celeste by my side. She was next to get her own T-shirt and we could not be prouder. Not only was working together creating solid results on-screen, but we were helping each other make a lot of money. At this point, it just seemed silly to do anything besides have the back of the woman you are working with. Ladies, you don't have to be friends. You don't have to like each other's clothes or disingenuously compliment each other's hair. But you have to know how to work together. Work together and watch yourselves get rich together.

When our title match finally came in 2013, I felt the pressure of fourteen years of a little girl's dreams on my shoulders. I had wanted to call myself the best women's wrestler since I was twelve, and at twenty-six I was about to be given the opportunity to make that dream a reality. I thought about every step I had taken to get to that moment, every obstacle that had been put in my way and the battles I had waged to overcome them.

I wanted to protect that little twelve-year-old's dreams—that girl with the knotty hair, the survivor who did not want to be a victim anymore—I owed her sanctuary and protection. I owed her the best moment of her life. I needed to make her dreams come true. It was the best match of my career.

Halfway through the bout, Celeste and I were told to wrap it up early, to help cut down on an already overrunning show. But women had endured having their matches shorted for time for years. And after delivering months of top-rated programming, I would be damned if we got screwed again. And so I grabbed Celeste's head and pressed my mouth against her ear as I lifted her before a move.

"They want us to 'go home.' Want to get in trouble and ignore them?"

"Hell, yeah, I do."

Our match went ten minutes over our allotted time and was one of the longest women's title bouts in history. But I think it was one of the best. And we didn't get into trouble. Because it was worth the wait.

I won my first championship. But it felt like more than just that. It felt like the culmination of a lifetime of hardship, work, and desire. I felt like I kept a promise to a little girl.

CHAPTER 14

CRAZY CHICKS DO IT BETTER

When I was sixteen, my dad wanted to do something special for my upcoming seventeenth birthday. He had found some consistent work as a doorman in a New York City high-rise, and for a wonderful moment in time, we were not scrounging to get by. When he found out WrestleMania was going to take place only a few days before my birthday, and only a few miles from home at Madison Square Garden, Dad worked overtime to save up two hundred and fifty dollars to give me the surprise of my life. But he didn't have a credit or debit card, so to buy tickets to the biggest wrestling show of the year, he would have to stand in line at the Garden to pay in cash. Instead of seeing that as a hole in his plan, he used it to create an adventure.

Dad and I took the train to Penn Station with a plastic bag full of water bottles and snacks. It was the first time just the two of us had been on an outing. Having his undivided attention brought me immeasurable joy.

We came prepared to stand in line among what would undoubtedly be a horde of people trying to score seats. The line was enormous, circling around the entire block. After four hours of spending the time talking, laughing, and sporadically shuffling two feet over, Dad left the line to grab us some

McDonald's and we nibbled on fries to get us through the next four. After standing in line for a grueling eight hours, we finally approached the ticket window.

"What are the best seats I can buy for two hundred fifty dollars?" Dad hesitantly asked the tired man behind the glass.

"Well, unfortunately, most everything has been bought up through Ticketmaster. Right now I have a few eighty-dollar seats left."

Dad was deflated. He had worked so hard to save and couldn't buy the seats he wanted me to have, but I was on cloud nine. I had tickets to my first live wrestling show, and it was the most monumental event of the whole year.

A few months later, when we took the train into the city for WrestleMania XX, I kept waiting for something to go wrong. I rarely received birthday presents, and I had never had a dream come to fruition. Everything always seemed out of reach, a destination for another distant day. *One day we'll have a nice house. One day you kids will get some nice clothes. One day we'll go to a wrestling show.* But one of those days was today. And I couldn't believe it was really happening.

As we entered the historic arena, my skin tingled with excitement. A few hours before showtime, the building was flooded with thousands of fans hectically trying to get to their seats. After riding three different escalators, we were sure we had made it to the top of the building and entered the cavernous arena bowl to hunt down our row. The place was lit up with bright lights and Jumbotrons, and at its center was a specially decorated wrestling ring.

"This is a pretty good view!" Dad was excited the seats seemed better than he had thought they would be. "Excuse me, sir," he called to an usher, "can you tell me where section 426 is?"

The usher illuminated our tickets with his flashlight and

studied them. "Hmm Row E . . . seats 17 and 18 . . . yeah, that's not here. You guys have to go up two more levels. Escalators are out that way."

He flippantly handed back what he clearly deemed to be lowly tickets and waved us away with the flick of his hand. I could see my dad grit his teeth to stop himself from socking the guy on the spot. I appreciated his restraint, on this, the day of his daughter's prebirthday. We hadn't realized this building even had two more levels. Craning my neck up, I squinted at the nosebleed section connected to the building's ceiling and read "426."

Fifteen minutes later, we finally found our seats, which were basically in New Jersey, and I quickly realized I had a fear of heights. As I tried to adjust to the steep row that made me feel like I was a second away from plummeting to my death, my eyes found the now minuscule ring. I looked over at Dad. He had tears in his eyes.

"I'm sorry I couldn't get you better seats, baby. I tried my best."

He had always tried his hardest to give us what he could. To make us happy with however little we had. I know deep in my heart, he tried his best our whole childhood. And I would try my best to one day make him proud of me.

"Don't worry, Daddy, this is perfect. Besides, one day I'm gonna be in that ring."

Ten years later, at 2014's WrestleMania XXX, I walked into that ring as champion, wrestled the entire female roster, and I walked out of that ring as champion.

And that was the day I knew my fight was over.

There could be no better full circle moment. After a decade, I had not only accomplished my goal of stepping foot inside of a WrestleMania ring, I had lived dreams I never even thought possible. Every goal had been checked off a list, every glass ceiling shattered within my first year and a half on television.

Every amazing moment that came after was an unexpected bonus. Frosting on top of a delicious Fudgy the Whale ice cream cake. I got to hold the title two more times and win the women's match at the next year's WrestleMania XXXI, as well. My cup runneth over. So when I had to have three surgeries for a health issue unrelated to the ring, and discovered ring-caused permanent damage to my cervical spine that occasionally makes my arms go numb and my fingers wiggle like an indecisive wizard, I felt the time was right to start planning the next chapter of my life. I began writing a new Ten-Year Life Plan that would pay forward the good fortune life had bestowed upon me. Maybe life made me work extra hard for that good fortune—made me truly earn it—but I still considered myself lucky. It was time to share the wealth. There were other strays like me out there, searching for someplace warm and safe. So I began working with animal rescue organizations and became an activist for animal rights. There were other little girls like I once was, out there in the world, worried about the clouds hanging over their heads. It was time to stop hiding my struggle and let them know they were not alone. And I began writing this book, this diary of the deranged.

My husband and I started toying with the idea of creating a family. Even if we ended up not wanting children, we had the desire to make for ourselves what we never had growing up—a peaceful, stable home. That place called "home" felt like a pot of gold at the end of one fucked-up rainbow. When Phil became embroiled in a dramatic breakup with the company, I worried the stress and chaos would test my mental fortitude and wreck the peace I had worked so hard to find within my mind. But surprisingly, I guess through years of practice under pressure, I managed to hold it together, for the most part. There were days I felt so overwhelmed I would cry in a bathroom stall mere moments before heading onto live TV. At times I felt caught in the middle, like a child of divorce. Trying to bridge the divide while getting inconsiderately trampled in the process. But despite what either side expected of me, what was more important to honor were my expectations of myself. The company gave me time off for surgeries, and I pushed my body through another year on the road. Just because my husband left didn't mean I had to follow. It was hard being newlyweds who only saw each other two days a week, but we were strong enough to handle it. I was going to wrestle for as long as it made me happy and as long as my body would

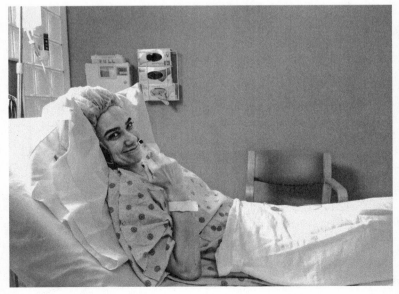

A delicate flower.

hold together. But in my heart I knew there was nothing left to prove. There were no more mountains to climb. No more history to make. My war was over. I had won.

It all felt so picture perfect. A career wrapped up in a tidy bow. I knew I had left the business better for women than when I had started and it would be fine without me. I had kicked down doors for the next generation, and I had faith they would deliver. You either go out on the top of your game, or watch yourself become less than your best. You either go out on your terms, or let someone else decide your fate. I didn't want to fade out. I wanted to go out with a bang. I publicly called out my bosses for not paying or treating most women equally even though I was proof that women could bring in just as much money and ratings for the company as men. All these years later and I still hadn't learned how to be a "good girl." I won at the biggest event of the year, "on the grandest stage of them all." I thanked Vince McMahon for every opportunity, and I retired.

All a woman needs to succeed is the guts to kick the door of opportunity open. All she needs is to be brave enough to be herself. For years people tried to quantify whatever formula had led to my unlikely success. How could a woman who wasn't conventionally attractive, who wasn't physically imposing, who didn't fit the mold set before her succeed where others had not? Was it the shoes? The clothes? Was it my smart mouth? Others have tried to replicate it all. But the answer was simple. I didn't try to be anything but me.

When looks fade, and your only value is your mind, will you still be beautiful? I figured out early on that investing in my heart, my personality, my mind, and my soul was going to be the key to success. Fans connected to me, they cheered for me, and they fought alongside me because I was genuine. When someone is honest and raw on-screen, the fans can see it. They can also tell when someone is not. Their bullshit meters are phenomenal. If you are the girliest girl in the world, then be that! If you are a freak or a geek, be that! Embrace it. And I promise the audience will embrace you too.

Sometimes I felt like the fans could see my soul through the screen. I have met many at autograph sessions and they have shared their gut-wrenching stories of depression, cutting, and suicide attempts. It is as if, without words, they understood my entire life story. Our struggles could sense a kinship in one another. And that connection is what made them a part of my revolution. I was honored to be their voice when they could not speak. Their fists when they could not fight. If I could make it out of a dark past, then so could they. Now it is their turn. I hope they will go on to be the superheroes they want to see in the world.

Trying to please everyone will appeal to no one. I was successful because I was willing not to be, in order to be true to my beliefs and myself. Being polarizing, giving people an extreme to connect to, that is where the magic happens. We all have extremes in our emotions and opinions; we just have to be unafraid in expressing them. And that is the gift being bipolar gave me.

I feel with every ounce of my body, and nothing can stop me from raising my voice. I do not fear fighting for what is right. I do not fear standing up, even if I have to stand alone. I am beautiful when I am confident enough to be ugly. I am stronger when I am vulnerable. And I will never apologize for any of that. There is endless power in giving zero fucks. There is endless power in being a crazy chick.

I was once told *crazy* was a bad word. Politically incorrect. Insensitive. Offensive. Closed-minded. Taboo. When I used it to facetiously describe my own mother's battle with mental illness, I was met with scandalized stares. How could I be so casual about something so serious? What kind of human could joke about something so terribly tragic? So I removed the word *crazy* from my vocabulary. I trained myself to fear it, to be ashamed of it. Society taught me mental illness was a burden to be carried solemnly and, more important, quietly.

Then I asked myself—why? Was mental illness Lord Voldemort and it should "not be named" aloud? Would I be able to summon it into existence by saying the words three times in front of a mirror like Bloody Mary? Could it be caught as easily as the dreaded cooties virus? No. It is nothing to be feared or embarrassed about. But yes—it is a struggle.

I was diagnosed with bipolar disorder in my early twenties after a lifetime of erratic, unexplained behavior. I had an answer to a long-plaguing question, but I struggled to figure out what came next. I fought to find the right path for treatment, experimenting with holistic methods and vacillating between being highly medicated to highly shrinked.

I lost sleep trying to accomplish the impossible task of finding the source of my illness. Was I born this way or was I made this way? Was nature or nurture to blame? I'm qualified for exactly three things: beating people up, remembering the entire "Pokérap," and wearing the hell out of a pair of jorts—so naturally, it's taken a while to come to a decisive conclusion on a widely contentious mystery of psychopathology.

Eventually, I made the decision to simply hide this self-discovery from the world's judgmental eyes. Bipolar disorder is the villain of this story. It has been a source of pain, but it has also been a fountain of strength. So save the pity. I am not a victim to mental illness. I am the hero of this story and I do not need to be saved.

This disorder is a pain in the ass and it is work. At times it is a cross to bear, and at others it is just a piece of the AJ-shaped puzzle. It is a part of me, as natural as the color of my eyes, but it is not all of me. Bipolar disorder does not define me. And I refuse to let a simple word be used as a weapon against me. There is no arrangement of letters that can make me feel inferior.

It wasn't long ago classmates called me a "nerd" in an attempt to hurt my feelings, and now that term is audaciously emblazoned on the front of T-shirts at Hot Topic. It is now a part of popular culture and it's suddenly cool to be a fan of all things "geek." Growing up I was mocked because I dressed "like a boy" and liked professional wrestling, and now we live in a world that celebrates the female athlete. Even so harsh a word as *bitch* has been adopted with a sense of pride by women refusing to let the world see their strong will as a handicap to feel guilty about.

It is my mission to demystify the world of mental illness. To show people it is not something to speak of in hushed tones. Mental illness is a bully and I refuse to let it intimidate, to give it power. I choose to drain its strength away. Stripping the stigma off of words like *crazy* and making them terms of endearment instead of hateful labels is my way of doing that.

Everything I was told should be my greatest insecurities, weaknesses, my biggest roadblocks—everything I've been labeled: SHORT, NERDY, SKINNY, WEAK, IMPULSIVE, UGLY, TOMBOY, POOR, REBEL, LOUD, FREAK, CRAZY—turned out to be my greatest strengths. I didn't become successful in spite of them. I became successful because of them. I am not afraid to be called crazy. Crazy is my superpower. Changing society's perception of the word is not going to happen overnight. But I've changed minds before. It took a lifetime to get here, but I know there are still miles to go before I sleep. This time I will reach farther. This time I will dream bigger. I am going to change the world, but first I'd like a nap.

ACKNOWLEDGMENTS

If someone had warned me that writing a book was going to involve crying into my hair and stress-eating an almost deadly amount of carbohydrates on a daily basis, I would've phoned it in to a ghostwriter. (Or at the very least a Ghost Rider, which come to think of it would've been pretty awesome.) But it's too late now, so I might as well just start thanking the people who inspired me to gain ten pounds in Thin Mints over the last few months.

Erica and Robbie, I wanted to dedicate this book to you guys, but I didn't, so let's move on. Robbie Rob, thank you for beating and peer-pressuring me into the person I am today. Thank you for serving our country and being the SuperDad to your twin daughters that all men should aspire to be. I think it's poetic that your children look exactly like me and spend their days beating the holy hell out of you. Homeskillz, thank you for being a second mother to me, always believing I was capable of anything, and happily reading every shitty thing I've ever written. You are so beautiful and talented and I can't wait for the world to hear the stories you have to tell. To my parents, thank you for allowing me to share our life together in print. Even though you did not give me permission and I forgot to ask for it. I love you both and I will always be your grouchy little baby. Thank you to the dogs who rescued me—Mugsy, Kagome, Señor Nacho Cheese, Pamela Beesly, and Larry Talbot—for teaching me that every life deserves a second chance, and for showing me what unconditional love should look like. You have all been bat-shit crazy, and I'm starting to think that maybe I'm the problem.

Papi, thank you for your butt. Thank you for loving my obnoxious snort laugh and snaggletooth and messy hair and boundless jokes about your being much, much older. Thank you for barging into my office several times a day, while I was locked away for hours writing this book, to let me know you were bored without me. It was superdistracting, but kind of adorable, and one time you brought me a grilled cheese sandwich, so we're cool. You are hilarious, brilliant, and brave. On an unrelated note, while you were getting your driver's license I was tracing hand turkeys with crayons in the first grade.

Thank you, Julie Klam, for the inspiration your work has given me as well as lending an invaluable helping hand to a perfect stranger. For your generosity and faith, I am forever indebted. Seriously, if you want my firstborn I think I legally have to give it to you. Lisa Leshne, thank you for taking a chance on a college dropout in short shorts and for holding my hand during every tiny, but very real panic attack I've had during this process. Thank you for your patience and guidance. You have both made me a better writer. Rob Guillory, thank you for your beautiful, moving, perfect art. You are insanely talented and I feel cooler just being associated with you. Thank you to my sisters from other misters, Jen Suarez and Kaidy Quiroz. Thank you to the amazing women who have been my partners in crime along the way, Jenny Quinn, Brittney Savage, Celeste Bonin Braun, Sarona Snuka, Eve Torres Gracie, Saraya Bevis, and Ettore Ewen. Thank you, Tricia Boczkowski, Mary Reynics, Jennifer Schuster, Julie

Cepler, Tammy Blake, Christopher Brand, Jenni Zellner, and every badass at the Crown Publishing Group for your hard work and belief in my story. Thank you to each and every fan for your years of support. You have all helped me attain the life I thought was only possible for my Sim.

Buffy Summers, Dana Scully, Daria, Kahlan Amnell, Jill Valentine, Meryl Silverburgh, Princess Kitana, Misty, Faye Valentine, Jean Grey, Chun-Li, Yuna and Lulu, Sydney Bristow, Lara Croft, Veronica Mars, and Harley Quinn—you helped a once weak little girl find her strength. Without you, there is no me.

ABOUT THE AUTHOR

AJ MENDEZ BROOKS is a New Jersey native, Florida
transplant, and Illinois resident who complains about
being cold literally every day. A former professional
wrestler with the WWE, she has won numerous wrestling awards and championships as well as inspired a
generation of young girls to wear sensible shoes. She
studied film and television production at NYU's Tisch
School of the Arts before they politely asked her to go
away. AJ currently works with several animal-rescue
and youth-oriented nonprofit organizations. She has
been the mom of numerous rescue dogs, and exclusively adopts the system's lost causes, because she is
attached to her stomach ulcers. She lives with her husband, their dog, and her PS4 in Chicago, Illinois.